"十三五"江苏省高等学校重点教材

U0685667

双语立体化教材

GMDSS COMMUNICATION SERVICES

GMDSS综合业务

主编 ◉ 张树奎 苏文明

主审 ◉ 汪龙生

大连海事大学出版社

DALIAN MARITIME UNIVERSITY PRESS

图书在版编目(CIP)数据

GMDSS 综合业务：英、汉／张树奎，苏文明主编.
大连：大连海事大学出版社，2024. 10. — ISBN 978-7
-5632-4565-9

Ⅰ. U676.8

中国国家版本馆 CIP 数据核字第 2024KS0551 号

大连海事大学出版社出版

地址：大连市黄浦路523号　邮编：116026　电话：0411-84729665(营销部)　84729480(总编室)
http://press.dlmu.edu.cn　E-mail：dmupress@dlmu.edu.cn

大连金华光彩色印刷有限公司印装　　　　　大连海事大学出版社发行
2024 年 10 月第 1 版　　　　　　　　　　2024 年 10 月第 1 次印刷
幅面尺寸：184 mm×260 mm　　　　　　　　　　　　印张：16
字数：364 千　　　　　　　　　　　　　　　印数：1~2000 册
出版人：刘明凯

责任编辑：高　颖　　　　　　　　　　　　责任校对：史云霞
封面设计：张爱妮　　　　　　　　　　　　版式设计：张爱妮

ISBN 978-7-5632-4565-9　　　定价：46.00 元

前 言
Preface

  GMDSS 是 1974 年《国际海上人命安全公约》规定的全球水上移动无线电通信系统,是国际海事组织(IMO)为了最大限度地保障海上人命与财产安全,并进一步完善常规海上通信手段,利用现代化的通信技术改善海上遇险与安全通信,建立新的搜救通信网络而开发的综合系统。该系统最重要功能的是提供一种全球化的实时搜救通信能力,并同时提供常规数据业务服务和海上安全信息广播,这对于促进船舶遇险通信和救助的现代化、增进船舶航行安全、提高船舶营运效率等,都具有深远的社会和经济意义。

  编者对国内外最新同类教材、文章进行了比较分析,并在此基础上将近年来有关 GMDSS 的最新国际公约、无线电规则以及相关规定的有关内容精心提炼和编排而成本书。本书比较系统地介绍了 GMDSS 的组成、基本原理及各个分系统的工作方式,符合中华人民共和国海事局公开发布的《海船船员培训大纲》对于 GMDSS 通信业务知识、技能的综合要求。在取材与编写上,本书注重实用性,采用英汉双语对照方式,并配有立体化学习资源,便于教学和培训的开展及读者的自学。

  本书可作为我国高等院校航海技术专业、海事管理专业 GMDSS 课程基础教材,也可作为高级海员 GMDSS 适任证书培训专用教材,还可作为海船船舶驾驶员、GMDSS 岸站无线电操作人员、搜救中心值班人员和其他有关人员业务学习、培训的参考用书。希望本书的出版能在航海教育和培训方面做出一定的贡献。

  本书由张树奎、苏文明担任主编。全书共分 7 章,其中第 1、2、3、7 章由苏文明编写,第 4、5、6 章由张树奎编写。本书的编写同时得到了江苏海事职业技术学院、大连海事大学航海学院有关同志的大力帮助以及大连海事大学出版社有关领导、编辑的积极支持,在此一并表示感谢!

  由于编者水平和资料来源有限,加之时间仓促,书中难免存在一些缺点和错误,殷切希望广大读者提出宝贵意见!

编者

2024 年 5 月

目 录
Contents

Chapter 1
Introduction of GMDSS 全球海上遇险和安全系统概论

Chapter 2
Distress, Urgency and Safety Communications 遇险、紧急和安全通信

Chapter 3
Satellite Communication Services 卫星通信业务

Chapter 4
Maritime Mobile Services 海上移动业务

Chapter 5
Maritime Safety Information in the GMDSS GMDSS 中的海上安全信息

Chapter 6
Ship Reporting Systems 船舶报告系统

Chapter 7
Modernization of GMDSS GMDSS 的现代化

Appendixes
附录

Introduction of GMDSS

全球海上遇险和安全系统概论

Chapter 1

1.1　General 概述

1.1.1　History 历史

Radio has been the foundation of the distress and safety systems used by ships at sea since the first instance of the use of radio to save lives at sea in 1899. It was soon realized that to be effective, a radio-based distress and safety system has to be founded on internationally agreed rules concerning the type of equipment, the radio frequencies used and operational procedures. The first international agreements were established under the auspices of the predecessor to the International Telecommunication Union (ITU). Many of the operational procedures for Morse telegraphy established at the turn of 20th century have been maintained to the present day.

无线电自 1899 年首次用于在海上拯救生命,自此以后便一直是海上船舶遇险和安全系统的基础。人们很快意识到,要想行之有效,基于无线电的遇险和安全系统必须建立在有关设备类型、使用的无线电频率和操作程序的国际商定规则之上。第一批国际协议是在国际电信联盟(ITU)的前身的主持下制定的,而 20 世纪初制定的许多莫尔斯电报操作程序一直沿用至今。

As more detailed regulations became necessary for the shipping industry, the most recent of International Convention for the Safety of Life at Sea (SOLAS) was adopted in 1974. The 1974 SOLAS Convention has become one of the main instruments of the International Maritime Organization (IMO).

随着航运业需要制定更详细的法规,最新的《国际海上人命安全公约》(SOLAS)于 1974 年通过。1974 年《国际海上人命安全公约》已成为国际海事组织的主要文书之一。

The distress and safety system used by most of the world's shipping companies until 1992, as

defined by Chapter Ⅳ of the 1974 SOLAS Convention and the ITU Radio Regulations, required a continuous Morse radiotelegraphy watch on 500 kHz for passenger ships, irrespective of size, and cargo ships of 1600 gross tonnage and upwards. The Convention also required a radiotelephone watch on 2182 kHz and 156.8 MHz (VHF channel) on all passenger ships and cargo ships of 300 gross tonnage and above. Although the system has proven itself reliable over many years, its limitations of short-range, manual alerting and aural watchkeeping have become a matter of increasing concern. Advances of technology led the IMO member governments to develop a new system based on modern technology and automation.

1974 年《国际海上人命安全公约》第四章和国际电信联盟《无线电规则》规定,在 1992 年之前,世界上大多数航运公司使用的遇险和安全系统都要求客船(无论大小)和 1600 总吨及以上的货船在 500 kHz 上持续进行莫尔斯无线电报值班。公约还要求所有客船和国际航线航行 300 总吨及以上的所有货船在 2182 kHz 和 156.8 MHz(VHF 频道)上进行无线电话值班。尽管该系统多年来已被证明相对可靠,但其距离短、需要手动报警和依赖听觉值班等局限性已经日益引发关注。技术的进步促使国际海事组织成员国政府开发了一种基于现代技术并且高度自动化的新系统。

The new system is called the Global Maritime Distress and Safety System (GMDSS). This system was adopted by IMO in 1988 and replaces the 500 kHz Morse code system. The GMDSS provides a reliable ship-to-shore communications path in addition to ship-to-ship alerting communications. The new system is automated and uses ship-to-shore alerting by means of terrestrial radio and satellite radio paths for alerting and subsequent communications.

这个新系统称为全球海上遇险和安全系统(GMDSS)。该系统于 1988 年被国际海事组织采用,并取代了 500 kHz 莫尔斯电码系统。GMDSS 除提供船对船报警通信外,还提供可靠的船对岸通信路径。新系统是高度自动化的,通过地面无线电和卫星无线电路径进行船对岸报警和后续通信。

1.1.2 Implementation of GMDSS GMDSS 的实施

The GMDSS requirements for radiocommunications are contained in Chapter Ⅳ of 1974 SOLAS Convention adopted at the GMDSS Conference held in 1988. There was a transition period from the old to the new system in order to allow industry time to overcome any unforeseen problems in implementation of the new system. The transition period began on 1 February 1992 continued to 1 February 1999.

1974 年《国际海上人命安全公约》第四章内容涉及 GMDSS 对无线电通信的要求,该公约在 1988 年举行的全球海上遇险和安全系统会议上得到通过。从旧系统到新系统有一个过渡期,以便让业界有时间克服在实施新系统过程中出现的任何不可预见的问题,过渡期从 1992 年 2 月 1 日开始,一直持续到 1999 年 2 月 1 日。

The GMDSS applies to all cargo ships of 300 gross tonnage and above, and to all passenger ships, regardless of size, on international voyages.

GMDSS 适用于从事国际航线航行 300 总吨及以上的货船和所有客船(不论大小)。

1.1.3 Basic Concept of GMDSS GMDSS 的基本概念

The basic concept of the GMDSS is that search and rescue authorities ashore as well as ships, or persons in the immediate vicinity of the ship in distress will be rapidly alerted to a distress incident so they can assist in a coordinated research and rescue operation with the minimum delay. The system also provides for urgency and safety communications and the promulgation of Maritime Safety Information (navigational and meteorological warnings and forecasts and other urgent safety information). In other words, every ship is able, irrespective of the sea area in which it operates, to perform those communication functions, which are essential for the safety of the ship itself and of other ships operating in the same sea area.

GMDSS 的基本概念是,遇险事件发生后,岸上的搜救机构以及遇险船舶附近的船舶或人员将迅速得到报警,以便他们能够在最短的时间内协助开展协调搜救行动。该系统还提供紧急和安全通信,并发布海上安全信息(航行警告、气象警告和预报以及其他紧急安全信息)。换句话说,船舶无论在哪个海区航行,都能使用该系统来完成本船和在同一海区航行的其他船舶的涉及安全的通信职能。

1.2 Sea Areas 海区

Because the different radio systems incorporated into GMDSS have individual limitations with respect to range and service provided, the equipment required to be carried by a ship is determined by the ship's area of operation. The GMDSS has divided the world's oceans into four distinct areas. All vessels are required to carry equipment appropriate to the sea area or areas in which they trade.

由于纳入 GMDSS 的不同无线电系统在覆盖范围和提供的业务方面都有各自的局限性,因此船舶需要携带的设备取决于船舶的航行区域。GMDSS 将世界海洋划分为四个不同的海区。所有船舶都必须配备与其航行海区相适应的设备。

Sea Area A1: within the radiotelephone coverage of at least one VHF coast station in which continuous VHF DSC alerting is available, such an area could extend typically 30–50 n mile from the coast station.

A1 海区：在至少一个 VHF 海岸电台(岸台)的无线电话覆盖范围内,在该区域可实现连续的 VHF DSC 报警,通常为海岸电台向外延伸 30~50 n mile。

Sea Area A2: within the radiotelephone coverage of at least one MF coast station in which continuous MF DSC alerting is available (excluding Sea Area A1). This area typically extends to up to 150–250 n mile offshore.

A2 海区:在至少一个 MF 海岸电台的无线电话覆盖范围内,在该区域可实现连续的 MF DSC 报警,但不包括 A1 海区。该区域通常延伸至离岸 150~250 n mile。

Sea Area A3: within the coverage area of an INMARSAT geostationary satellite in which con-

tinuous alerting is available. This area lies between about latitudes 70° north and south but excludes Sea Areas Al and A2.

A3 海区:在国际海事卫星组织(INMARSAT)地球同步静止卫星覆盖区内且可实现连续报警。该区域位于北纬 70°和南纬 70°之间,但不包括 Al 和 A2 海区。

Sea Area A4: the remaining sea areas outside Sea Areas A1, A2 and A3, this is essentially the polar regions north and south of about 70° of latitude.

A4 海区:指全球海域除 A1、A2 和 A3 海区以外的海区,主要是指纬度约 70°以北和以南的极区。

1.3　Functional Requirements 功能要求

Each Government Contracting to the amendments to the 1974 SOLAS Convention concerning radiocommunications for the GMDSS undertake to make available appropriate shore-based facilities for space and terrestrial radiocommunications services, as recommended by the International Maritime Organization, and all ships, while at sea, must be capable of:

a.Transmitting ship-to-shore distress alerts by at least two separate and independent means, each using a different radiocommunication service;

b.Receiving shore-to-ship distress alerts;

c.Transmitting and receiving ship-to-ship distress alerts;

d.Transmitting and receiving search and rescue coordinating communications;

e.Transmitting and receiving on-scene communications;

f.Transmitting and receiving signals for locating;

g.Transmitting and receiving Maritime Safety Information;

h.Transmitting and receiving general radiocommunications from shore-based radio systems or networks;

i.Transmitting and receiving bridge-to-bridge communications.

参加 1974 年《国际海上人命安全公约》关于 GMDSS 无线电通信修正案的各缔约国政府承诺,按照国际海事组织的建议,为卫星和地面无线电通信业务提供适当的岸基设施,所有船舶在海上航行时必须能够实现以下功能:

a.通过至少两种独立且互不依赖的方式,分别使用不同的无线电通信业务,发送船对岸遇险报警;

b.接收岸对船遇险报警;

c.发送和接收船对船遇险报警;

d.发送和接收搜救协调通信;

e.发送和接收现场通信;

f.发送和接收定位信号;

g.发送和接收海上安全信息;

h.发送和接收岸基无线电系统或网络的常规无线电通信;

i.发送和接收驾驶台间通信。

1.3.1 Ship-to-shore Distress Alert 船对岸遇险报警

Ship-to-shore distress alert is a basic and vital function of the GMDSS. GMDSS ship must have the ability of sending ship-to-shore distress alerts by at least two separate and independent means, each using a different radiocommunication service. For instance, on a Sea Area A1 ship, which always remains within DSC range of a VHF shore station, the primary means would be the VHF DSC and the secondary means could be an Emergency Position Indicating Radio Beacon (EPIRB). In the case of a Sea Area A4 ship, the primary means would have to be HF DSC and the secondary means would be a 406 MHz EPIRB.

船对岸遇险报警是 GMDSS 的一项基础且重要功能。符合要求的船舶必须能够通过至少两种独立且互不依赖的方式发送船对岸遇险报警,每种方式应能使用不同的无线电通信业务。例如,A1 海区的船舶始终处于 VHF 岸基站的 DSC 覆盖范围内,其主要报警手段是 VHF DSC,次要手段可以使用紧急无线电示位标(EPIRB)。如果是 A4 海区的船舶,则必须以 HF DSC 为主要报警手段,以 406 MHz EPIRB 为辅助报警手段。

1.3.2 Ship-to-ship Distress Alert 船对船遇险报警

Ship-to-ship distress alert is a short-medium range communication. A ship in distress can alert other ships in the vicinity by sending a DSC distress alert on VHF and MF, simultaneously if desired, and follow it up with a distress (MAYDAY) voice message on Channel 16 or 2182 kHz. Note that HF DSC is for long-range work and is intended primarily for alerting the shore-based authorities rather than ships at sea.

船对船遇险报警是一种中短程通信。遇险船舶可通过 VHF 和 MF(如需要可同时发送)发送 DSC 遇险报警,并在 16 频道或 2182 kHz 上发送遇险(MAYDAY)语音电文,以提醒附近的其他船舶。需要注意的是,HF DSC 用于远距离工作,主要用于向岸上机构而非海上船舶进行报警。

1.3.3 Shore-to-ship Distress Alert 岸对船遇险报警

The shore authorities could relay the distress details by directing a DSC call and/or a satellite call to all ships within a defined area in order to make these ships, especially the ships in the vicinity, become aware of the distress.

岸上机构可以通过 DSC 呼叫和/或卫星呼叫向指定区域内的所有船舶转发遇险详情,以便让这些船舶,尤其是遇险船舶附近的船舶了解遇险情况。

1.3.4　Search and Rescue Coordinating（SAR）Communications 搜救协调通信

For the coordination and control of SAR operations, Rescue Coordination Centers（RCCs）require communications with the ship in distress as well as with units participating in the operation. The methods and types of communication（terrestrial/satellite, telephone/telex）used will be determined by the equipment available onboard the ship in distress as well as those onboard assisting units.

为了协调和控制搜救行动,搜救协调中心（RCC）需要与遇险船舶以及参与行动的单位进行通信。所使用的通信方式和类型（地面/卫星、电话/电传）将取决于遇险船舶以及救助单位配备的设备。

1.3.5　On-scene Communications 现场通信

On-scene communications are those between the ship in distress and assisting vessels and between SAR vessels and the on-scene commander（OSC）or the coordinator of the surface search（CSS）. These communications are normally short, medium range communications which will be generally made on the VHF or MF distress and safety frequencies in the GMDSS. However, ships fitted with INMARSAT Ship Earth Station could, if necessary, use satellite communications as a supplement to their VHF and MF facilities.

现场通信是指遇险船舶与救助船舶之间,以及搜救船舶与现场指挥官（OSC）或水面搜救协调员（CSS）之间的通信。这些通信通常为中短程通信,一般使用 GMDSS 中的 VHF 或 MF 遇险和安全频率。不过,如果有必要,装有 INMARSAT 船舶地球站（船站）的船舶可以使用卫星通信作为 VHF 和 MF 设备的补充。

Control of on-scene communications is the responsibility of the unit coordinating search and rescue operations. Simplex communications shall be used so that all on-scene mobile stations may share relevant information concerning the distress incident. If direct-printing telegraphy is used, it shall be in the Forward Error Correcting（FEC）mode.

现场通信的控制由协调搜救行动的单位负责。应使用单工通信,以便所有现场移动电台都能共享遇险事件的相关信息。如果使用直接印字电报,则应采用前向纠错（FEC）模式。

On-scene communication frequencies for radiotelephone are:

- VHF（F3E）: Channel 16（distress & safety communications）and Channel 6（inter-ship and ship-aircraft communications）;

- VHF（A3E）: 121.5 & 123.1 MHz（ship-aircraft communications—compulsory for passenger vessels）;

- MF（J3E）: 2182 kHz（distress & safety communications）;

- HF（J3E）: 3023 kHz（ship-aircraft）, 4125 kHz（ship-shore, ship-ship）and 5680 kHz（ship-aircraft）.

现场无线电话通信频率为：

- 16 频道（遇险和安全通信）和 6 频道（船间和船舶-飞机通信）；

- 121.5 和 123.1 MHz（船舶-飞机通信——此项客船必须使用）；

- 2182 kHz（遇险和安全通信）；

- 3023 kHz（船舶-飞机）、4125 kHz（船-岸、船-船）和 5680 kHz（船舶-飞机）。

The frequency 2174.5 kHz may also be used for ship-to-ship on-scene communications using Narrow Band Direct Printing(NBDP) telegraphy in the FEC mode.

2174.5 kHz 的频率也可用于在 FEC 模式下使用窄带直接印字（NBDP）电报进行船对船现场通信。

1.3.6 Locating Signals 定位信号

Locating and homing signals in the GMDSS are provided by radar Search and Rescue Radar Transponders (SARTs) and EPIRBs. SARTs are intended for use on board ship in distress or survival craft and enable ships and aircrafts engaged in a search and rescue operation to locate survivors using 9 GHz (3 cm or X-band) radar. Most EPIRBs in current manufacture also incorporate some form of locating function. The COSPAS-SARSAT system only detects and locates distress beacons operating at 406 MHz. The COSPAS-SARSAT 406 MHz EPIRBs once provided for an additional transmission on 121.5/243 MHz, which suitably equipped ships and aircrafts can use as a homing signal. 121.5/243 MHz processing by COSPAS-SARSAT ceased on 1 February 2009.

GMDSS 的定位和寻位信号由搜救雷达应答器（SART）和 EPIRB 提供。SART 用于定位遇险船舶或救生船舶，使参与搜救行动的船舶和飞机能够利用 9 GHz（3 cm 或 X 波段）雷达确定幸存者的位置。目前制造的大多数 EPIRB 也具有某种形式的定位功能。全球卫星搜救系统（COSPAS-SARSAT 系统）只能探测和定位工作频率为 406 MHz 的遇险信标。COSPAS-SARSAT 406 MHz EPIRB 曾在 121.5/243 MHz 频率上为配备该系统的船舶和飞机额外提供寻位信号。COSPAS-SARSAT 系统于 2009 年 2 月 1 日停止处理 121.5/243 MHz 信号。

1.3.7 Maritime Safety Information 海上安全信息

MSI is short for Maritime Safety Information. In the GMDSS, MSI broadcast will be mainly made on two dedicated systems providing near-continuous automated reception on board ships. The two systems are INMARSAT SafetyNET Service and NAVTEX. However, in Sea Area A4, HF NBDP radiotelex is the only method for transmission and reception of MSI.

MSI 是海上安全信息的简称。在 GMDSS 中，MSI 广播主要通过两个专用系统进行，这两个系统可在船上提供近乎不间断的自动接收。这两个系统是 INMARSAT 安全网业务和航行警告电传系统（NAVTEX）。但在 A4 海区，HF NBDP 无线电传是发送和接收 MSI 的唯一手段。

1.3.8 General Radiocommunications 常规无线电通信

The GMDSS provides facilities for all types of commercial and personal communications.

GMDSS radio operators can make telephone and telex calls to shipping agents, port authorities, the public telephone network, etc. through commercial telecommunication networks.

GMDSS 为各类商业和个人通信提供设施。GMDSS 无线电操作员可通过商业电信网络与船运代理、港口当局、公共电话网等进行电话和电传呼叫。

1.3.9　Bridge-to-bridge Communications 驾驶台间通信

Bridge-to-bridge communications are inter-ship VHF radiotelephone communications for the purpose of assisting the safe movement of ships.

驾驶台间通信是指船舶之间的 VHF 无线电话通信,目的是协助船舶的安全航行。

1.4　Radio Personnel Certificate Requirements 无线电人员证书要求

The provisions of the Radio Regulations define four classes of radio personnel certificate in GMDSS. Every ship shall carry personnel qualified for distress and safety radiocommunication purposes to the satisfaction of the administration. The personnel shall be holders of certificates specified in the Radio Regulations, any one of whom shall be designated to have primary responsibility for radiocommunications during distress incidents.

- · First-Class Radio Electronic Certificate (includes full on-board maintenance);
- · Second-Class Radio Electronic Certificate(includes limited on-board maintenance);
- · General Operator's Certificate (world-wide operation, but not including maintenance);
- · Restricted Operator's Certificate (for Sea Area A1 ships).

《无线电规则》的条款规定了 GMDSS 的四类无线电人员证书。每艘船舶均应配备合格的遇险和安全无线电通信人员以满足管理部门要求。这些人员应持有《无线电规则》规定的证书,其中任何一人应被指定在遇险事件中主要负责无线电通信。

- · 一级无线电电子员证书(包括全套船载设备维修);
- · 二级无线电电子员证书(包括有限的船载设备维修);
- · 通用操作员证书(全球通用,但不包括维修职能);
- · 限用操作员证书(适用于 A1 海区船舶)。

The Radio Regulations requires that the personnel of ship stations and ship earth stations for which a radio installation is compulsory under international agreements and which use the frequencies and techniques of the GMDSS shall include at least:

- · For stations on-board vessels which sail beyond the range of VHF coast stations (Sea Areas A2, A3 and A4), taking into account the provisions of 1974 SOLAS Convention: a holder of a First- or Second-Class Radio Electronic Certificate or two General Operator's Certificates (GOC);

- For stations on-board vessels which sail within the range of VHF coast stations (Sea Area A1), taking into account the provisions of 1974 SOLAS Convention: a holder of a First-or Second-Class Radio Electronic Certificate or a General Operator's Certificate or a Restricted Operator's Certificate (ROC).

《无线电规则》规定,根据国际协议,必须安装无线电设备并使用 GMDSS 频率和技术的船舶电台(船台)和船站,其人员至少应包括:

- 根据 1974 年《国际海上人命安全公约》的规定,对于在 VHF 海岸电台覆盖范围以外,即 A2、A3 和 A4 海区航行的船舶上:配备一名一级或一名二级无线电电子员或两名通用操作员;

- 根据 1974 年《国际海上人命安全公约》的规定,对于在 VHF 海岸电台即 A1 海区范围内航行的船舶上:配备一名一级或一名二级无线电电子员或一名通用操作员或一名限用操作员。

1.5 GMDSS Equipment Requirements GMDSS 设备要求

GMDSS equipment requirements for all passenger ships in international trade as well as cargo ships of 300 gross tonnage and above in international trade are indicated as follow.

所有从事国际航线航行的客船和 300 总吨及以上货船的 GMDSS 设备要求如下。

1.5.1 GMDSS Equipment for All Ships 所有船舶的 GMDSS 设备

406 EPIRB

A 406 Satellite EPIRB is a requirement of GMDSS for the purpose of transmitting a distress alert signal ashore and transmitting a locating signal. This EPIRB must be mounted in a float free location.

406 卫星 EPIRB 是 GMDSS 的要求,用于向岸上发射遇险报警信号和发射定位信号。该 EPIRB 必须安装在能自由浮起的位置。

SART

- Cargo ships >300GT but <500GT are required to only carry one SART.

- Cargo ships >500GT and all passenger ships are required to carry two SARTs, one on each side of vessel, ready to be taken to survival craft.

- On ships carrying at least two SARTs and equipped with free-fall lifeboats, one of the SARTs shall be stowed in a free-fall lifeboat and the other located in the immediate vicinity of the navigation bridge.

- 大于 300GT 但小于 500GT 的货船需携带一个 SART。

- 大于 500GT 的货船和所有客船都必须携带两个 SART,船的两侧各一个,随时准备送

往救生艇。

- 在至少装有两个 SART 并配有自由落体式救生艇的船上,其中一个 SART 应存放在自由落体式救生艇中,另一个应位于驾驶台附近。

Survival Craft Radiotelephone 救生艇无线电话

- Emergency VHF transceivers that operate on VHF Channel 16 and one other channel (VHF Channel 06 is recommended).

- Cargo ships >300GT but <500GT are only required to carry two VHF transceivers.

- Cargo ships >500GT and all passenger ships are required to carry three VHF transceivers.

- A transceiver permanently installed in a survival craft may count towards this requirement.

- 使用 VHF 16 频道和一个其他频道(建议使用 VHF 06 频道)的应急 VHF 无线电话。

- 大于 300GT 但小于 500GT 的货船需携带两台 VHF 无线电话。

- 大于 500GT 的货船和所有客船必须携带三台 VHF 无线电话。

- 永久性安装在救生艇上的无线电话可计入数量要求。

VHF Installation VHF 设备

- Capable of operating on VHF Channels 06, 13 and 16.

- Capable of maintaining continuous DSC monitoring on VHF Channel 70.

- Capable of initiating DSC distress alert transmissions on Channel 70.

- 可使用 VHF 06、13 和 16 频道。

- 能够通过 VHF 70 频道持续守听 DSC。

- 能够在 70 频道上启动 DSC 遇险报警传输。

NAVTEX 航行警告系统电传

- One NAVTEX receiver is required. Where NAVTEX service is not available, the vessel must have INMARSAT Enhanced Group Calling system, or HF NBDP telegraphy to receive MSI.

- 需要一个 NAVTEX 接收机。在没有 NAVTEX 业务的情况下,船舶必须配备 INMARSAT 增强群呼(EGC)系统或 HF NBDP 电报才能接收 MSI。

1.5.2 GMDSS Equipment Summarized per Sea Area 按海区汇总的 GMDSS 设备

Sea Area A1 A1 海区

- VHF Installation VHF 安装

- 406 EPIRB 406 EPIRB

Sea Area A2　A2 海区

- VHF Installation　VHF 安装

- MF Installation　MF 安装

- 406 EPIRB　406 EPIRB

Sea Area A3　A3 海区

- VHF Installation　VHF 安装

- MF/HF Installation or INMARSAT Installation　MF/HF 安装或者 INMARSAT 安装

- 406 EPIRB　406 EPIRB

Sea Area A4　A4 海区

- VHF Installation　VHF 安装

- MF/HF Installation　MF/HF 安装

- 406 EPIRB　406 EPIRB

1.6　Availability of Ship Station Equipment 船舶电台设备的可用性

A ship should not depart from any port unless and until the ship is able to perform all distress and safety communications. In addition, ships shall ensure the availability of their GMDSS equipment.

在船舶能够进行所有遇险和安全通信之前,船舶不得离开任何港口。此外,船舶应确保其 GMDSS 设备的可用性。

1.6.1　Methods of Ensuring the Availability 确保可用性的方式

Ships sailing in Sea Areas A1 and A2, shall ensure the availability by using at least one of the following methods; On ships sailing in Sea Areas A3 and A4, this availability shall be ensured by using a combination of at least two of the following methods:

- Duplication of equipment (DOE);

- Shore-based maintenance (SBM); and

- At-sea maintenance (ASM).

在 A1 和 A2 海区航行的船舶,应至少使用以下一种方法确保可用性;在 A3 和 A4 海区航行的船舶,应至少结合使用两种方法来确保这种可用性:

- 双套设备 (DOE);

- 岸基维修(SBM);和

- 海上维修(ASM)。

Within the GMDSS, if availability is ensured by using a combination of methods which includes shore-based maintenance, an arrangement acceptable to the administration should be established to ensure adequate sort of the ship for the maintenance and repair of its radio installations.

在 GMDSS 内,如果使用包括岸基维修在内的多种方法来确保可用性,则应做出主管机关可接受的安排,以确保船舶有足够的能力来维修和修理其无线电设备。

Where ASM is used as an option to ensure availability of radio equipment through a maintenance capability, the arrangements made must be acceptable to the relevant authorities concerned.

如果海上维修被用作通过维修能力确保无线电设备可用性的一种选择,所做的安排必须符合主管机关要求。

Duplication of Equipment 双套设备

Duplication of equipment may be used as a means of contributing to the inability of equipment in the GMDSS. In order to satisfy the requirement of the Convention where there is no onboard maintainer, vessels will be required to carry duplicate equipment as follows.

· Sea Area A1 DSC VHF Radio;

· Sea Area A2 DSC VHF Radio and either MF or HF Radio, or SES;

· Sea Area A3 DSC VHF Radio and either HF Radio, or SES;

· Sea Area A4 DSC VHF Radio, HF Radio.

双套设备可作为一种手段,以提高 GMDSS 设备的可用性。为了满足公约的要求,在船上没有维修人员的情况下,船舶必须携带以下双套设备。

· A1 海区 DSC VHF 无线电;

· A2 海区 DSC VHF 无线电和 MF 或 HF 无线电,或 SES;

· A3 海区 DSC VHF 无线电和 HF 无线电,或 SES;

· A4 海区 DSC VHF 无线电,HF 无线电。

Separate antennas are required for duplicate radio installations.

双套无线电设备需要有单独的天线。

1.6.2 Test of GMDSS Equipment GMDSS 设备测试

On all GMDSS ships, usually a person holding an appropriate Radio Operator's Certificate, shall while the ship is at sea, carry out the daily, weekly and monthly tests required by both international and national regulations. If any of the radio equipment required by these regulations is not in working order, the nominated person shall inform the Master and record details of the deficiencies in the radio log.

在所有符合 GMDSS 要求的船舶上,通常应由一名持有无线电操作员适任证书的人员在船舶出海时进行国际和国家规定所要求的每日、每周和每月测试。如果这些规定所要求的任何无线电设备出现故障,测试人员应通知船长,并在无线电日志中记录故障详情。

The testing of compulsorily fitted radio equipment should be carried out according to the following.

对强制安装的无线电设备的测试应按以下要求进行。

Daily Tests 每日测试

a.The proper functioning of the DSC facilities shall be tested without radiation of signals, by use of the means provided by equipment.

b.Batteries providing a source of energy for any part of the radio stations shall be tested daily and, where necessary, brought up to the fully charged condition.

c.Printer(s) shall be checked daily to ensure there is an adequate supply of paper.

a.应使用设备提供的方法,在没有信号发射的情况下,测试 DSC 设备的正常功能。

b.对为无线电台的任何部分提供能源的电池,应每天进行测试,必要时应确保满电状态。

c.应每天检查打印机,确保纸张充足。

Weekly Tests 每周测试

a.The proper operation of the DSC facilities shall be tested at least once per week by means of a test call, when within communication range of a coast station fitted with DSC equipment.

b.Where a ship has been out of communication range of coast station fitted with DSC equipment for a period longer than a week, a test call shall be made on the first opportunity the ship is in communication range of such a coast station.

c.Where the reserve source of energy is not a battery (for example, a motor generator), the reserve source of energy shall be tested weekly.

d.Each survival craft two-way VHF equipment shall be tested at least once a week on a frequency besides Channel 16.

a.在装有 DSC 设备的海岸电台的通信范围内,应至少每周一次通过测试呼叫对 DSC 设备进行测试。

b.如果船舶离开海岸电台 DSC 设备覆盖范围的时间超过一周,则应在首次进入海岸电台覆盖范围时马上进行测试呼叫。

c.如果备用电源不是蓄电池(如电动发电机),则应每周对备用电源进行测试。

d.每艘救生艇的双向 VHF 设备应至少每周在 16 频道以外的频率上进行一次测试。

Monthly Tests 每月测试

a.Each EPIRB shall be tested at least once per month to determine its capability to operate properly using the means provided on the device and without using the satellite system.

b.Each SART shall be checked at least once per month for security and signs of damage.

c.A check shall be made at least once per month on the security and condition of all batteries providing a source of energy for any part of a radio installation. The battery connections and compartment shall also be checked.

d.Each survival craft two-way VHF equipment shall be tested at least once per month on a frequency other than Channel 16.

a.应至少每月测试一次 EPIRB 设备,以确定其在不使用卫星系统的情况下,能够使用设备提供的方法正常运行。

b.应至少每月一次检查每个 SART 的安全状况和标志损毁情况。

c.应至少每月一次检查为无线电设备任何部分提供能源的所有电池的安全和状态。还应对电池的连接和电池盒进行检查。

d.每艘救生艇的双向 VHF 设备应每月至少测试一次 16 频道以外的频道。

1.7 Summary Notes of GMDSS Equipment GMDSS 设备要点总结

a.VHF radiotelephone（RT）must be capable of transmitting and receiving DSC on Channel 70 and RT on Channel 06, Channel 13 and Channel 16.

b.The DSC Channel 70 VHF watchkeeping equipment may be separated or combined with item（a）above.

c.Ships sailing exclusively in Sea Area A1 may carry in lieu of a 406 MHz satellite EPIRB, an EPIRB which is capable of transmitting a DSC distress alert on Channel 70 VHF and providing location by means of a 9 GHz transponder.

d.MF radio installation must be capable of transmitting and receiving DSC on 2187.5 kHz and RT on 2182 kHz for distress purposes.

e.The dedicated 2187. 5 kHz DSC watchkeeping receiver may be separated with DSC equipment in item（d）above.

f.MF/HF installations must be capable of transmitting and receiving on all distress and safety frequencies in the 1605−27500 kHz range using DSC, RT and NBDP.

g.MF/HF DSC watchkeeping receivers must be capable of receiving on the frequencies of 2187.5 kHz and 8414.5 kHz and at least one of the other HF DSC frequencies（4207.5, 6312, 12577 or 16804.5 kHz）. The watchkeeping receiver may be separated or combined with DSC equipment in item（f）above.

a.VHF 无线电话(RT)必须能够发射和接收 70 频道上的 DSC 以及 06 频道、13 频道和 16 频道上的无线电话。

b.DSC 70 频道 VHF 值守设备可与上述第(a)项分开或合并使用。

c.仅在 A1 海区航行的船舶可以配备一个 406 MHz 卫星 EPIRB,该 EPIRB 能够通过 VHF 70 频道发送 DSC 遇险报警,并通过 9 GHz 转发器提供位置。

d.MF 无线电设备必须能够发射和接收 2187.5 kHz DSC 和 2182 kHz 无线电话,以备遇险之用。

e.专用的 2187.5 kHz DSC 值守机可与上述第(d)项中的 DSC 设备分开。

f.MF/HF 设备必须能够使用 DSC、无线电话和 NBDP 在 1605~27500 kHz 范围内发射和接收所有遇险和安全频率。

g.MF/HF DSC 值守机必须能够接收 2187.5 kHz 和 8414.5 kHz 频率以及至少一个其他 HF DSC 频率(4207.5、6312、12577 或 16804.5 kHz)。值守机可以是单独的,也可以与上述第(f)项中的 DSC 设备结合使用。

Distress，Urgency and Safety Communications
遇险、紧急和安全通信

Chapter 2

2.1 Distress Frequencies 遇险频率

2.1.1 Distress and Safety Frequencies in Terrestrial Services 地面业务中的遇险和安全频率

Within GMDSS a number of frequencies are specifically allocated for distress communication purposes depending on the communication medium being used. These frequencies should be used by ships，aircrafts or survival crafts when seeking assistance in the maritime mobile service. They should be used for the distress call and distress traffic and for calls preceded by either the urgency signal or the safety signal.

在 GMDSS 中，根据所使用的通信手段，专门分配了一些频率用于遇险通信。船舶、飞机或救生艇在海上移动业务中寻求救助时应使用这些频率。这些频率应用于遇险呼叫和遇险通信，以及紧急或安全呼叫。

Frequencies in Table 2.1 may be used for distress purposes in the GMDSS terrestrial services. Frequencies in column one is DSC frequencies，frequencies in columns two and three are to be used for subsequent communications.

表 2.1 中的频率可用于 GMDSS 地面业务中的遇险通信。第一栏中的频率为 DSC 频率，第二栏和第三栏中的频率用于后续通信。

Table 2.1 Maritime Distress Communication Frequencies

表 2.1 海上遇险通信频率

	DSC	RT	TELEX
VHF	Channel 70 (156.525 MHz)	Channel 16 (156.800 MHz)	Not used 未使用
MF	2187.5 kHz	2182 kHz	2174.5 kHz
HF 4M	4207.5 kHz	4125 kHz	4177.5 kHz
HF 6M	6312 kHz	6215 kHz	6268 kHz
HF 8M	8414.5 kHz	8291 kHz	8376.5 kHz
HF 12M	12577 kHz	12290 kHz	12520 kHz
HF 16M	16804.5 kHz	16420 kHz	16695 kHz

The aeronautical carrier frequencies 3023 kHz, 4125kHz and 5680 kHz may be used for inter-communication between mobile stations engaged in coordinated search and rescue operations, and for communication between these stations and participating land stations.

3023 kHz、4125 kHz 以及 5680 kHz 航空频率可用于参与协调搜救行动的移动电台之间的通信,以及这些移动电台与参与搜救行动的陆地电台之间的通信。

The emergency frequency is 121.5 MHz in the aeronautical VHF radiotelephony service. Survival craft can also use this frequency for distress and urgency communications. The auxiliary aeronautical frequency of 123.1 MHz which is used by the service and by other mobile and land stations engaged in coordinated SAR operations. Maritime mobile stations may communicate with aircraft stations on 121.5 MHz and 243 MHz for distress and urgency purposes. Class A3E emissions are used on these frequencies.

应急频率为航空 VHF 无线电话业务中的 121.5 MHz。救生艇也可使用该频率进行遇险和紧急通信。辅助航空频率为 123.1 MHz,由该业务以及参与协调搜救行动的其他移动电台和陆地电台使用。海上移动电台可使用 121.5 MHz 和 243 MHz 与航空电台进行遇险和紧急通信。这些频率使用 A3E 类发射。

2.1.2 Usage of VHF Channels VHF 频道的使用

VHF Channel 06 (156.3 MHz) VHF 06 频道(156.3 MHz)

The frequency 156.3 MHz may be used for communication between ship stations and aircraft stations engaged in coordinated search and rescue operations. It may also be used by aircraft stations to communicate with ship stations for other safety purposes.

156.3 MHz 频率可用于参与协调搜救行动的船舶电台和航空电台之间的通信。航空电台也可使用该频率与船舶电台进行其他以安全为目的的通信。

VHF Channel 70 (156.525 MHz) VHF 70 频道(156.525 MHz)

The frequency 156.525 MHz is used in the maritime mobile service for distress and safety calls using DSC.

156.525 MHz 频率用于海上移动业务,通过 DSC 进行遇险和安全呼叫。

VHF Channel 13（156.650 MHz） VHF 13 频道(156.650 MHz)

The frequency 156.650 MHz is used for ship-to-ship communications relating to the safety of navigation.

156.650 MHz 频率用于与航行安全有关的船对船通信。

VHF Channel 16（156.8 MHz） VHF 16 频道(156.8 MHz)

The frequency 156.8 MHz is used for distress and safety communications by radiotelephony. Additionally, the frequency 156.8 MHz may be used by aircraft stations for safety purposes only.

156.8 MHz 频率用于无线电话的遇险和安全通信。此外,156.8 MHz 频率也可由航空电台使用,但仅限于安全目的。

AIS-SART VHF Channel AIS 1（161.975 MHz）and AIS 2（162.025 MHz） AIS-SART VHF AIS 1(161.975 MHz)和 AIS 2 频道(162.025 MHz)

AIS 1 and AIS 2 are used for AIS search and rescue transmitter（AIS-SART）for use in search and rescue operations.

搜救应答器(AIS-SART)的 AIS 1 与 AIS 2 频道用于搜索和救援行动。

2.1.3 Special Frequencies in Satellite Services 卫星业务中的特殊频率

There are some special frequencies used in satellite service in Table 2.2, such frequencies must also be protected strictly to avoid harmful interference.

表 2.2 列出了卫星业务中使用的一些特殊频率,这些频率也必须严格保护,以避免有害干扰。

Table 2.2 Special Frequencies Used in Satellite Services
表 2.2 卫星业务中使用的特殊频率

Frequency（MHz）	Description of usage	Notes
406~406.1	406-EPIRB	This frequency band is used exclusively by satellite emergency position-indicating radio beacons in the earth-to-space direction 该频段专门用于地球对卫星方向的卫星紧急无线电示位标
1530~1544	Satellite communication	In addition to its availability for routine non-safety purposes, the band 1530~1544 MHz is used for distress and safety purposes in the space-to-earth direction in the maritime mobile-satellite service. GMDSS distress, urgency and safety communications have priority in this band 1530~1544 MHz 频段除了用于日常非安全外,还用于海上移动卫星业务卫星对地球方向的遇险和安全。GMDSS 的遇险、紧急和安全通信优先使用这一频段

Continued　续表

Frequency (MHz)	Description of usage	Notes
1544−1545	Distress and safety	Use of the band 1544−1545 MHz (space-to-earth) is limited to distress and safety operations, including feeder links of satellites needed to relay the emissions of satellite emergency position indicating radio beacons to earth stations and narrow-band (space-to-earth) links from space stations to mobile earth stations 1544~1545 MHz 频段(卫星对地球)的使用仅限于遇险和安全操作，包括向地球站转发卫星紧急无线电示位标所需的卫星馈送链路，以及空间站到移动地球站的窄带(卫星对地球)链路
1626.5−1645.5	Satellite communication	In addition to its availability for routine non-safety purposes, the band 1626.5−1645.5 MHz is used for distress and safety purposes in the earth-to-space direction in the maritime mobile-satellite service. GMDSS distress, urgency and safety communications have priority in this band 1626.5~1645.5 MHz 频段除了用于日常非安全外，还用于海上移动卫星业务地球对卫星方向的遇险和安全。GMDSS 的遇险、紧急和安全通信优先使用该频段
1645.5−1646.5	Distress and safety	Use of the band 1645.5−1646.5 MHz (earth-to-space) is limited to distress and safety operations 1645.5~1646.5 MHz 频段(地球对卫星)的使用仅限于遇险和安全操作
9200−9500	SART	This frequency band is used by SART to facilitate search and rescue 这一频段使用 SART 为搜索和救援提供便利

2.1.4　Protection of Distress Frequencies 遇险频率的保护

Any emission capable of causing harmful interference to distress, urgency or safety communications on any of the MF/HF and VHF radiotelephone DSC and NBDP distress and safety channels is prohibited by the ITU Radio Regulations. Unnecessary conversations, non-essential remarks and all profane or obscene words are forbidden. Test transmissions on distress frequencies shall be kept to a minimum, and wherever practicable be carried out using artificial antennas or with reduced power.

国际电联《无线电规则》禁止在 MF/HF 和 VHF 无线电话 DSC 和 NBDP 遇险和安全频道上进行任何可能对遇险、紧急或安全通信造成有害干扰的发射，并禁止不必要的对话、非必要的言论和所有冒犯的词语。应尽量减少在遇险频率上的测试呼叫，并在可行的情况下使用假负载或降低功率进行测试呼叫。

Operators should take every precaution to ensure that their transmissions will not cause harmful interference to other stations. It is important that all operators：

·　When using terrestrial communications, listen on the frequency before transmitting；

·　Where possible, use the minimum power necessary for reliable communications；

- Strictly observe the purpose for which a frequency is allocated; and

- Keep test signal's time to a minimum.

操作员应采取一切预防措施,确保其传输不会对其他电台造成有害干扰。所有操作员必须遵守:

- 使用地面通信时,在发射前监听频率;

- 尽可能使用可靠通信所需的最小功率;

- 严格遵守频率分配的目的;以及

- 尽量减少测试信号时间。

The ITU Radio Regulations establish a guard band on either side of the 2 MHz radiotelephony distress frequency of 2182 kHz. This band extends from 2173.5−2190.5 kHz. Transmission on any frequency except 2177 kHz, 2189.5 kHz, 2182 kHz, 2187.5 kHz (DSC) and 2174.5 kHz (NBDP) within this band is prohibited.

国际电联《无线电规则》在 2 MHz 无线电话遇险频率 2182 kHz 的两侧各设置了一个保护频段。该频段从 2173.5 kHz 延伸至 2190.5 kHz。除 2177 kHz、2189.5 kHz、2182 kHz、2187.5 kHz (DSC)和 2174.5 kHz(NBDP)外,禁止在此频段内进行任何通信。

All emissions in the frequency band 156.7625−156.8375 MHz are forbidden which might cause interference to VHF Channel 16 (156.8 MHz).

禁止在 156.7625~156.8375 MHz 频段内进行可能对 VHF 16 频道(156.8 MHz)造成干扰的所有发射。

2.2 General Operational Procedures 一般操作程序

Distress procedures under the GMDSS can be described as consisting of two elements or phases:

a.Alerting phase. Essentially, this involves alerting other maritime mobile stations and shore stations that a distress situation exists.

b.Communication phase. This requires the broadcasting of detailed information concerning the distress incident by radiotelephony or radiotelex.

GMDSS 下的遇险程序可分为两个阶段:

a.报警阶段。这主要是向其他海上移动电台和岸基站发出报警,告知存在遇险情况。

b.通信阶段。这需要通过无线电话或电传广播有关遇险事件的详细信息。

The two phases of the distress procedure are common to both the terrestrial communication bands and the satellite communication bands used in the GMDSS for distress and safety.

遇险程序的两个阶段对 GMDSS 系统中遇险和安全相关的地面通信和卫星通信频段都是

通用的。

Distress alerts are transmitted either：

a.Via satellite with absolute priority using the general communication channels； or

b.Via satellite using exclusive distress and safety frequencies； or

c.Using DSC on the appropriate distress and safety frequencies in the MF, HF or VHF bands； and

d.The distress call shall be sent on the distress and safety frequencies in the MF, HF or VHF bands for radiotelephony.

发送遇险报警的方式有：

a.通过卫星,在一般通信频道中具有绝对优先权;或

b.通过卫星,使用专用遇险和安全频率;或

c.在 MF、HF 或 VHF 频段遇险和安全频率上使用 DSC;以及

d.遇险信号应通过无线电话的 MF、HF 或 VHF 频段的遇险和安全频率发送。

When transmitting distress, urgency or safety messages by radiotelephony, transmissions should be made slowly and distinctly with clear pronunciation. The use of the International Code of Signals (ICS) is recommended, including the use of abbreviations and the phonetic alphabet, particularly in situations in which language difficulties arise. It should be noted that all stations receiving a DSC distress alert must immediately cease any transmission that may interfere with distress traffic.

在通过无线电话发送遇险、紧急或安全电文时,应缓慢、清晰地发音。建议使用《国际信号规则》(ICS),包括使用缩写词和码语,特别是在语言出现困难的情况下。应注意的是,所有收到 DSC 遇险报警的电台必须立即停止可能干扰遇险通信的任何传输。

2.2.1　Authority of the Master 船长的权力

Before the transmission of a distress alert by whatever method, an operator must obtain authority from the Master or person responsible for the ship, aircraft or other vehicle. Therefore, GMDSS operators must receive a formal command from the Master or person responsible for the ship, aircraft or other vehicle before sending a distress alert. This rule also applies to distress relay situations. The GMDSS Operating Guidance for Masters of Ships in Distress is shown in Figure 2.1.

在以任何方式发送遇险报警之前,操作员必须获得船长或船舶、飞机或其他交通工具负责人的授权。因此,GMDSS 操作员在发送遇险报警前必须收到船长或船舶、飞机或其他交通工具负责人的正式命令。这一规则也适用于遇险转发情况。图 2.1 为 GMDSS 遇险船舶船长操作指南。

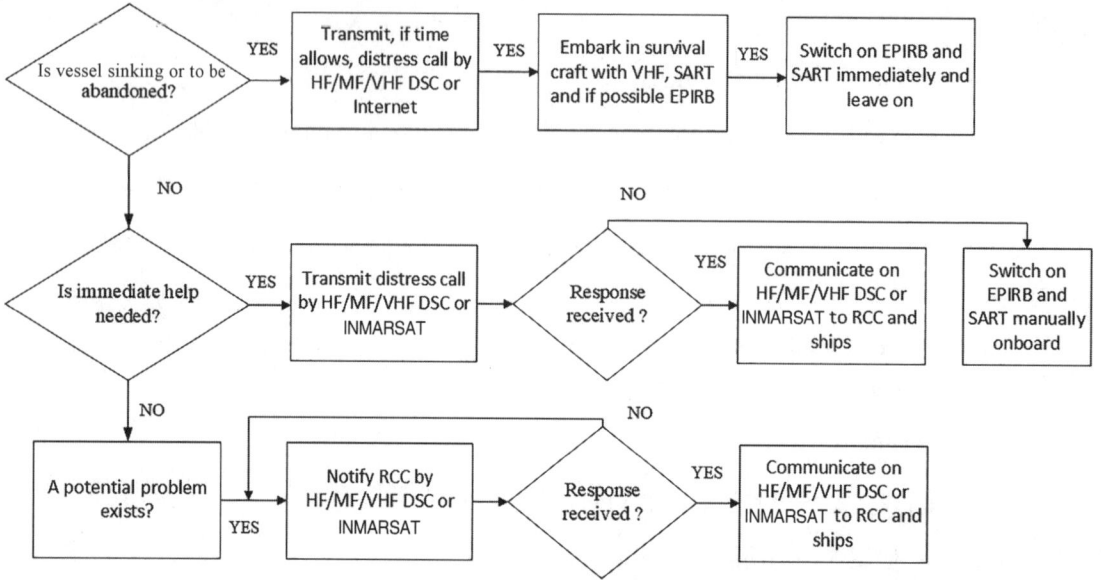

Figure 2.1   GMDSS Operating Guidance for Masters of Ships in Distress

图 2.1   GMDSS 遇险船舶船长操作指南

2.3 Distress Alerting 遇险报警

Distress alerting is defined as the rapid and successful reporting of a distress situation to author-ities that can provide coordinated assistance to the station in distress. A distress alert transmission in-fers that a mobile unit (ship, aircraft or other vehicle) or a person is in distress or imminent danger and requires immediate assistance. In general, distress incidents fall into two main categories:

a.Coastal, in which some or all of the following may be available to assist—ships, aircraft, helicopters and shore-based life-saving facilities; or

b.Oceanic, in which ships and long-range aircraft may be available, although in the more re-mote sea areas only ships may be available.

遇险报警的定义是遇险电台迅速、成功地向能为其提供协调援助的有关机构报告遇险情况。遇险报警意味着移动设备(船舶、飞机或其他交通工具)或人员遇险或面临迫在眉睫的危险,需要立即援助。一般来说,遇险事件分为两大类:

a.在沿海地区遇险。在这种情况下,其中下列部分或者全部可以提供援助:船舶、飞机、直升机和岸上救生设施;或

b.在大洋中间遇险。可能有船舶和远程飞机的援助,但在较偏远的海区可能只有船舶。

In either case, a distress alert may be defined as:

a.In the terrestrial radiocommunication bands, a DSC alert using the distress;

b.In the satellite service: an alert using the distress format for relay through space stations.

无论哪种情况,遇险报警都可定义为:

a.在地面无线电通信频段,使用 DSC 设备以遇险信号报警;

b.在卫星业务中,使用通过空间站转发的遇险格式发出报警。

The distress alert must include the identification of the station in distress and its position. The alert may contain the course and speed of the mobile unit, and the time that this information was recorded, other information, such as the nature of the distress and type of assistance required, or in the case of a person in distress, the applications of the following procedures may need to be adapted to meet anything else that may facilitate rescue, may be included in the alert.

遇险报警必须包括遇险电台的标识及其位置。报警中可包括移动船舶的航向和速度,以及记录这些信息的时间。报警中还可包括其他信息,如遇险的性质和所需援助的类型,或者在人员遇险的情况下,可能需要对以下程序的应用进行调整,以满足可能有助于救援的其他任何条件。

Ship-to-shore distress alerts are used to warn Maritime Rescue Coordination Centers (MRCCs) that a vessel is in distress. This alerting is routed via Land Earth Station (LES) using satellite transmissions from Mobile Earth Station (MES) or Emergency Position Indicating Radio Beacon (EPIRB).

船对岸遇险报警用于向海上搜救协调中心(MRCC)发出船舶遇险的报警。这种报警是通过移动地球站(MES)或紧急无线电示位标(EPIRB)的卫星传输向陆地地球站(LES)发送报警的。

Ship-to-shore DSC distress alerts warn MRCCs of a distress situation, and the terrestrial MF, HF and VHF bands are used for this purpose.

船对岸的 DSC 遇险报警向 MRCC 发出遇险报警,地面 MF、HF 和 VHF 波段均可用于此目的。

Ship-to-ship alerts warn other vessels in the vicinity of the distressed vessel about a distress situation using DSC techniques in the MF and VHF terrestrial bands.

船对船报警使用 MF 和 VHF 地面波段的 DSC 技术向遇险船舶附近的其他船舶发出遇险报警。

Most modern equipment will automatically switch the transmitter/receiver to the correct radio-telephony frequency or channel once the DSC distress alert has been acknowledged. It should be noted that the DSC distress alert will be repeated automatically approximately every 4 min until the acknowledgement is received by the equipment or it is manually switched off.

一旦 DSC 遇险报警得到确认,大多数现代设备都会自动将发射机/接收机切换到正确的无线电话频率或频道。应注意的是,DSC 遇险报警将大约每 4 min 自动重复一次,直到设备收到确认或被手动关闭为止。

2.3.1　Distress Alert by DSC 通过 DSC 发出遇险报警

In order to increase the probability of a DSC distress alert being received, all MF/HF controllers automatically repeat a DSC distress alert either 5 times on a single frequency (single frequency

call attempt) or the operator may initiate up to 6 consecutive DSC distress alerts are spread over 6 DSC distress frequencies (multi-frequency call attempts). During the process of sending a DSC distress using the single frequency call attempt or the multi-frequency call attempts, or a combination of the two, stations should be able to receive acknowledgements continuously on all distress frequencies.

为了增加 DSC 遇险报警被接收的可能性,所有 MF/HF 控制器都会自动在单个频率上重复发送 DSC 遇险报警 5 次(单频呼叫尝试),或者操作员最多可在 6 个 DSC 遇险频率上连续发送 6 次 DSC 遇险报警(多频呼叫尝试)。在使用单频呼叫尝试、多频呼叫尝试或两者结合的方式发送 DSC 遇险报警的过程中,各电台应能在所有遇险频率上连续收到确认。

To avoid call collision and loss of acknowledgements, call attempts will be repeated after a random delay of between 3.5 and 4.5 min, unless stopped by switching off the transceiver, receiving an acknowledgement via DSC or when DSC equipment is rendered unserviceable due to sinking.

为避免呼叫拥挤和确认丢失,呼叫尝试将在随机延迟 3.5~4.5 min 后重复,除非关闭接收机、通过 DSC 收到确认或 DSC 设备因下沉而无法使用。

On VHF DSC only a single DSC distress call is used since there is only one VHF DSC frequency (Channel 70).

由于只有一个 VHF DSC 频率(70 频道),因此 VHF DSC 只能进行单个 DSC 遇险呼叫。

2.3.1.1 Transmission of DSC Distress Alert by Ship Station 船舶电台发送 DSC 遇险报警

A DSC distress alert should as far as possible include the ship's last known position and the time (in UTC) when it was valid. The position and the time may be included automatically by the ship's navigational equipment or may be inserted manually. The DSC distress alert is transmitted as follows:

a.Tune the transmitter to the DSC distress channel.

b.If time permits key in or select on the DSC equipment keyboard:

- The nature of distress;
- The ship's last known position (latitude and longitude);
- The time (in UTC) when the position was valid;
- Type of subsequent distress communication (radiotelephony).

c.Transmit the DSC distress alert in accordance with the DSC equipment manufacturer's instructions.

d.Prepare for the subsequent distress traffic by tuning the radiotelephony transmitter and the receiver to the distress traffic channel in the same band, while waiting for DSC distress acknowledgement.

e.Send the following spoken message on the radiotelephone channel.

DSC 遇险报警应尽可能包括船舶最后的已知位置和有效时间(UTC)。该位置和时间可由船舶导航设备自动输入,也可手动输入。DSC 遇险报警的发送方式如下:

a.将发射机调至 DSC 遇险频道。

b.如果时间允许,在 DSC 设备键盘上键入或选择:

· 遇险性质;

· 船舶最后的已知位置(纬度和经度);

· 位置有效的时间(UTC);

· 随后的遇险通信(无线电话)类型。

c.按照 DSC 设备制造商的说明发送 DSC 遇险报警。

d.在等待 DSC 遇险确认的同时,将无线电话发射机和接收机调谐到同一波段的遇险通信频道,为随后的遇险通信做好准备。

e.在无线电话频道上发送以下口语电文。

Distress Call 遇险呼叫

Distress signal (×3)	MAYDAY MAYDAY MAYDAY
Words "THIS IS"	THIS IS
Name of vessel (×3)	ROSE ROSE ROSE
Call sign or other identification	Call sign PBUB/ MMSI 246227000

Distress Message 遇险电文

Distress signal	MAYDAY
Name of vessel	ROSE
Call sign or other identification	VJEK
MMSI	503123000
Position	POSITION 5 MILES EAST OF GREEN CAPE
Nature of distress	ON FIRE OUT OF CONTROL
Other information	VESSEL IS A GAS TANKER, NOBODY HURT
To signify end of message	OVER

2.3.1.2 Actions on Receipt of a Distress Alert by Ship Station 船舶电台收到遇险报警后的行动

Ships receiving a DSC distress alert from another ship should normally not acknowledge the alert by DSC, since the acknowledgement of a DSC distress alert by use of DSC is normally made

by coast stations only.

收到另一艘船发出 DSC 遇险报警的船舶通常不应通过 DSC 确认报警,因为通常只有海岸电台才会通过 DSC 确认 DSC 遇险报警。

Only if no other station seems to have received the DSC distress alert, and the transmission of the DSC distress alert continues, should the ship acknowledge the DSC distress alert by use of DSC to terminate the call. The ship should then, in addition, inform a coast station or a Coast Earth Station (CES) by any practicable means.

只有在似乎没有其他电台收到 DSC 遇险报警,且 DSC 遇险报警的发射仍在继续的情况下,船舶才应使用 DSC 确认 DSC 遇险报警,以终止呼叫。此外,船舶还应以任何可行的方式通知海岸电台或者海岸地球站(CES)。

In those areas where reliable communications with a coast station is possible ships should delay acknowledgement for a short period to permit coast stations to acknowledge first. Ships may be sailing in areas where reliable communication with a coast station is not practicable. In these circumstances if they receive a distress alert from a ship station which is beyond doubt in their vicinity, they must acknowledge receipt as soon as possible. They must also, if so equipped, inform an RCC of the alert via a coast station or LES.

在那些可能与海岸电台进行可靠通信的地区,船舶应在短时间内延迟确认,以便海岸电台先行确认。船舶可能会在无法与海岸电台进行可靠通信的地区航行,在这种情况下,如果船舶收到了来自其附近船舶电台的遇险报警,则必须尽快确认收到报警。如果有相关设备,他们还必须通过海岸电台或陆地地球站(LES)将报警通知区域搜救协调中心。

If a ship station continues to receive a DSC distress alert on an MF or VHF channel, a DSC acknowledgement should be transmitted to terminate the call only after consulting with an RCC or a coast station and being directed to do so.

如果船舶电台在 MF 或 VHF 频道上继续接收到 DSC 遇险报警,则应在与区域 RCC 或海岸电台协商并得到指示后,发送 DSC 确认以终止呼叫。

Ships receiving an HF distress alert do not need to acknowledge it but should set watch on the RT frequency indicated in the distress alert, they may also set watch on the telex (NBDP) frequency associated with the distress alert frequency. If, however the alert is not acknowledged by a coast station within 3 min, then the receiving ship station must relay the distress alert.

接收到 HF 遇险报警的船舶无须确认报警,但应在遇险报警中指示的无线电话频率上设置值守,也可在与遇险报警频率相关的电传(NBDP)频率上设置值守。但是,如果海岸电台在 3 min内未确认报警,则接收船舶电台必须转发遇险报警。

Ships receiving a DSC distress alert from another ship should also defer the acknowledgement of the distress alert by radiotelephony for a short interval, if the ship is within an area covered by one or more coast stations, in order to give the coast station time to acknowledge the DSC distress alert first.

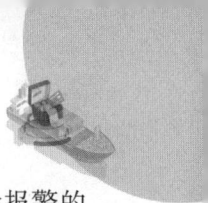

如果船舶位于一个或多个海岸电台覆盖的区域内,则收到另一艘船发出 DSC 遇险报警的船舶也应将通过无线电话确认遇险报警的时间推迟一小段时间,以便让海岸电台有时间先确认 DSC 遇险报警。

A ship receiving a DSC distress alert from another ship shall:

a.Watch for the reception of a distress acknowledgement on the distress channel.

b.Prepare for receiving the subsequent distress communication by tuning the radiotelephony receiver to the distress traffic frequency in the same band in which the DSC distress alert was received.

c.Acknowledge the receipt of the distress alert by transmitting the following by radiotelephony on the distress traffic frequency in the same band in which the DSC distress alert was received:

- MAYDAY;

- The 9-digit MMSI of the ship in distress, repeated 3 times;

- THIS IS;

- The 9-digit MMSI or the call sign or other identification of own ship, repeated 3 times;

- RECEIVED MAYDAY.

收到另一艘船发出的 DSC 遇险报警的船舶应:

a.留意遇险频道是否收到遇险确认。

b.将无线电话接收机调到与收到 DSC 遇险报警相同波段的遇险通信频率,为接收随后的遇险通信做好准备。

c.在收到 DSC 遇险报警的同一波段的遇险交通频率上,通过无线电话发送以下内容,以确认收到遇险报警:

- MAYDAY;

- 遇险船舶的 9 位 MMSI,重复 3 次;

- 这是;

- 本船的 9 位 MMSI 或呼号或本船其他标识,重复 3 次;

- 呼救收到。

The NBDP radiotelex services can also be used:

也可使用 NBDP 无线电传:

- MAYDAY;

- BXXX (Call sign of the distress ship)(遇险船舶的呼号);

- DE (This is);

- BAAA（Acknowledging ship call sign）（确认船舶呼号）；

- RRR MAYDAY.

2.3.1.3　Distress Traffic 遇险通信

The distress traffic is defined as all messages relating to the immediate assistance required by the ship in distress. It also includes search and rescue（SAR）communications and on-scene communications as well as locating signals. All distress traffic should take place as far as possible on the frequencies set aside in band for this purpose.

遇险通信是指与遇险船舶所需的紧急援助有关的所有电文。它还包括搜救(SAR)通信和现场通信以及定位信号。所有遇险通信都应尽可能使用为此目的在波段中预留的频率。

On receipt of a DSC distress acknowledgement, the ship in distress should commence the distress traffic by radiotelephony on the distress traffic frequency as follows：

- MAYDAY；

- THIS IS；

- The 9-digit MMSI, call sign or other identification of the ship in distress；

- The ship's position in latitude and longitude or other references to a known geographical location；

- The nature of distress and assistance wanted；

- Any other information which might facilitate the rescue.

在收到 DSC 遇险确认后,遇险船舶应通过遇险通信频率上的无线电话开始遇险通信,具体做法如下：

- MAYDAY；

- 这是；

- 遇险船舶的 9 位 MMSI、呼号或其他标识；

- 以经纬度或其他已知地理位置为参照的船位；

- 遇险性质和希望得到的援助；

- 任何其他有助于救援的信息。

Distress traffic by NBDP telegraphy should normally be established by the ship in distress and should be in the FEC broadcast mode. The ARQ mode may subsequently be used when it is advantageous to do so.

通常应由遇险船舶建立 NBDP 电报的遇险通信,并应采用 FEC 广播模式,但如果有必要,可随后使用 ARQ 模式。

2.3.1.4 Transmission of a DSC Distress Relay Alert 发送 DSC 遇险转发报警

A ship knowing that another ship is in distress shall transmit a DSC distress relay alert if：

· The ship in distress is not itself able to transmit the distress alert；

· The Master of the ship considers that further help is necessary.

在下列情况下,明知另一船舶遇险的船舶应发送 DSC 遇险转发报警：

· 遇险船舶本身无法发送遇险报警；

· 船长认为有必要提供进一步援助。

The DSC distress relay alert is transmitted as follows：

a.Tune the transmitter to the DSC distress channel；

b.Select the distress relay call format on the DSC equipment；

c.Key in or select on the DSC equipment keyboard：

· The call ALL SHIPS or the 9-digit MMSI of the appropriate coast station；

· The 9-digit MMSI of the ship in distress（if known）；

· The nature of distress；

· The latest position of the ship in distress（if known）；

· The time（in UTC）when the position was valid（if known）；

· Type of subsequent distress communication（radiotelephony）；

· Transmit the DSC distress relay call.

DSC 遇险转发报警的发送方式如下：

a.将发射机调至 DSC 遇险频道；

b.在 DSC 设备上选择遇险转发呼叫格式；

c.在 DSC 设备键盘上键入或选择：

· 所有船舶呼叫或相应海岸电台的 9 位 MMSI；

· 遇险船舶的 9 位 MMSI(如果知道)；

· 遇险性质；

· 遇险船舶的最新位置(如果知道)；

· 位置有效的时间(UTC)(如果知道)；

· 随后的遇险通信(无线电话)类型；

· 发送 DSC 遇险转发呼叫。

Prepare for the subsequent distress traffic by tuning the radiotelephony transmitter and the receiver to the distress traffic channel in the same band, i. e. 2182 kHz on MF and Channel 16 on VHF, while waiting for the DSC distress acknowledgement.

在等待 DSC 遇险确认的同时,将无线电话发射机和接收机调至同一波段的遇险通信频道,即 MF 的 2182 kHz 和 VHF 16 频道,为随后的遇险通信做好准备。

Coast stations, after having received and acknowledged a DSC distress alert, may if necessary, retransmit the information received as a DSC distress relay call, addressed to all ships, all ships in a specific geographical area, a group of ships or a specific ship.

海岸电台在收到并确认 DSC 遇险报警后,必要时可将收到的信息作为 DSC 遇险转发呼叫重新发送给所有船舶、特定地理区域内的所有船舶、一组船舶或特定船舶。

Ships receiving a distress relay call transmitted by a coast station shall not use DSC to acknowledge the call, but should acknowledge the receipt of the call by radiotelephony on the distress traffic channel in the same band in which the relay call was received, i.e. 2182 kHz on MF, Channel 16 on VHF.

收到海岸电台转发的遇险转发呼叫的船舶不应使用 DSC 确认呼叫,而应在收到遇险转发呼叫的同一波段的遇险通信频道(即 MF 2182 kHz,VHF 16 频道)上通过无线电话呼叫确认收到呼叫。

2.4　Distress Alert by INMARSAT INMARSAT 遇险报警

The INMARSAT system provides priority access to satellite communication channels in emergency situations. Each Ship Earth Station (SES) is capable of initiating a "request message" with distress priority. This is automatically recognized and a satellite channel assigned immediately. In the event of all satellite channels being busy with routine communications, one of them will be preempted and allocated to the SES which initiated the distress priority call.

INMARSAT 系统在紧急情况下提供优先使用卫星通信信道。每个船舶地球站(SES)都能发出具有遇险优先等级的"请求电文"。该电文会被自动识别,并立即分配一个卫星信道。在所有卫星信道都被日常通信占用的情况下,其中一个信道将被抢占并分配给发出遇险优先呼叫的 SES。

The English language is used for international maritime distress messages.

国际海上遇险电文使用英语。

The distress priority applies not only with respect to allocation of satellite channels but also to automatic routing of the alert to the appropriate rescue authority. Each Land Earth Station (LES) is required to provide reliable telecommunication connections with an associated MRCC.

遇险优先等级不仅适用于卫星信道的分配,也适用于将报警自动转发给相关救援机构。每个陆地地球站(LES)都需要为相关的 MRCC 提供可靠的通信连接。

2.4.1 Initiation of a Distress Alert 启动遇险报警

Initiation of a distress alert from most SESs is made simple by the provision of one distress button or more distress buttons, or in some cases, the input of a brief keyboard code. This simple operation provides an automatic, direct and assured connection to the MRCC associated with the LES which has been contacted. The need for the operator to enter the telephone or telex number (if used) of the MRCC is thus avoided. The establishment of the connection is completely automatic and should take only a few seconds.

大多数 SES 的遇险报警启动都很简单,只需提供一个或多个遇险按钮,或在某些情况下输入一个简短的键盘代码。这种简单的操作可自动、直接并确保与被联系的 LES 相关的 MRCC 连接。操作员无须输入 MRCC 的电话号码或电传号码,连接可完全自动建立,只需要几秒钟。

2.4.2 INMARSAT-B/F77 Ship Earth Stations INMARSAT-B/F77 船舶地球站

The issue of an INMARSAT-B/F77 distress alert by a ship may be made by using either the telex (INMARSAT-B only) or telephony communication channels.

船舶可通过电传(仅限 INMARSAT-B)或电话通信信道发出 INMARSAT-B/F77 遇险报警。

If a distress alert is issued on a telex channel, the ship's operator should pause until receiving the answerback of the MRCC, then type essential details of the distress including the ship's callsign, name, position, nature of distress and type of assistance required.

如果通过电传信道发出了遇险报警,船舶操作员应暂停,直到收到 MRCC 的回话,然后键入遇险的基本细节,包括船舶的呼号、名称、位置、遇险性质和所需援助类型。

A distress alert issued on a telephony channel will be automatically routed to the LES's associated MRCC. The process usually takes less than 1 min. On being connected to the duty officer at the MRCC, the ship's operator should clearly state details of the distress, using the voice MAYDAY procedures.

通过电话信道发出的遇险报警将自动转发到与 LES 相关的 MRCC。这一过程通常不超过 1 min。在与 MRCC 的值班人员接通电话后,船舶操作员应在电话里根据遇险程序清楚地说明遇险详情。

2.4.3 INMARSAT-C Ship Earth Stations INMARSAT-C 船舶地球站

An INMARSAT-C Ship Earth Station allows an operator to send two different types of distress call—a brief distress alert, or a detailed message with distress priority.

INMARSAT-C 船舶地球站允许操作员发送两种不同类型的遇险呼叫——简短的遇险报警或详细的遇险优先等级电文。

Both types of distress call are automatically routed through a LES to its associated MRCC. Initially, the brief distress alert should be sent and, if time permits, a detailed distress priority message

should follow.

这两种遇险信号都会通过 LES 自动发送到相关的 MRCC。首先应发送简短的遇险报警，如果时间允许,随后应发送详细的遇险优先等级电文。

The brief distress alert only requires the operation of one or two controls and results in a distress message containing the following pre-programmed information being transmitted:

- The identity of the SES;

- The nature of the distress (chosen from a menu or "maritime unspecified" if not chosen); and

- The ship's position, course and speed (from the most recent entry to the equipment).

简短的遇险报警只需操作一到两个控制器,就能发送包含以下预设信息的遇险电文:

- SES 的识别码;

- 遇险的性质(从菜单中选择,如未选择,则为"海事未指定");以及

- 船舶的位置、航向和速度(从设备的最近一次输入开始)。

A distress alert may be initiated even when an SES is engaged in sending or receiving a message. Routine communications will be abandoned immediately and the distress alert transmitted.

即使 SES 正在发送或接收电文,也可发出遇险报警。SES 将立即放弃例行通信,转而发送遇险报警。

If an acknowledgment is not received from both the LES and the MRCC within 5 min, the distress alert should be repeated. Some SES equipment provides its own indication to the operator that the distress alert is being transmitted and of its receipt at the LES.

如果在 5 min 内未收到 LES 和 MRCC 的确认,则应重复发送遇险报警。有些 SES 设备会自行向操作员显示正在发送遇险报警以及 LES 收到报警的情况。

A detailed distress message may be typed into the equipment using the text editor facility in the same way as a normal message. However, distress priority must be selected by the operator before transmission.

详细的遇险电文可以与正常电文一样使用文本编辑器输入设备。不过,在发送之前,操作员必须选择遇险优先等级。

Some SES equipment will send a distress alert to the "preferred LES" (a stored entry in the distress message generator) or, if this entry has not been made, to the LES most recently in communication with the SES.

有些 SES 设备会向 "首选 LES"(遇险电文生成器中的一个存储条目)发送遇险报警,如果没有该条目,则会向最近与 SES 通信的 LES 发送遇险报警。

Other types of SES require the operator to select a LES through which to send a distress alert or

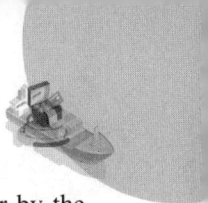

call. This should be the nearest LES to the distressed vessel. If a LES is not specified either by the equipment or the operator, the distress alert will be routed via the Network Coordination Station (NCS) and may result in an unnecessary delay.

其他类型的 SES 要求操作员选择一个 LES,通过它发送遇险报警或呼叫。这应该是距离遇险船舶最近的 LES。如果设备或操作员没有指定 LES,遇险报警将通过网络协调站（NCS）发送,可能会造成不必要的延误。

Usually a shipboard INMARSAT-C terminal will be interfaced with the vessel's satellite navigator to provide an accurate and current position for automatic transmission in a distress alert.

通常,船上的 INMARSAT-C 终端将与船舶的卫星导航仪连接,以便在遇险报警中为自动发送提供准确的当前位置。

On ships where this interfacing is not possible, it is essential that the ship's position, course and speed are entered manually at intervals not exceeding 4 h.

在无法实现这种连接的船舶上,必须以不超过 4 h 的间隔手动输入船位、航向和航速。

The regular entry of position information to INMARSAT-C equipment is also vital to ensure that the integral enhanced group calling (EGC) facility responds to Maritime Safety Information which is relevant to the ship's position.

定期向 INMARSAT-C 设备输入位置信息对于确保集成的增强群呼(EGC)设施响应与船舶位置相关的海上安全信息也至关重要。

All INMARSAT-C equipment is required to be fitted with a device for generating a distress alert from a position remote from which the vessel is normally navigated. This equipment is known as a Remote Distress Initiation Device (RDID), and is usually installed in either the Master's cabin, or a suitable remote location. Upon activation of the RDID, the INMARSAT-C equipment will transmit a pre-programmed distress alert.

所有 INMARSAT-C 设备都必须安装一个装置,用于从船舶正常航行的远处位置发出遇险报警。这种设备称为远程遇险启动装置(RDID),通常安装在船长室或适当的远程位置。一旦启动该装置,INMARSAT-C 设备将发送预先编程的遇险报警。

2.4.4   INMARSAT 505 Emergency Calling (Fleet Broadband) INMARSAT 505 紧急呼叫(船队宽带)

INMARSAT has recently introduced a new non-GMDSS service called 505 Emergency Calling. It is intended as a free-of-charge service for smaller vessels that do not require GMDSS-compatible equipment. It can only be used via Fleet Broadband 500250 and 150 terminals. 505 calls can only be made whilst there is an Internet Protocol (IP) connection, not an Integrated Services Digital Network (ISDN) connection.

INMARSAT 最近推出了一项新的非 GMDSS 业务,名为 505 紧急呼叫。该业务旨在为不需要 GMDSS 兼容设备的小型船舶提供免费业务。它只能通过船队宽带 500、250 和 150 终端

使用。505 呼叫只能在互联网协议(IP)连接状态下进行,而不能在综合业务数字网(ISDN)连接状态下进行。

It is a short code dialling facility that provided direct access to maritime relief. In time of distress a seafarer dials 505 (selected for its similarity to SOS) to contact a MRCC. This service is NOT GMDSS-compliant and GMDSS-compliant equipment should be used in the first instance if fitted.

这是一个短码拨号设施,提供直接的海上救援。遇险时,海员可拨打 505(因其与 SOS 相似)与 MRCC 取得联系。这项业务不符合 GMDSS 标准,如果安装了符合 GMDSS 标准的设备,应首先使用 GMDSS 设备。

2.5　Distress Alert by EPIRB 通过 EPIRB 发出遇险报警

When ship is in distress, the EPIRB shall be activated manually, or released automatically by Hydrostatic Release Unit, in order to send distress alert. 406 MHz beacons transmit a one-half second burst every 50 s. The distress signals are detected by COSPAS-SARSAT polar-orbiting satellites equipped with suitable receivers/processors. The signals are then relayed to a ground receiving station, termed a Local User Terminal (LUT), which processes the signals. An alert is then relayed, together with location data and other information as available through an Mission Control Center (MCC), either to a national RCC, or another MCC or to the appropriate SAR authority to initiate SAR activities.

当船舶遇险时,应手动启动 EPIRB 或通过静水压力释放设备自动释放 EPIRB,以发出遇险报警。406 MHz 信标每 50 s 发射一次时长为半秒的脉冲串。装有接收机/处理器的 COSPAS-SARSAT 极轨道卫星会检测到遇险信号。信号随后被转发到地面接收站,即本地用户终端(LUT),由其对信号进行处理。然后通过任务控制中心(MCC)向国家 RCC 或其他 MCC 或相应的搜救机构发出报警以及位置数据和其他信息,以启动搜救活动。

2.6　On-scene Communications 现场通信

On-scene communications are those between the mobile unit in distress and other mobile units assisting in the distress. They also include communications between mobile units and the unit coordinating SAR operations. On-scene communications could be the responsibility of the on-scene coordinator (OSC). The commander of a rescue unit designated to coordinate SAR operations within a specified search area by the appropriate MRCC to locate and rescue survivors. Until such time as an OSC has been designated, the first rescue unit arriving at the scene of the action should automatically assume the duties and responsibilities of an OSC.

现场通信是指遇险的移动单位与协助救援的其他移动单位之间的通信。它们还包括移动单位与协调搜救行动的单位之间的通信。现场通信可以由现场协调员(OSC)负责。OSC 是由相关的 MRCC 指定的在指定搜索区域内协调搜救行动以寻找和营救幸存者的救援单位的指挥官。在指定现场协调员之前,第一个到达行动现场的救援单位应自动承担现场协调员的职责和责任。

To ensure that all on-scene mobile stations may share relevant information concerning the distress incident, all communications must be transmitted using simplex mode of emission. If NBDP is used, it shall be in the FEC mode.

为确保所有现场移动电台都能共享遇险事件的相关信息,所有通信都必须使用单工发射模式。如果使用 NBDP,则应使用 FEC 模式。

The preferred frequencies for RT on-scene communications are 2182 kHz and Channel 16 VHF, using simplex transmissions so that all on-scene mobiles share the relevant distress information.

无线电话现场通信的首选频率为 2182 kHz 和 VHF 16 频道,使用单工发射,以便所有现场移动电话共享相关的遇险信息。

The radiotelex (NBDP) frequency of 2174.5 kHz may also be used for ship-to-ship on-scene communications, but if telex is selected, then FEC mode must be used.

2174.5 kHz 的无线电传(NBDP)频率也可用于船对船现场通信,但如果选择电传,则必须使用 FEC 模式。

In addition to 2182 kHz and Channel 16 VHF, the following frequencies may be used for on-scene communications between ships and aircraft:

除 2182 kHz 和 VHF 16 频道外,以下频率也可用于船舶和飞机之间的现场通信:

- 3023 kHz;

- 4125 kHz;

- 5680 kHz;

- Channel 6 VHF;

- 123.1 MHz.

Ships can listen only to aircraft using these frequencies.

船舶只能监听使用这些频率的飞机。

The selection or designation of on-scene frequencies is the responsibility of the unit coordinating the SAR operations—that is, the OSC. All participating on-scene mobile units must maintain a continuous aural or teleprinter watch once an on-scene frequency has been established.

现场频率的选择或指定由协调搜救行动的单位(即 OSC)负责。一旦确定了现场频率,所有参与现场行动的移动单位都必须保持持续电话或电传守听。

The OSC shall be responsible for undertaking the following actions:

a.Coordinate operations of all SAR facilities on-scene.

b.Receive the search action plan or rescue plan from the SAR mission coordinator (SMC), or plan the SAR operation, if no plan is otherwise available.

c.Modify the search action or rescue action plan as the situation on-scene dictates, keeping the SMC advised (doing so in consultation with the SMC where practicable).

d.Coordinate on-scene communications.

e.Monitor the performance of other participating facilities.

f.Ensure that operations are conducted safely, paying particular attention to maintaining safe separations among all facilities, both surface and air.

g.Make periodic situation reports (SITREPs) to the SMC, to include, but not be limited to：

·　weather and sea conditions；

·　the results of search to date；

·　any actions are taken；and

·　any future plans or recommendations.

h.Maintain a detailed record of the operations, including on-scene arrival and departure time of SAR facilities；other vessels and aircraft engaged in the operation areas searched；track spacing used；sighting and leads reported；actions taken；results obtained.

i.Advise the SMC to release facilities no longer required.

j.Report the number and names of survivors to the SMC.

k.Provide the SMC with the names and designations of facilities with survivors aboard.

l.Report which survivors are in each facility.

m.Request additional SMC assistance when necessary (for example, medical evacuation of seriously injured survivors).

OSC 应负责采取以下行动：

a.协调现场所有搜救设施的行动。

b.从搜救任务协调员(SMC)处接收搜索行动计划或救援计划,如果没有其他计划,则制订搜救行动计划。

c.根据现场情况修改搜索行动或救援行动计划,并随时告知 SMC(在可行的情况下与 SMC 协商)。

d.协调现场通信。

e.监测其他设施设备。

f.确保行动安全进行,特别注意保持地面和空中所有设施之间的安全隔离。

g.定期向 SMC 提交情况报告(SITREP),包括但不限于：

·　天气和海况；

- 迄今为止的搜索结果；

- 采取的任何行动；以及

- 未来的计划或建议。

h.保留一份详细的行动记录，包括搜救设施到达和离开现场的时间；参与行动的其他船舶和飞机搜索的区域；使用的轨道间距；报告的发现和线索；采取的行动；取得的结果。

i.建议 SMC 取消占用不再需要的设施。

j.向 SMC 报告幸存者的人数和姓名。

k.向 SMC 提供载有幸存者的设施的名称和编号。

l.报告每个设施中有哪些幸存者。

m.必要时请求 SMC 提供额外援助（例如，对重伤幸存者进行医疗后送）。

2.7　Imposing Silence 强制静默

While the MRCC responsible for controlling SAR operations also coordinates the distress traffic relating to the incident, it may appoint another coast station to do this. Controlling stations, the OSC, or the coast station may impose silence on stations that interfere with distress or SAR traffic. Depending on individual circumstances, this may be addressed to all stations or to an individual station. The procedure used is:

a. In radiotelephone, the signal SEELONCE MAYDAY, pronounced as in the French expression "silence, maider";

b.In radiotelex (NBDP) normally using FEC mode, the signal SILENCE MAYDAY.

虽然负责控制搜救行动的 MRCC 也协调与事故有关的遇险通信，但它可以指定另一个海岸电台来做这项工作。控制电台、OSC 或海岸电台可对干扰遇险或搜救通信的移动电台实施静默。根据具体情况，静默可以对所有电台或个别电台实施。使用的程序是：

a.在无线电话中，SEELONCE MAYDAY 信号的发音与法语中的"silence, maider"的发音相同；

b.在通常使用 FEC 模式的无线电传(NBDP)中，信号为 SILENCE MAYDAY。

All stations that are aware of distress traffic, but are not taking part in the communications, are forbidden to transmit on the frequencies being used for distress traffic until they receive a signal indicating that normal working may be resumed.

在收到可以恢复正常工作的信号之前，所有知道有遇险通信但没有参与通信的电台都不得在用于遇险通信的频率上进行信息发送。

A station in the mobile service that is able to continue its normal service while following distress traffic may do so. This is when the distress traffic is well established and provided that the mo-

bile station does not interfere with the distress traffic as previously indicated.

移动电台如果能够在跟踪遇险通信的同时继续提供正常业务,则可以这样做。但前提是遇险通信已经被确定,而且移动电台不会干扰遇险通信(如前所述)。

2.7.1 Resumption of Normal Working 恢复正常工作

When distress traffic has ceased on frequencies that have been used for distress traffic, the MRCC or station controlling SAR operations must initiate a message for transmission on those frequencies indicating that distress traffic has finished.

当用于遇险通信的频率上的遇险通信停止后,MRCC 或控制搜救行动的电台必须在这些频率上发出电文,表明遇险通信已经结束。

In radiotelephone, this message consists of:

- · The distress signal MAYDAY;
- · The call ALL STATIONS, spoken three times;
- · The words THIS IS;
- · The name of the station sending the message, spoken three times;
- · The call sign or other identification of the station sending the message;
- · The time of handing in the message;
- · The MMSI (if the initial alert was sent by DSC), the name and call sign of the mobile station that was in distress;
- · The words SEELONCE FEENEE.

在无线电话中,该电文包括:

- · 遇险信号 MAYDAY;
- · 呼叫 "ALL STATIONS",连说三遍;
- · "这是"字样;
- · 发送电文的电台名称,连说三遍;
- · 发送电文的电台的呼号或其他标识;
- · 提交电文的时间;
- · MMSI(如果最初的报警是通过 DSC 发送的),遇险移动电台的名称和呼号;
- · SEELONCE FEENEE 字样。

For example:

例如:

MAYDAY

ALL STATIONS, ALL STATIONS, ALL STATIONS

THIS IS

CLYDE COASTGUARD, CLYDE COASTGUARD, CLYDE COASTGUARD

MMSI 002320022

1536 UTC

YUCATAN/XCGC MMSI 345862190

SEELONCE FEENEE

When using radiotelex（NBDP）, the message consists of:

· The distress signal MAYDAY;

· The call CQ;

· The word DE;

· The call sign or other identification of the station sending the message;

· The time of handing in the message;

· The name and call sign of the mobile station that was in distress;

· The words SILENCE FINI.

在使用无线电传(NBDP)时,电文内容包括:

· 遇险信号 MAYDAY;

· 呼叫 CQ;

· DE 字样;

· 发送电文的电台的呼号或其他标识;

· 提交电文的时间;

· 遇险移动电台的名称和呼号;

· SILENCE FINI 字样。

For example:

例如:

MAYDAY

CQ

DE OXZ

1536 UTC

YUCATAN/XCGC

SILENCE FINI

2.8 False Alert 误报警

False alerts caused by the inadvertent of incorrect operation of GMDSS equipment can put a significant burden on search and rescue centers. So, search and rescue forces could be delayed in responding to a real distress. Most false alerts are caused as a result of human error. A station transmitting an inadvertent distress alert shall cancel the distress alert using the following procedure. Figure 2.2 shows the correct procedures of false distress alert cancellation.

对 GMDSS 设备操作不当而造成的误报警,会给搜救中心带来沉重负担。搜救机构可能会因误报警而延误对真正的遇险事件做出反应。大多数误报警都是由人为错误造成的。不慎发送遇险报警的电台应按以下程序取消遇险报警。图 2.2 显示了取消遇险误报警的正确程序。

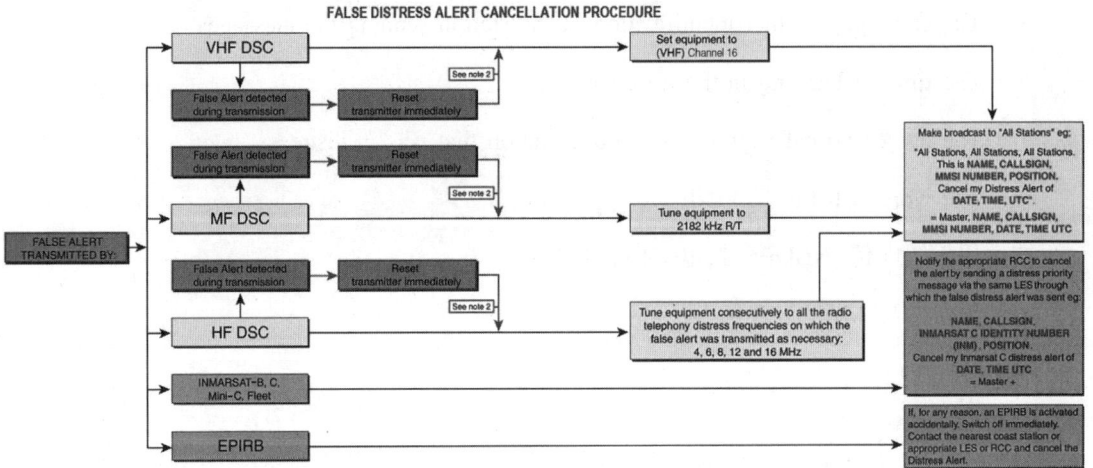

Figure 2.2   Procedure of False Distress Alert Cancellation

图 2.2   取消遇险误报警程序

2.8.1 DSC

VHF

a.Switch off transmitter immediately;

b.Switch equipment on and set to Channel 16; and

c.Make broadcast to "ALL STATIONS" giving the ship's name, call sign and DSC number, and cancel the false distress alert.

This applies when the false alert is detected during transmission.

a.立即关闭发射机;

b.打开设备并设置为 16 频道；以及

c.向"所有电台"广播,告知船名、呼号和 DSC 号码,并取消遇险误报警。

这适用于在发送过程中检测到误报警的情况。

Example：

例如：

ALL STATIONS, ALL STATIONS, ALL STATIONS

This is NAME, CALL SIGN

DSC NUMBER, POSITION

Cancel my distress alert of

DATE, TIME UTC

Master

MF

a. Switch off equipment immediately；

b. Switch equipment on and tune for radiotelephony transmission on 2182 kHz；and

c. Make broadcast to "ALL STATIONS" giving the ship's name, call sign and DSC number, and cancel the false distress alert.

This applies when the false alert is detected during transmission.

a.立即关闭设备；

b.打开设备并调谐,以便在 2182 kHz 上进行无线电话发送；以及

c.向各电台播报船名、呼号和 DSC 号码,并取消错误的遇险报警。

这适用于在发送过程中检测到误报警的情况。

Example：

例如：

ALL STATIONS, ALL STATIONS, ALL STATIONS

This is NAME, CALL SIGN

DSC NUMBER, POSITION

Cancel my distress alert of

DATE, TIME UTC

Master NAME

HF

As for MF, but the alert must be cancelled on all the frequency bands on which it was transmitted. The transmitter should tune consecutively to the radiotelephony distress frequencies in the 4, 6, 8, 12 and 16 MHz bands, as necessary.

与 MF 一样,但必须在发出报警的所有频段上取消报警。发射机应根据需要连续调谐到 4、6、8、12 和 16 MHz 频段的无线电话遇险频率。

2.8.2　INMARSAT-C

Notify the appropriate RCC to cancel the alert by sending a distress priority message via the same CES through which the false distress alert was sent.

由发送误报警的同一海岸地球站发送遇险优先等级电文,通知相关 RCC 取消报警。

Example of message：

电文示例：

NAME, CALL SIGN, IDENTITY NUMBER

POSITION

Cancel my INMARSAT-C distress alert of

DATE, TIME UTC

Master

2.8.3　EPIRB

If for any reason an EPIRB is activated accidentally, the ship should contact the nearest coast station or an appropriate CES or RCC and cancel the distress alert.

如果因任何原因意外启动 EPIRB,船舶应联系最近的海岸电台或适当的 CES 或 RCC,并取消误报警。

Notwithstanding the above, ships may use any means available to them to inform the appropriate authorities that a false distress alert has been transmitted and should be cancelled.

尽管有上述规定,船舶仍可使用任何可用手段通知有关机构已发出误报警,并应取消该报警。

No action will normally be taken against any ship or mariner for reporting and cancelling a false distress alert. However, in view of the serious consequences of false alerts, and the strict ban on their transmission, Governments may prosecute in cases of repeated violations.

通常不会对报告和取消误报警的船舶或海员采取任何行动。然而,鉴于误报警的严重后果以及对其传播的严格禁止,各国政府可能会对屡次违反规定的情况进行起诉。

2.9   Urgency and Safety Communications 紧急和安全通信

Urgency and safety communications relate to：

a.Navigational and meteorological warnings；

b.Ship-to-ship safety of navigation；

c.Ship reporting；

d.Support communications for SAR operations；

e.Medical advice and transports；

f.Other urgent or safety messages.

紧急和安全通信涉及：

a.航行和气象警告；

b.船对船航行安全；

c.船舶报告；

d.为搜救行动提供通信支持；

e.医疗咨询和转运；

f.其他紧急或安全电文。

2.9.1   Urgency Communiction 紧急通信

The urgency signal PAN PAN indicates that a very important message is to follow concerning the safety of a ship, aircraft or other vehicle, or the safety of a person. The urgency signal and the message which follows are sent on a distress frequency. However, in the case of a long message or a medical call in an area of a heavy traffic, or when the message is being repeated, then it is sent on a working frequency after an announcement using the urgency signal on an appropriate distress frequency.

紧急信号 PAN PAN 表示随后将发出有关船舶、飞机或其他交通工具安全或人员安全的重要电文。紧急信号和随后的电文都是在遇险频率上发送的。但是，如果是在通信繁忙区域发送长电文或医疗呼叫，或者电文正在重复发送，则在使用紧急信号在适当的遇险频率上发布公告后，再在工作频率上发送。

Transmission of urgency messages shall be carried out in two steps：

a.Announcement of the urgency message；

b.Transmission of the urgency message.

紧急电文的发送应分两步进行:

a.发布紧急电文;

b.发送紧急电文。

The announcement is carried out by transmission of a DSC urgency call on the DSC distress calling channel (2187. 5 kHz on MF,Channel 70 on VHF).

通过在 DSC 遇险呼叫频道(MF 2187. 5 kHz,VHF 70 频道)上发送 DSC 紧急呼叫发布公告。

The urgency message is transmitted on the distress traffic channel (RT:2182 kHz on MF, Channel 16 on VHF. Telex:2174.5 kHz on MF).

紧急电文通过遇险通信频道发送(无线电话:MF 2182 kHz,VHF 16 频道。电传:MF 2174.5 kHz)。

The DSC urgency call may be addressed to all stations or a specific station. The frequency on which the urgency message will be transmitted shall be included in the DSC urgency call.

DSC 紧急呼叫的对象可以是所有电台,也可以是某个特定电台。DSC 紧急呼叫中应包括发送紧急电文的频率。

The urgency call format using RT is:

PAN PAN (three times);

ALL STATIONS (three times) or NAMED STATION (three times);

THIS IS;

CALL SIGN or IDENTIFICATION (three times).

使用无线电话的紧急呼叫格式为:

PAN PAN(三次);

所有电台(三次)或指定电台(三次);

这是;

呼号或身份识别(三次)。

The format of the message should then be similar to the example shown.

电文格式应与所示示例类似。

PAN PAN, PAN PAN, PAN PAN

ALL STATIONS, ALL STATIONS, ALL STATIONS

THIS IS NONSUCH, NONSUCH, NONSUCH

ONE ZERO MILES WEST OF SKERRIES

LOST PROPELLER DRIFTING WEST SOUTH AT THREE KNOTS

REQUIRE TOW URGENTLY

OVER

When using NBDP, the urgency message is preceded by the urgency signal PAN PAN and the identification of the transmitting station.

使用 NBDP 时,紧急电文前会有紧急信号 PAN PAN 和发射站标识。

PAN PAN

DE BACD

PAN PAN, PAN PAN, PAN PAN

ALL STATIONS, ALL STATIONS, ALL STATIONS

THIS IS NONSUCH, NONSUCH, NONSUCH

PAN PAN

DE BACD

Urgency communication using NBDP should be established in the broadcast FEC mode. ARQ mode may subsequently be used where it is advantageous to do so.

使用 NBDP 的紧急通信应在广播 FEC 模式下建立。在有利的情况下,可随后使用 ARQ 模式。

All messages must be preceded by at least one carriage return (CR), a line feed signal (LF), and the urgency signal (PAN PAN).

所有电文前必须至少有一个回车符(CR)、一个换行信号(LF)和一个紧急信号(PAN PAN)。

Medical Advice 医疗建议

Most coast stations around the world provide a medical advice service.

全球大多数海岸电台都提供医疗咨询业务。

When using RT, the urgency signal PAN PAN (three times) should be used for the call. The message which then follows should be addressed to the nearest coast station, using the published preamble shown in the ITU List of Radiodetermination and Special Service Stations. In many instances, though, it may be preferable to place a telephone call to a doctor.

使用无线电话时,呼叫应使用紧急信号 PAN PAN(三次)。随后的电文应使用国际电信联盟《无线电定位和特别业务电台表》中公布的电报报头,发送给最近的海岸电台。但在许多情况下,最好还是给医生打电话。

Charges 收费

As noted in Recommendation ITU-T D90 (see in the ITU Manual for Use by the Maritime

Mobile and Maritime Mobile-Satellite Services), no charge is raised, against the originating maritime Mobile Earth Station, for communications using the maritime mobile service which relate to medical advice provided to both:

a. They are exchanged directly between mobile stations and land stations shown in the ITU List of Radiodetermination and Special Service Stations as providing such a service;

b. They are addressed in accordance with the conditions published in the above list, or as specified by the satellite service operator.

如 ITU-T D90 号建议(见《国际电信联盟海上移动和海上移动卫星业务使用手册》)所述,对于使用海上移动业务进行的与向双方提供医疗建议有关的通信,不向初始海上移动地球站收取费用:

a. 它们在移动电台和国际电信联盟《无线电定位和特别业务电台表》中显示的提供此类业务的陆地电台之间直接通信;

b. 它们将根据上述清单中公布的条件或卫星业务运营商的规定进行处理。

Any land station and landline charges for medical advice communications will be billed to the appropriate shore authority.

任何陆地电台用于医疗建议通信的陆线费用都将由相应的岸上机构支付。

The medical message should contain:

Ship's name/call sign, and nationality, position;

Next or nearest port with ETA;

Patient's details (i.e., name, age, sex, medical history, etc.);

Patient's symptoms;

Advice required medication carried on board.

医疗电文应包括:

船名/呼号和国籍、位置;

下一个或最近的停靠港口及预计到达时间;

患者资料(如姓名、年龄、性别、病史等);

患者症状;

建议船上携带的所需药品。

Example:

例如:

To contact Shanghai Radio CN, use: MEDICO SHANGHAI RADIO.

联系 Shanghai Radio CN,请使用:MEDICO SHANGHAI RADIO。

When using telex, the prefix MED+ should be used to gain priority.

使用电传时,应使用前缀 MED+ 以获得优先权。

Worldwide, medical advice and assistance can be obtained via coast stations or via INMARSAT CESs. Further information will be found in the ITU List of Radiodetermination and Special Service Stations, and the INMARSAT Communications Handbook.

在世界范围内,可通过海岸电台或 INMARSAT 海岸地球站获得医疗建议和援助。更多信息可参阅国际电信联盟《无线电定位和特别业务电台表》和《INMARSAT 通信手册》。

The IMO International Code of Signals contains medical (3-letter) codes. Use of such codes should be proceeded by the word INTERCO, which indicates that such codes are about to be used.

IMO《国际信号代码》包含医用(3 个字母)代码。在使用此类代码时,应先使用 INTERCO 字样,表示即将使用此类代码。

Medical Transports 医疗转运

Distinctive signals may be used by medical units or transports for communications relating to persons protected in time of war. The term Medical Transports, as defined by the Geneva Conventions and Additional Protocols, 12 August 1949, refers to any means of transportations by land, sea or air used to assist the wounded, the sick and the shipwrecked. Neutral vessels should provide such assistance when requested by one or other of warring parties and are afforded protection from any hostile actions.

医疗单位或运输工具可使用特殊信号进行与战时受保护人员有关的通信。根据 1949 年 8 月 12 日《日内瓦公约》及《附加议定书》的定义,"医疗转运"一词系指用于救助伤病员和遇险者的任何陆、海、空运输工具。中立船舶应根据交战一方或另一方的请求提供此类援助,并应受到保护,使其免受任何敌对行动的影响。

For the purpose of announcing and identifying medical transports which are protected by the Geneva Convention, the radio signal shall consist of the urgency signal as described by Radio Regulations followed immediately by the addition of the single word Medical in NBDP mode and by the addition of the simple word MAY-DEE-CALL, i.e., pronounced as in French "medical", in radiotelephone.

为宣布和识别受《日内瓦公约》保护的医疗转运,无线电信号应包括《无线电规则》所述的紧急信号,紧接着在 NBDP 模式下加上单词 "Medical"(医疗),在无线电话模式下加上简单的单词 "MAY-DEE-CALL"(即法文"医疗"的发音)。

When using radiotelephone, the urgency signal PAN PAN (three times) should be used for the call.

当使用无线电话时,呼叫应使用紧急信号 PAN PAN(三次)。

The radio message, preceded by the urgency signal, must convey the following data relating to the medical transports concerned:

a. Call sign or other means of identification;

b. Position;

c. Number and type of units;

d. Intended route;

e. Estimated time en route and of departure and arrival, as appropriate;

f. Any other information, such as flight altitude, radio frequencies guarded, languages used and secondary surveillance radar modes and codes.

在发出紧急信号之前,无线电电文必须传送与相关医疗转运有关的下列资料:

a. 呼号或其他识别手段;

b. 位置;

c. 单位数量和类型;

d. 计划航线;

e. 途中、出发和抵达的预计时间(视情况而定);

f. 任何其他信息,如飞行高度、守听的无线电频率、使用的语言以及二次监视雷达的模式和代码。

In order to facilitate communications, one or more of the parties to a conflict may designate frequencies to be used for such communications.

为便于通信,冲突一方或多方可指定用于此类通信的频率。

2.9.2 Safety Communication 安全通信

The safety signal SECURITE indicates that an important meteorological or navigational warning is about to follow. The message is sent on a working frequency after an announcement on the distress frequency. Most safety calls and messages are sent upon receipt and at the end of the next silence period. As well as the distress frequencies already mentioned, VHF Channel 13 is used as an intership navigation safety channel. Other channels may be designated by local maritime administrations for inshore warnings.

安全信号 SECURITE 表示即将发出重要的气象或航行警告。该电文在遇险频率上发布后在工作频率上发送。大多数安全呼叫和电文在收到后和下一个静默期结束时发送。除上述遇险频率外,VHF 13 频道也被用作内部航行安全频道。地方海事主管机关可指定其他频道用于近岸报警。

Transmission of safety messages shall be carried out in two steps as urgency messages.

安全电文应作为紧急电文,分两步进行发送。

An example of a safety call format and signal would be illustrated as follows:

SECURITE（three times）；

ALL STATIONS（three times）；

THIS IS（three times）；

CALL SIGN/IDENTIFICATION（three times）；

LISTEN FOR NAVIGATIONAL WARNING ON FREQUENCY/CHANNEL…

安全呼叫的格式和信号的举例如下：

SECURITE(三次)；

所有台(三次)；

这是(三次)；

呼叫信号/身份识别(三次)；

收听……频率/频道上的航行警告。

On a GMDSS ship you should send a "ALL SHIPS" safety call on DSC Channel 70 or 2187.5 kHz indicating the working frequency could be.

在 GMDSS 船舶上，您应通过 DSC 70 频道或 2187.5 kHz 发送"所有船舶"安全呼叫，并指明工作频率。

An example of the safety message sent on the working frequency could be illustrated as follows.

在工作频率上发送安全电文的举例如下。

SECURITE, SECURITE, SECURITE

ALL STATIONS, ALL STATIONS, ALL STATIONS

THIS IS NONSUCH, NONSUCH, NONSUCH

LARGE RED CONTAINER SPOTTED AT 1030 UTC IN POSITION

52.02 NORTH 003.36 WEST

VESSELS KEEP SHARP LOOKOUT AND REPORT

OUT

2.10　SART 搜救雷达应答器

SARTs are the main means in the GMDSS for locating ships in distress or their survival craft, and their carriage on board ships is mandatory. The SART is a small, battery powered, omni-directional radar receiver and transmitter. They may also be incorporated into a float-free satellite EPIRB. The batteries fitted to a SART allow operation in the standby condition for at least 96 h, plus a fur-

ther 8 h whilst being interrogated. IMO Safety of Navigation Circular 197 provides guidance on using X-band radar for the detection of SARTs.

SART 是 GMDSS 确定遇险船舶或其救生艇位置的主要手段,必须在船上安装。SART 是一种小型、电池供电的全方位雷达接收机和发射机。它们也可与自浮式卫星 EPIRB 结合使用。SART 的电池可在待机状态下工作至少 96 h,在接受雷达信号触发时还可再工作 8 h。国际海事组织航行安全通告 197 为使用 X 波段雷达探测 SART 提供了指导。

2.10.1 Purpose and Method of Operation of a SART SART 的使用目的及操作方式

A SART operates in the 9 GHz (3 cm or "X-band") radar frequency band and, on receiving a signal from a ship or aircraft radar, transmits a series of response (homing) signals. The SART can be activated manually or automatically (in some cases) so that it will thereafter respond when interrogated. The method of using and activating SARTs varies over the type available, but instructions are marked on the sides of all SARTs.

SART 在 9 GHz(3 cm 或 "X 波段")雷达频段内工作,在接收到船舶或飞机雷达发出的信号后,会发射一系列响应(寻位)信号。SART 可以手动激活或自动激活(在某些情况下),以便在受到询问时做出响应。使用和激活 SART 的方法因型号而异,但所有 SART 的侧面都标有说明。

These response signals will be seen on the ship or aircraft radar screen as a line of 12 dots (0.64 n mile apart) extending approximately 8 n mile outward from the SART's position along its line of bearing. This unique radar signal is easily recognized and allows the rescue vessel or aircraft to locate the survival craft. As the SART becomes closer, another 12 dots are produced, also 0.64 n mile apart.

这些响应信号会在船舶或飞机的雷达屏幕上显示为一条由 12 个点(相距 0.64 n mile)组成的线,从 SART 的位置沿其方位线向外延伸约 8 n mile。这种独特的雷达信号很容易识别,并使救援船舶或飞机能够确定救生艇的位置。随着 SART 越来越近,会产生另外 12 个点,间距也是 0.64 n mile。

A SART will not respond to 3 GHz (also referred to as 10 cm or "S-band") radar.

SART 不会对 3 GHz (也称为 10 cm 或"S 波段")雷达做出响应。

Indication of Operation and Interrogation 指示操作和询问

On activation the SART will provide a visible and/or audible indication of its correct operation. It will also provide an indication when it is being interrogated by radar signals from a searching ship or aircraft.

一旦启动,SART 就会发出视觉和/或听觉的指示,说明其操作正确。当搜索船或飞机的雷达信号对其进行询问时,它也会发出指示。

2.10.2   **Location Distances 位置距离**

A SART should respond when interrogated by a shipborne X-band radar with a scanner height of 15 m within 8 n mile. A SART should also respond when interrogated by a compatible X-band radar fitted to an aircraft operating at a height of 3000 ft at a distance of at least 30 n mile.

当扫描高度为 15 m 的船载 X 波段雷达在 8 n mile 范围内询问 SART 时,SART 应做出响应。SART 还应在距离至少 30 n mile、高度为 3000 ft 的飞机上接收兼容 X 波段雷达的询问时做出响应。

As height is the key to improving the distance that a SART will respond to a radar signal, survivors should endeavor to mount the SART as high as possible in a lifeboat or life raft, by lashing it to an oar, etc. Some models of SART incorporate mounting poles for this purpose. The vertical polar diagram of the antenna and the characteristics of the device will permit the SART to respond to radars under heavy swell conditions. SART transmission is substantially omni-directional in the horizontal plane.

由于高度是提高 SART 对雷达信号响应距离的关键,幸存者应尽量将 SART 安装在救生艇或救生筏上的高处,如将其绑在船桨上等。有些型号的 SART 还为此配备了安装杆。天线的垂直极化图和设备的特性可使 SART 在大浪条件下对雷达做出响应。SART 在水平面上的发射基本上是全向的。

2.10.3   **Location Errors 定位错误**

When a SART is being interrogated by a search radar, the SART's receiver is sweeping the radar band continuously, and searching for radar signals. Once interrogated (or triggered) by an X-band radar in range, the sweeps become alternately slow and fast. As all marine radars do not operate on exactly the same frequency within the 9 GHz radar band, there may be a small delay in SART response as the SART receiver locks onto the searching radar signal. Once the SART receiver has locked onto the searching radar, there is also a delay as the SART switches from receive to transmit mode, and it continues to sweep.

当搜索雷达询问 SART 时,SART 的接收机会连续扫描雷达波段,搜索雷达信号。一旦被射程内的 X 波段雷达询问(或触发),扫描速度就会时慢时快。由于在 9 GHz 雷达波段内,所有海事雷达的工作频率并不完全相同,因此当 SART 接收机锁定搜索雷达信号时,SART 的响应可能会有少许延迟。一旦 SART 接收机锁定搜索雷达,当 SART 从接收模式切换到发射模式并继续扫描时,也会出现延迟。

When the range closes so that the fast sweep responses are seen, the first dot of the SART response displayed will be no more than 150 m distant from the true location of the SART.

当测距范围缩小到可以看到快速扫描图像时,所显示的 SART 图像的第一个点距离 SART 的真实位置将不超过 150 m。

When the range is such that only the slow sweep responses are seen (range approximately

greater than 1 n mile), the first dot of the SART response displayed will be as much as 0.64 n mile beyond the true position of the SART.

当测距范围仅能看到慢速扫描图像时(测距范围约大于 1 n mile),所显示的 SART 图像的第一个点将超出 SART 真实位置 0.64 n mile。

2.10.4　GMDSS Carriage Requirement GMDSS 的配备要求

The GMDSS regulations require vessels between 300 and 500 GRT to carry one SART (or AIS-SART). Vessels over 500 GRT must carry two. As for the passenger ship, one SAR locating device (i.e. SART or AIS-SART) on each side of the ship capable of being rapidly placed in any survival craft.

GMDSS 规定,总吨位在 300 至 500 的船舶必须携带一个 SART(或 AIS-SART)。500 总吨以上的船舶必须携带两个。至于客船,则需要在船的两侧各安装一个 SAR 定位设备(即 SART 或 AIS-SART),该设备可迅速放置在任何救生艇上。

The SART(s) or AIS-SART(s) must be stowed in locations from where they can be rapidly placed in survival craft. Most GMDSS vessels have SARTs stowed on the bridge, near the bridge wing doors. Alternatively, they may be stowed in survival craft.

SART 或 AIS-SART 必须存放在可以迅速放入救生艇的位置。大多数使用 GMDSS 的船舶都将 SART 安装在靠近侧门的驾驶台上,也可以将其放置在救生艇上。

2.10.5　AIS-SARTs

Since 1 January 2010, AIS-SARTs can be carried in lieu of SARTs on vessels subject to the 1974 SOLAS Convention.The AIS-SART is designed to transmit AIS messages that indicate the position, static and safety information of a unit in distress. An AIS-SART has an integral position source (e.g. a GPS receiver) and accordingly, AIS stations receiving the AIS-SART signal are able to display the range and bearing to the AIS-SART.

自 2010 年 1 月 1 日起,受 1974 年《国际海上人命安全公约》约束的船舶可携带 AIS-SART,以代替 SART。AIS-SART 用于发射 AIS 电文,显示遇险单位的位置、静态和安全信息。AIS-SART 具有完整的位置源(如 GPS 接收机),因此,接收 AIS-SART 信号的 AIS 站能够显示 AIS-SART 的范围和方位。

AIS-SARTs can only be detected by AIS installations. They cannot be interrogated, and transmit autonomously once activated. AIS-SARTs use the Self-organizing Time Division Multiple Access (SOTDMA) protocol in the similar way to a Class A mobile AIS station.

AIS-SART 只能被 AIS 设备探测到。它们不能被询问触发,一旦被激活就会自主发送电文。AIS-SART 使用自组织时分多址(SOTDMA)协议,与 A 级移动 AIS 站类似。

An AIS-SART is designed to be deployed in a similar way to a SART in that it is designed to operate from a survival craft at a height of 1 m above sea level. It may be fitted as an integral part of a survival craft, and can be manually activated or deactivated. Automatic activation may be pro-

vided. It is supplied with a buoyant lanyard of highly visible yellow/orange colour to secure it to the survival craft.

AIS-SART 的部署方式与 SART 类似，都是在海平面以上 1 m 高的救生艇上操作。它可以作为救生艇的一个组成部分安装，可以手动启动或关闭，也可提供自动启动功能。该设备配有一根高度可见的黄色/橙色浮力绳，用于将其固定在救生艇上。

2.10.5.1　Technique Features 技术特点

An AIS-SART, being an AIS transmitter, has a unique identifier (an MMSI), using the format 970 xxyyyy, where xx is the manufacturer ID from 01 to 99 and yyyy is the sequence number assigned by the manufacturer from 0000 to 9999. (The manufacturer ID xx = 00 is reserved for test purposes.) The MMSIs of AIS-SARTs are not recorded by the ITU or rescue authorities, nor are they tied to a particular ship.

作为 AIS 发射机，AIS-SART 有一个唯一的标识符（MMSI），格式为 970 xxyyyy，其中 xx 是制造商 ID，从 01 到 99，yyyy 是制造商分配的序列号，从 0000 到 9999。（保留制造商 ID xx = 00 是为了进行测试。）AIS-SART 的 MMSI 不被国际电联或救援机构记录，也不与特定船舶绑定。

An AIS-SART is to be equipped with a means which is either visual or audible, or both visual and audible, to indicate correct operation locally and be provided with test facilities for all functionalities using specific test information. An indication will be provided to show that the AIS-SART has been activated, is undergoing test and has completed test. There will also be an indication of the position fixing system status when the AIS-SART is activated.

AIS-SART 应配备一种可视或可听或可视可听的设备，以指示当地的正确操作。该设备能使用特定检测数据为所有功能提供检测便利。当 AIS-SART 已经启动、正在测试和已经完成测试时，该设备会发出提示。当 AIS-SART 启动时，该设备还将显示定位系统的状态。

The pre-set broadcast messages of SART TEST or SART ACTIVE should be seen as text adjacent to an AIS-SART target symbol on AIS installations fitted on vessels or shore stations in VHF reception range of the unit in distress, and is to be clearly distinguished from an AIS installation (i.e. a ship, AIS A to N, etc.). In ships fitted with an AIS MKD (Minimum Keyboard and Display), the text only will be seen, together with range and bearing.

在遇险单位 VHF 接收范围内的船舶或岸基站上安装的 AIS 设备上，SART TEST 或 SART ACTIVE 的预设广播电文应作为文本显示在 AIS-SART 目标符号旁，并应与 AIS 设备（即船舶、AIS A 至 N 等）明显区分开来。在安装了 AIS MKD（最小键盘和显示器）的船舶上，只能看到文字以及范围和方位。

Detection range of an AIS-SART 1 m above the sea surface by a Class A mobile AIS station antenna at 15 m above the sea surface over water is at least 5 n mile, but have been found to be 9.5 n mile in tests. Detection ranges are much greater from aircraft, and tests have shown detection of an AIS-SART from a fixed wing aircraft at 115-129 n mile (at 20000 feet), 81-95 n mile (at

10000 ft），60 n mile（at 5000 ft）and 25 n mile（at 1000 ft）.

A 级移动 AIS 站天线在海面以上 15 m 处探测距离海面 1 m 高度的 AIS-SART 的距离至少为 5 n mile，但在测试中发现可达 9.5 n mile。从飞机上探测的距离要大得多，测试表明，从固定翼飞机上探测的 AIS-SART 的距离为 115~129 n mile（20000 ft 高度）、81~95 n mile（10000 ft 高度）、60 n mile（5000 ft 高度）和 25 n mile（1000 ft 高度）。

2.10.5.2 Operations of AIS-SART AIS-SART 的操作

The AIS-SART will have two modes when activated：ACTIVE or TEST. In ACTIVE mode, messages are transmitted in a burst of 8 messages once per minute. The duration of the burst is 14 s（beginning to end）. A burst consists of 8 messages, split between AIS 1 and AIS 2. Only one burst is necessary to be detected from time to time for a rescue vessel to locate the AIS-SART. The multiple messages are designed to maximize detection in a seaway. The position shall be determined every minute.

AIS-SART 启动时有两种模式：激活或测试。在激活模式下，电文以每分钟一次、每次 8 条的频率发送。脉冲持续时间为 14 s（从开始到结束）。一次脉冲由 8 条电文组成，分别由 AIS 1 和 AIS 2 发送。只需检测到一次脉冲，救援船舶就能找到 AIS-SART。多条电文的设计是为了最大限度地在航道上探测。位置应每分钟确定一次。

The AIS-SART will start transmitting within 1 min after activation. If the position is unknown, a default position will be used（+91；+181）. If time is not established, operation will commence unsynchronized but shall begin synchronized transmission with correct position within 15 min.

AIS-SART 将在激活后 1 min 内开始发送电文。如果位置未知，将使用默认位置（+91；+181）。如果时间未确定，则将以非同步方式开始运行，但将在 15 min 内以正确位置开始同步发射。

If the AIS-SART cannot obtain time and position within 15 min, the AIS-SART shall attempt to obtain one for at least 30 min in the first hour and at least 5 min in each subsequent hour.

如果 AIS-SART 无法在 15 min 内获得时间和位置，AIS-SART 应尝试在第一小时内至少 30 min 获得时间和位置，并在其后每小时内至少 5 min 获得时间和位置。

Message 1（Position Report）is transmitted with the Navigational Status set to 14（SART ACTIVE）.

发送电文 1（位置报告）时，导航状态设置为 14（SART ACTIVE）。

Message 14（Broadcast safety related message）is transmitted with the text SART ACTIVE.

电文 14（广播安全相关电文）的发送文字为"SART ACTIVE"。

Message 14 is transmitted every 4 min, and replaces one of the position reports on both channels. So, in a burst of 8 messages, the first 4 messages will be position reports, then 2 messages of SART ACTIVE, then 2 messages of position reports. This sequence is then repeated.

电文 14 每 4 min 发送一次，并取代两个频道上的其中一个位置报告。因此，在 8 条电文中,前 4 条电文是位置报告,然后是 2 条 SART ACTIVE 电文,接着是 2 条位置报告电文。然后以这一顺序重复。

If position and time synchronization is lost, the AIS-SART continues to transmit with the last known position and indicates that the position system is inoperative.

如果位置和时间同步丢失,AIS-SART 将继续发送最后的已知位置,并显示定位系统无法工作。

In TEST mode, the AIS-SART will broadcast Message 14 with the text SART TEST. The operation can be summarized in sequence as below:

· In TEST mode, there shall be only one burst of 8 messages, 4 on each channel.

· The first and last messages of the sequence will be Message 14 with the text SART TEST.

· The remaining messages will be Message 1 with Navigational Status set to 15 (undefined).

· The test messages shall be transmitted in one burst after position, SOG (speed over ground), COG (course over ground) and time are available.

· If the AIS-SART does not acquire position, SOG, COG and time within 15 min it will transmit anyway, but with appropriate default values (i.e. lat = 91°, long = 181°, COG and SOG = unavailable, time = position system inoperative).

· After the test transmission burst has completed, the test facility will reset automatically.

在测试模式下,AIS-SART 将广播电文 14,内容为 SART TEST。操作顺序可概括如下:

· 在测试模式下,只能有一次 8 条电文的脉冲,每个频道 4 条。

· 该序列的第一条和最后一条电文将是电文 14,文字为 SART TEST。

· 其余电文为导航状态设置为 15(未定义)的电文 1。

· 测试电文应在获得位置、SOG(对地速度)、COG(对地航向)和时间后一次性发送。

· 如果 AIS-SART 在 15 min 内未获取位置、SOG、COG 和时间,它仍将发送,但会使用适当的默认值(即纬度 = 91°,经度 = 181°,COG 和 SOG = 不可用,时间 = 位置系统无法使用)。

· 测试发射结束后,测试设备将自动复位。

2.10.5.3 AIS-SART Carriage Requirements AIS-SART 的配备要求

GMDSS carriage requirement for AIS-SARTs are the same as for SARTs, in that they can be used in lieu of (radar) SARTs.

GMDSS 对 AIS-SART 的配备要求与对 SART 的要求相同,即可以用 AIS-SART 代替(雷达)SART。

The environmental and basic requirements are rugged and similar to a SART. It is to be water-tight to a depth of 10 m for 5 min, float (not necessarily in an operating position), survive a drop into water from 20 m, not be unduly affected by sea water or oil and be of a highly visible yellow/orange colour, etc.

AIS-SART 对环境和基本要求都很苛刻,与 SART 类似。它必须在 10 m 深的水下保持 5 min 不进水,能够漂浮(不一定处于工作位置),从 20 m 高处掉入水中后仍能使用,不会受到海水或油类的影响,以及具有高度可见的黄色/橙色等。

Nominal radiated transmit power of an AIS-SART shall be 1 W, and each transmission shall alternate between the frequencies of AIS 1 and AIS 2.

AIS-SART 的标称辐射发射功率应为 1 W,每次发射应在 AIS 1 和 AIS 2 频率之间交替进行。

The AIS-SART should have sufficient battery capacity to operate for 96 h (−20 ℃ to + 55 ℃).

AIS-SART 应有足够的电池容量,可工作 96 h(−20 ℃ 至 +55 ℃)。

The unit will be having a durable label with brief operating and test instructions, expiry date (battery replacement date) for the primary (i.e. non-rechargeable) battery used, and the unique identifier (MMSI).

设备将有一个耐用标签,上面有简短的操作和测试说明、所用主电池(即非充电电池)的有效期(电池更换日期)和海上移动业务识别码(MMSI)。

AIS-SARTs should be done sparingly, in order to prolong battery life, avoid mis-activation. If testing is required in port, the port authorities should be informed prior to activation, who can also confirm whether the testing is successful. The AIS-SART should be physically examined at least once per month with a view to ensure there is no obvious physical damage, battery expiry date and the support cradle is intact.

AIS-SART 应尽量少用,以延长电池寿命,避免误激活。如果需要在港口进行测试,应在启动前通知港口机构,他们也可以确认测试是否成功。应至少每月对 AIS-SART 进行一次外观检查,以确保没有明显的物理损坏、电池未过期和支座完好无损。

Satellite Communication Services

卫星通信业务

Chapter 3

3.1 General Information of INMARSAT INMARSAT 一般信息

INMARSAT（International Maritime Satellite Organization）is a partnership of member countries. These countries cooperate to provide global mobile communications, via geostationary satellites, to and from ships, portable/transportable terminals, land-based vehicles and aircraft.

INMARSAT(国际海事卫星组织)是一个由成员国组成的合作伙伴组织。这些国家相互合作,通过地球同步静止卫星向船舶、便携式/可移动终端、陆基车辆和飞机提供全球移动通信。

INMARSAT's primary satellite constellation consists of four satellites in geostationary orbit, covering the surface of the earth up to latitude 76° North/South, comprising IMO Sea Area A3. The INMARSAT system provides voice, E-mail, telex, data and facsimile services to shipping. The system also incorporates distress and safety communications services.

INMARSAT 的主要卫星星座由地球静止轨道上的四颗卫星组成,覆盖南纬 76°至北纬 76° 以内的地球表面,包括 IMO A3 海区。INMARSAT 系统为航运提供语音、电子邮件、电传、数据 和传真业务。该系统还包括遇险和安全通信业务。

The INMARSAT communications structure comprises three major components:

· The Space Segment;

· The Ground Segment;

· The Ship Earth Stations.

INMARSAT 的通信结构由三个主要部分组成：

- 空间段；

- 地面段；

- 船舶地球站。

3.1.1　Space Segment 空间段

The Space Segment is provided by INMARSAT, and consists of four geostationary communications satellites, with backup satellites in orbit ready to be used if necessary.

空间段由 INMARSAT 提供，由四颗地球静止通信卫星组成，后备卫星在轨道上，必要时可随时使用。

Geostationary communications satellites are launched into the geostationary orbit（GSO），which is a circular orbit 35700 km above the equator and lying in the plane of the equator. Satellites in the GSO earth at exactly the same rate as the earth rotates about its axis and therefore appear to be stationary above a fixed point on the earth's equator, thus eliminating the need to track the satellite from fixed earth stations.

地球静止通信卫星被发射到地球静止轨道(GSO)上，这是一个在赤道上方 35700 km、位于赤道平面上的圆形轨道。地球静止轨道上的卫星绕地球运行的速度与地球绕地轴旋转的速度完全相同，因此看起来就像静止在地球赤道上的一个固定点上方，从而无须从固定的地球站跟踪卫星。

Solar panels provide communications satellites with their electrical power requirements and the gas motors provide the means to perform minor positional corrections in orbit.

太阳能电池板为通信卫星提供所需的电力，发动机则可以使卫星在轨道上进行微小位置校正。

The INMARSAT satellites are controlled from the Satellite Control Center（SCC）based in the INMARSAT headquarters in London, United Kingdom.

INMARSAT 的卫星由设在英国伦敦 INMARSAT 总部的卫星控制中心(SCC)控制。

The satellites mainly used are INMARSAT-4（I-4）satellites, which were launched in 2005 and 2008. The I-4 satellites have set a new benchmark for mobile satellite communications in terms of their power, capacity and flexibility. One I-4 satellite is sixty times more powerful than an INMARSAT-3 satellite. The three in orbit I-4 satellites deliver broadband on a global basis except for the extreme polar regions. Each I-4 satellite generates hundreds of high-power spot beams, which can be re-configured in real-time so that network capacity is available in areas of high service demand.

目前主要使用的卫星是 2005 年和 2008 年发射的 INMARSAT-4（I-4）卫星。I-4 卫星在功率、容量和灵活性方面为移动卫星通信设定了新的基准。一颗 I-4 卫星的功率是 INMARSAT-3 卫星的 60 倍多。除极区外，三颗在轨 I-4 卫星可在全球范围内提供宽带业务。每颗 I-4 卫星可

产生数百个高功率点波束,这些点波束可实时重新配置,以便在业务需求高的地区提供网络容量。

I-4 satellite traffic is mostly carried as Internet Protocol (IP) packet-switched data. This extends our network's ability to provide enhanced digital mobile communications. It also supports traditional circuit-switched services, such as voice and ISDN, supporting legacy back-office systems, while providing a clear migration path to IP.

I-4 卫星通信主要以互联网协议(IP)分组交换数据的形式传输。这扩展了我们网络提供增强型数字移动通信的能力。它还支持传统的电路交换业务,如语音和 ISDN,支持传统的后台系统,同时为向 IP 转移提供了明确的途径。

Managed by Satellite Control and Network Operations centers in London, I-4 satellite system is linked to the internet and the world's terrestrial telephone networks via three INMARSAT-owned Satellite Access Stations (SAS) in Italy, the Netherlands and Hawaii. INMARSAT has also entered into agreement with the European Space Agency (ESA) to become the commercial operator of a new satellite called Alphasat. The satellite is part of an ESA initiative to develop a new spacecraft platform capable of carrying a large communications payload. Table 3.1 shows the operational status of INMARSAT systems.

I-4 卫星系统由位于伦敦的卫星控制和网络运营中心管理,通过位于意大利、荷兰和夏威夷的三个 INMARSAT 所属卫星接入站（SAS）与互联网和世界地面电话网络连接。INMARSAT 还与欧洲航天局(ESA)达成协议,成为名为"阿尔法"的新卫星的商业运营商。这颗卫星是欧洲航天局开发的能够携带大型通信有效载荷的新航天器平台计划的一部分。表 3.1 显示了 IN-MARSAT 系统的运行状况。

Table 3.1   The Operational Status of INMARSAT Systems

表 3.1   INMARSAT 系统的运行状况

Satellite 卫星	Coverage 覆盖范围	Longitude 经度	Launch year 发射年份	Services 业务
I-3 F1	IOR	64.5° E	1996	Existing and evolved services only 仅限现有业务和发展中业务
I-3 F2	AOR-E	15.5° W	1996	Existing and evolved services only 仅限现有业务和发展中业务
I-3 F3	POR	178° E	1996	Existing and evolved services only 仅限现有业务和发展中业务
I-3 F4	AOR-W	54° W	1997	Existing and evolved services only 仅限现有业务和发展中业务
I-3 F5	I-3 Europe, Middle-East, Africa I-3 欧洲、中东、非洲	24.6° E	1998	Various leases 各种租赁
I-4 F1	I-4 Asia-Pacific I-4 亚太地区	143.5° E	2005	BGAN family, SPS and lease services BGAN 系列、SPS 和租赁业务

Continued　续表

Satellite 卫星	Coverage 覆盖范围	Longitude 经度	Launch year 发射年份	Services 业务
I-4 F2	I-4 Middle-East, Asia I-4 中东、亚洲	64.4° E	2005	BGAN family, SPS and lease services, Fleet Broadband, Swift Broadband Transferred from 25° east to 63° east in mid-2015 BGAN 系列、SPS 和租赁业务、船队宽带、海上宽带 2015 年年中从东经 25° 转至东经 63°
I-4 F3	I-4 Americas I-4 美洲	98° W	2008	BGAN family and lease services BGAN 系列和租赁业务
I-4A F4 （Alphasat） I-4A F4 （阿尔法卫星）	I-4 Europe, Middle-East, Africa I-4 欧洲、中东、非洲	24.8° E	2013	BGAN family, SPS and lease services BGAN 系列、SPS 和租赁业务
I-5 F1 （GX-1）	I-5 Europe, Middle East, Africa I-5 欧洲、中东、非洲	62.6° E	2013	Ka-Band global data services, Global Xpress Ka 波段全球数据业务,Global Xpress
I-5 F2 （GX-2）	I-5 Americas I-5 美洲	55° W	2015	Ka-Band global data services, Global Xpress Ka 波段全球数据业务,Global Xpress
I-5 F3 （GX-3）	I-5 Pacific, Asia, West Americas I-5 太平洋、亚洲、西美洲	179.6° E	2015	Ka-Band global data services, Global Xpress Ka 波段全球数据业务,Global Xpress
I-5 F4 （GX-4）	I-5 Europe in-orbit spare I-5 欧洲在轨备用	56.5° E	2017	Ka-Band global data services, Global Xpress Ka 波段全球数据业务,Global Xpress
I-5 F5 （GX-5）	First of additional Global Xpress satellites 第一颗新增的 Global Xpress 卫星	11° E	2019	Ka-Band global data services, first Global Xpress satellite after the 4 first generation satellites Ka 波段全球数据业务,继四颗第一代卫星之后的首颗 Global Xpress 卫星

3.1.2　Ocean Regions 海洋区域

The coverage area of each satellite is defined as the area on the earth's surface within which a mobile or fixed antenna can obtain reliable line-of-sight communications with the satellite. Each INMARSAT satellite is engineered to provide complete coverage of the visible face of the earth. The line-of-sight condition is not, however, satisfied over the polar regions, and communications start to become unreliable for locations above 76° North or South.

每颗卫星的覆盖范围是指移动或固定天线能够与卫星进行可靠视距通信的地球表面区域。每一颗 INMARSAT 卫星的设计都是为了提供对地球可见表面的完整覆盖。然而,在极区无法与通信卫星进行视距通信,在北纬 76°或南纬 76°以上的区域,通信变得异常困难。

The four INMARSAT satellites, corresponding to the four Oceans Regions, provide overlapping coverage and are positioned thus.

INMARSAT 的四颗卫星与四大洋区相对应,提供重叠的覆盖范围和定位。

3.1.3 **Ground Segment 地面段**

The ground segment comprises a network of Land Earth Stations (LESs) which are operated by Land Earth Station operators, Network Coordination Stations (NCSs), and a Network Operation Center (NOC).

地面段包括一个由陆地地球站运营商运营的陆地地球站(LES)网络、网络协调站(NCS)和一个网络运行中心(NOC)。

Each LES operator provides a link between the satellite network and the international telecommunication network. An LES is capable of handling many calls to and from MESs simultaneously, over the different INMARSAT networks. LESs are owned by telecommunications operators which act as LES operators and provide a wide range of communications services to the MES user. At present, there are 52 INMARSAT-B/F and 32 INMARSAT-C LESs located at various sites worldwide. These figures include also virtual LESs (hosted services) and illustrate the total number of points of access to the INMARSAT network. Many LES operators now offer service in all four ocean regions, through a global sharing agreement with other LES operators in ocean regions which cannot be seen from their own location.

每个 LES 运营商提供卫星网络和国际电信网络之间的连接。一个 LES 能够通过不同的 INMARSAT 网络同时处理多个与 MES 之间的呼叫。LES 由电信运营商拥有,这些电信运营商作为 LES 运营商,为 MES 用户提供广泛的通信业务。目前,共有 52 个 INMARSAT-B/F 和 32 个 INMARSAT-C LES 分布在世界各地。这些数字还包括虚拟 LES(托管业务),并说明了 INMARSAT 网络接入点的总数。许多 LES 经营者现在通过与其他 LES 经营者签订全球共享协议,在所有四大洋区提供业务,因为这些 LES 所处位置无法通过所在洋区卫星覆盖这些洋区。

For each INMARSAT system and ocean region there is a NCS which monitors and controls all communications. Each NCS communicates with the LES operators in its ocean region, the other NCSs and the NOC located at INMARSAT's London headquarters, making it possible to transfer operational information throughout the system.

INMARSAT 的每个系统和每个洋区都有一个 NCS,负责监控和控制所有通信。每个 NCS 与所在洋区的 LES 运营商、其他 NCS 和设在 INMARSAT 伦敦总部的 NOC 进行通信,从而使整个系统的运行信息传输成为可能。

The NCSs are involved in setting up calls between an MES and a LES operator.

NCS 负责在 MES 和 LES 运营者之间建立呼叫。

Figure 3.1 illustrates in general terms how the NCS responds to a request from an MES for a communications channel, by assigning a channel to which both the MES and LES operator must tune for the call to proceed.

图 3.1 概括说明了 NCS 如何响应 MES 对通信信道的请求，即分配一个信道，MES 和 LES 运营商必须调谐到该信道才能进行呼叫。

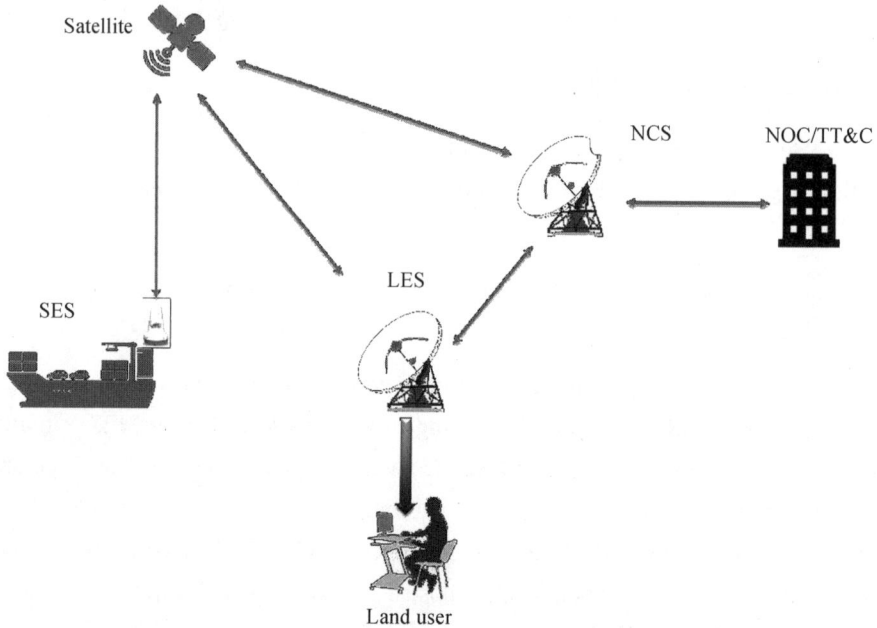

Figure 3.1　The basic system structure of INMARSAT
图 3.1　INMARSAT 的基本系统结构

In order to call a Ship Earth Station（SES）in one of the four ocean regions, the following telex and telephone access codes, corresponding to the country codes in the public telex and telephone networks, should be used as shown in Table 3.2.

如表 3.2 所示，要呼叫四大洋区之一的船舶地球站（SES），应使用下列电传和电话接入代码，这些代码与公共电传和电话网络中的国家代码相对应。

Table 3.2　The Access Country Code of INMARSAT Services
表 3.2　INMARSAT 业务的接入国家代码

	AOR-E	POR	IOR	AORW
Telephone	871	872	873	874
Telex	581	582	583	584
Data	1111	1112	1113	1114

The country codes 871, 872, 873 and 874 phased out on 31 December 2008.

国家代码 871、872、873 和 874 已经于 2008 年 12 月 31 日停止使用。

The permanent telephone country code for calling INMARSAT destinations is：870 SNAC (Single Network Access Code).

呼叫 INMARSAT 目的地的永久性电话国家代码为：870 SNAC(单一网络访问代码)。

The 870 number is an automatic locator; it is not necessary to know to which satellite the destination INMARSAT terminal is logged in. SNAC is now usable by all INMARSAT services.

870 号码是一个自动定位器；无须知道目的地 INMARSAT 终端登录的是哪颗卫星。现在 SNAC 可用于所有 INMARSAT 业务。

3.1.4   Ship Earth Station 船舶地球站

An SES is a device installed on a ship (or a fixed installation in a maritime environment) to enable the user to communicate to and from shore-based subscribers, via a selected satellite and CES.

SES 是一种安装在船上的设备(或在海洋环境中的固定设备)，使用户能够通过选定的卫星和 CES 与岸基用户进行通信。

There is a range of different GMDSS shipboard satellite terminal equipment available, each having its own particular features：

- · INMARSAT-B (was decommissioned in December 2016);
- · INMARSAT-C (including Mini-C);
- · INMARSAT-Fleet 77 (abbreviated as F77);
- · Fleet Safety (Fleet One).

有一系列不同的 GMDSS 船载卫星终端设备可供选择，每种设备都有自己的特点：

- · INMARSAT-B(已于 2016 年 12 月退役);
- · INMARSAT-C(包括 Mini-C);
- · INMARSAT-F77(简称 F77);
- · 船队安全网(Fleet One).

3.1.5   INMARSAT Priority INMARSAT 优先权

There are four levels of GMDSS priority within the INMARSAT system：

- · Level 0 Routine priority;
- · Level 1 Safety priority;
- · Level 2 Urgency priority;

· Level 3 Distress priority.

INMARSAT 系统内的 GMDSS 优先级分为四级：

· 0 级常规；

· 1 级安全；

· 2 级紧急；

· 3 级遇险。

These priority levels are used particularly within the F77 service to comply with IMO GMDSS rules regarding distress, urgency and safety.

这些优先级专用于 F77 业务，以遵守 IMO GMDSS 有关遇险、紧急和安全的规则。

Level 3 has the highest priority and is reserved for distress. Pressing and holding the distress button for 5 s selects Level 3. A Level 3 call will pre-empt all other communications in both ship-to-shore and shore-to-ship directions, hence guaranteeing a connection.

3 级具有最高优先级，专门用于遇险。按住遇险按钮 5 s 可选择 3 级。3 级呼叫将优先于船对岸和岸对船方向上的所有其他通信，从而保证连接。

A Level 2 call will pre-empt safety and routine calls.

2 级呼叫优先于安全和常规通信。

A Level 1 call will pre-empt routine communications.

1 级呼叫优先于常规通信。

F77 data services (ISDN and MPDS) are recognized as routine priority and are liable for pre-emption if voice call using a higher priority is initiated. If the F77 is currently being used in either of the data modes, MPDS or ISDN, and a telephone call using a higher priority than routine, is either initiated by an operator on board the vessel or by the land users, the F77 terminal will connect the incoming call automatically.

F77 数据业务(ISDN 和 MPDS)被视为常规优先级，如果更高优先级的语音呼叫被启动，则可优先使用。如果 F77 目前正在使用 MPDS 或 ISDN 中的一种数据模式，而船上的操作员或陆地用户发起了优先级高于常规优先级的电话呼叫，则 F77 终端将自动接通来电。

3.1.6 Special Access Codes（SACs）特别接入码

Table 3.3 shows 2-digit codes (SACs) designated for P1/P2 calls, as recommended by INMARSAT Safety services.

表 3.3 列出了根据 INMARSAT 安全业务部门的建议为 P1/P2 呼叫指定的两位数代码（SAC）。

Table 3.3　2-Digit Codes Used in INMARSAT

表 3.3　INMARSAT 使用的两位数代码

2-digit code 两位数代码	Service 业务	Remarks 备注
00	Automatic 自动	Use this code to make automatic telex calls using the international telex country codes 使用此代码可使用国际电传国家代码拨打自动电传电话
11	International operator 国际运营商	Use this code to obtain information from the international operator about the country where the service provider is located 使用此代码可从国际运营商处获取业务提供商所在国家的信息
12	International information 国际信息	Use this code to obtain information about a subscriber in a country other than that where the service provider is located 使用此代码可获取业务提供商所在国以外国家的用户信息
13	National operator 国内运营商	Use this code to obtain assistance to connect to a subscriber in a country where the service provider is. In any country which does not have an international operator, use this code instead of Code 11 使用此代码可获得帮助,以连接业务提供商所在国家的用户。在任何没有国际运营商的国家,请使用此代码代替代码 11
14	National information 国内信息	Use this code to obtain information about subscribers in the country where the service provider is located 使用此代码可获取业务提供商所在国家的用户信息
15	Radio-telegram service 无线电报业务	This code will connect the caller to the radio-telegram service position for the transmission of radio-telegrams originated via telex 此代码将把呼叫方连接到无线电报业务位置,以便通过电传传送无线电报
17	Telephone call booking 电话预订	This code may be used via some LES operators to book telephone calls 此代码可通过某些 LES 运营商预订电话时使用
21	Store-and-forward (international) 存储转发(国际)	This code is used to gain access to a Store-and-Forward Unit (SFU) for international calls 此代码用于接入国际呼叫的存储转发单元(SFU)
22	Store-and-forward (national) 存储转发(国内)	This code is used to gain access to a Store-and-Forward Unit (SFU) for national calls 此代码用于接入国内呼叫的存储转发单元(SFU)
24	Telex letter service 电传信函业务	This code is used for directly transmitting a message originated from an MES to a selected telegraph office for delivery by mail or other appropriate means (INMARSAT-C only) 此代码用于直接传输从 MES 发送到选定的电报局的原始信息,以便通过邮件或其他适当方式投递(仅限 INMARSAT-C)

Continued 续表

2-digit code 两位数代码	Service 业务	Remarks 备注
31	Maritime enquiries 海事查询	This code may be used for special enquiries such as ship location, authorisation, etc. 此代码可用于特殊查询,如船舶位置、授权等
32	Medical advice 医疗建议	Use this code to obtain medical advice. Some LES operators have direct connections with local hospitals for use with this code 使用此代码可获得医疗建议。一些 LES 运营商与当地医院有直接联系,可使用此代码
38	Medical assistance 医疗援助	This code should be used if the condition of an ill or injured person on board the vessel requires urgent evacuation ashore or the services of a doctor board the vessel. This code will ensure that the call is routed to the appropriate agency or authority ashore to deal with the situation 如果船上的病人或伤员需要紧急撤离到岸上或需要医生上船服务,则应使用此代码。此代码将确保呼叫被转接到岸上的适当机构或部门,以处理有关情况
39	Maritime assistance 海事援助	This code should be used to obtain maritime assistance if the vessel requires assistance or a tow or has encountered oil pollution etc. 如果船舶需要援助或拖带,或遇到油污等情况,应使用此代码获得海事援助
41	Meteorological reports 气象报告	This code should be used by weather-observing vessels to send their observations. In most cases where this service is free of charge to the vessel, the national weather authority paying the relevant charges 气象观测船舶应使用此代码发送观测数据。在大多数情况下,这项业务对船舶是免费的,由国家气象机构支付相关费用
42	Navigational hazards and warnings 航行危险和警告	This code provides a connection to a navigational office for transmission of information from the vessel about any hazards which could endanger the safety of navigation (e.g. wrecks, derelicts, floating obstructions, defective radio beacons or light vessels, icebergs, floating mines etc.) 此代码提供了与航道管理部门的连接,以便从船上传输任何可能危及航行安全的危险信息(如沉船、废弃物、漂浮障碍物、有缺陷的无线电信标或照明船、冰山、漂浮水雷等)
43	Ship position reports 船位报告	This code provides a connection to an appropriate national or international ship reporting center collecting ship movement information for search and rescue (or other) purposes e.g. AMVER or AUSREP etc. 此代码提供与适当的国家或国际船舶报告中心(如 AMVER 或 AUSREP 等)的连接,这些中心收集用于搜救(或其他)目的的船舶移动信息,如 AMVER 或 AUSREP 等
51	Meteorological forecasts 气象预报	This code is used for the retrieval of meteorological forecasts 此代码用于检索气象预报

Continued   续表

2-digit code 两位数代码	Service 业务	Remarks 备注
52	Navigational warnings 航行警告	This code is used for the retrieval of navigational warnings 此代码用于检索航行警告
6(x)	Administration specialised use 行政专用	For specialised use by administrations. Often used for leased lines, etc. The "x" digit following the 6 is allocated on a national basis and is not usually given to the same service or leased line for more than one LES operators 供行政部门专门使用。通常用于专线等。6 后面的用"x"代表的数字按国家分配,通常不会分配给多个运营商的同一业务或专线
70	Databases 数据库	This code is normally used by a LES operators to allow automatic access to its information retrieval database 此代码通常由 LES 运营商使用,以允许自动接入其信息检索数据库
91	Automatic line tests 自动线路测试	This code should be used to obtain a telex receiver check 使用此代码可获得电传接收机检查
92	Commissioning tests 调试测试	This code should be used when a vessel is ready to commence its INMARSAT commissioning tests. The code should be used for this purpose only, and then solely via the LES operators through which the commissioning has been arranged 当船舶准备开始 INMARSAT 设备调试测试时,应使用此代码。此代码只能用于此目的,而且仅供已通过安排调试的 LES 运营商使用

3.2   INMARSAT-F INMARSAT-F 船站

3.2.1   INMARSAT-F Services INMARSAT-F 业务

There were three Fleet terminals in INMARSAT system which can be defined by the diameter of antenna, F77, F55 and F33. F77 does not support telex however, which is rarely used now, and in some countries is no longer available. F55/33 offers a combination of voice and data communications and is suited for vessels which require a small antenna, lightweight deck equipment and simple hardware. The summary of INMARSAT-F77/55/33 services can be described as Table 3.4.

INMARSAT 系统中有三个船队终端,可根据天线直径来定义,即 F77、F55 和 F33。但 F77 不支持电传,现在很少使用,在一些国家已无法使用。F55/33 结合了语音和数据通信功能,适用于需要小型天线、轻型甲板设备和简单硬件的船舶。INMARSAT-F77/55/33 服务概要见表 3.4。

Table 3.4 The Summary of INMARSAT-F77/55/33 Services

表 3.4 INMARSAT-F77/55/33 服务概要

Services 业务	Coverage 覆盖范围	Data 1 数据 1	Data 2 数据 2	Fax 传真	GMDSS 全球海上遇险和安全系统	Antenna 天线
F77	Global 全球	64 kbit/s ISDN	MPDS	2.4 kbit/s 9.6 kbit/s 64 kbit/s G4 Fax	Voice 声音	75~90 cm
F55	Global voice Spot beam data and fax 全球语音 点波束数据和传真	64 kbit/s ISDN	MPDS	9.6 kbit/s 64 kbit/s G4 Fax	N/A	50~60 cm
F33	Global voice Spot beam data and fax 全球语音 点波束数据和传真	96 kbit/s data variant option from 2003 从 2003 年起可选 96 kbit/s 数据	data variant option from 2003 从 2003 年起的可选数据	9.6 kbit/s Fax only with 9.6 kbit/s data variant	N/A	30~40 cm

Note：The MPDS service has been shut down on 31 December 2017. F33 and F55 were closed on 31 December 2018, while F77 has been out of line since 1 December 2020.

注：MPDS 业务已于 2017 年 12 月 31 日关闭。F33 和 F55 已于 2018 年 12 月 31 日关闭,而 F77 于 2020 年 12 月 1 日关闭。

F77 is fully compliant with GMDSS, with four levels of pre-emption and voice prioritization for distress, urgency and safety applications. It provides INMARSAT mobile ISDN at 64 kbit/s, enabling large volumes of data to be transferred efficiently, and a mobile packet data service (MPDS) with always-on connectivity when charges are based on the volume of traffic transferred. Access to the Internet, E-mail services, telemedicine, local area networks (LAN) and private networks are possible. Voice, fax and data services are available via the global beams. Mobile ISDN of 128 kbit/s is available via spot beams.

F77 完全符合 GMDSS 的要求,具有四级优先级抢占和语音优先级功能,适用于遇险、紧急和安全通信。它提供 64 kbit/s 的 INMARSAT 移动 ISDN,可有效传输大量数据,还提供移动包交换数据业务(MPDS),在根据传输量收费的情况下可始终保持连接。可接入互联网、电子邮件业务、远程医疗、局域网(LAN)和专用网络。可通过全球波束提供语音、传真和数据业务。通过点波束可提供 128 kbit/s 的移动 ISDN 业务。

F77 does not support telex, but using Internet-based providers, it is possible to send messages to telex terminals. This type of terminal is generally preferred by vessel operators over INMARSAT-B now, due to increased functionality (apart from not supporting telex).

F77 不支持电传,但利用基于互联网的供应商,可以向电传终端发送电文。由于功能增加(除不支持电传外),船舶运营商现在一般更倾向于使用这种终端而不是 INMARSAT-B。

3.2.2   F77 LES Access Codes F77 LES 接入码

In each ocean region there is a Network Coordination Station（NCS）, which manages and coordinates the telecommunications traffic in that region. The NCS assigns available communication channels to the Mobile Earth Stations（MESs）. When a channel is no longer required, it is released to be allocated later to another MES when required. Typically, the NCS function is performed at a particular Land Earth Station（LES）under contract to INMARSAT. Of all the INMARSAT systems, INMARSAT-M, INMARSAT-B, Mini-M, F77 and F55 actually all use the same NCS in each ocean region. The Network Operation Center（NOC）at INMARSAT's headquarters in London, England performs coordination of the network 24 hours a day. The LESs and NCSs of INMARSAT-F77 are shown in Table 3.5 and Table 3.6.

每个洋区都有一个网络协调站（NCS）, 负责管理和协调该区域的电信通信。NCS 将可用的通信信道分配给移动地球站（MES）。当不再需要某个信道时, 该信道就会被释放, 以便以后需要时再分配给另一个 MES。通常情况下, NCS 的功能是在与 INMARSAT 签订合同的特定陆地地球站（LES）上执行的。在 INMARSAT 的所有系统中, INMARSAT-M、INMARSAT-B、Mini-M、F77 和 F55 实际上在每个洋区都使用同一个 NCS。位于英国伦敦 INMARSAT 总部的网络运行中心（NOC）每天 24 小时对网络进行协调。INMARSAT-F77 的 LES 和 NCS 见表 3.5 和表 3.6。

Table 3.5   The LESs of INMARSAT-F77

表 3.5   INMARSAT-F77 的 LES

Country 国家	LES provider LES 提供商	AOR-E	AOR-W	IOR	POR
Algeria 阿尔及利亚	Telecom d' AlgQrie	777			
Australia 澳大利亚	Stratos Mobile			022	022
China 中国	MCN	868	868	868	868
France 法国	Vizada	011	011	011	011
Greece 希腊	OTESAT	005	005	005	005
India 印度	VSNL		306		
Israel 以色列	RRSat	711	711		
Italy 意大利	Telecom Italia	555	555	555	

Continued　续表

Country 国家	LES provider LES 提供商	AOR-E	AOR-W	IOR	POR
Japan 日本	KDDI	003	003	003	003
Republic of Korea 韩国	Korea Telecom	006	006	006	006
Malaysia 马来西亚	Telecom Malaysia	060	060	060	060
Netherlands 荷兰	Stratos Mobile	012	012	012	
Norway 挪威	Vizada	004	004	004	004
Singapore 新加坡	Singapore Telecom	210	210	210	210
UK（Ex） 英国(前)	Stratos Mobile	002	002	002	002
United States 美国	Stratos Mobile	013		013	
United States 美国	Vizada	001	001	001	001

Table 3.6　The NCSs of INMARSAT-F77

表 3.6　INMARSAT-F77 的 NCS

	AOR-E	AOR-W	IOR	POR
Main NCS 主用网络协调站	Goohilly, UK 英国,贡希利	Goohilly, UK 英国,贡希利	Yamaguchi, Japan 日本,山口	Yamaguchi, Japan 日本,山口
Standby NCS 备用网络协调站	Eik, Norway 挪威,艾伊克	Eik, Norway 挪威,艾伊克	Sentosa, Singapore 新加坡,圣淘沙	Sentosa, Singapore 新加坡,圣淘沙

3.2.3　F77 Distress Procedure F77 遇险程序

An F77 distress call is a quick automated method of making a voice connection with the operator at a Maritime Rescue Coordination Center（MRCC）. Once connected, the vessel's position, from the GPS or other electronic positioning system, and MES identity are automatically sent to the MRCC.

F77 遇险呼叫是一种与海上搜救协调中心（MRCC）接线员进行语音连接的快速自动方式。连接后,GPS 或其他电子定位系统提供的船舶位置和 MES 身份信息将自动发送至 MRCC。

The following are the actions that should be taken to initiate a distress priority call.

a.Press and hold the "Distress" button (usually under a protective flap) for 5 s.

b.Select the nearest LES and press the # key (Some MES equipment will automatically select a default distress LES for each ocean region if the "#" key is not pressed within a short period of time.)

c.When the MRCC operator responds, give the following information：

MAYDAY；

Ship's name and/or call sign and Fleet IMN；

Position；

Nature of distress；

Assistance required；

Other information.

d.The ship operator should be prepared to confirm the vessel's own 9-digit IMN, the ocean region satellite currently being used, and details of present course and speed.

e.Follow the instructions given by the MRCC operator.

以下是启动遇险优先呼叫应采取的行动。

a.按住 "遇险"按钮(通常在保护盖下面)5 s。

b.选择最近的 LES 并按"#"键(如果短时间内未按"#"键,某些 MES 设备会自动为每个洋区选择一个默认的遇险 LES)。

c.当 MRCC 接线员回复时,请提供以下信息：

MAYDAY；

船名和/或呼号以及船站识别码(IMN)；

船位；

遇险性质；

所需援助；

其他信息。

d.船舶操作员应准备好确认船舶自身的 9 位 IMN、当前使用的洋区卫星以及当前航向和航速的详细信息。

e.听从 MRCC 接线员的指示。

3.2.4   INMARSAT-F77 Equipment INMARSAT-F77 设备

The INMARSAT-F77 equipment can be divided into two parts as shown in Figure 3.2, which are Above Deck Equipment (ADE) and Below Deck Equipment (BDE). The antenna, stabilization mechanism, antenna control electronic and the VHF transmit/receive equipment are usually referred to as the "Above Deck Equipment" or ADE. Typical all-up mass of the ADE is 27–150 kg.

如图 3.2 所示,INMARSAT-F77 设备可分为两部分,即甲板上设备(ADE)和甲板下设备(BDE)。天线、稳定机构、天线控制电子设备和 VHF 发射/接收设备通常称为"甲板上设备"或 ADE。ADE 的全重为 27~150 千克。

The Below Deck Equipment consists of the actual satcom terminal, usually with a computer type monitor and keyboard attached, and peripherals such as telephones, facsimile machines and call alarms. Most systems support multiple extension telephones, and it is common practice to site one on the bridge, one in the radio room and one in the Master's office or cabin. Interfacing to the ship's internal telephone exchange is also possible with some terminals.

甲板下设备包括实际的卫星通信终端,通常配有计算机型显示器和键盘,以及电话、传真机和呼叫报警器等外围设备。大多数系统支持多部分机电话,通常的做法是在驾驶台、无线电室和船长办公室或船舱各安装一部。有些终端还可以与船上的内部电话交换机连接。

Directional Antenna 定向天线

Because of the range of communications provided by INMARSAT-F77 equipment and the consequent requirement for wide radio spectrum bandwidth and high power, it is necessary for the transmitted energy to be concentrated to a narrow beam by the use of a dish antenna. This antenna is protected by a fiberglass housing.

由于 INMARSAT-F77 设备提供的通信范围很大,因此需要更宽的无线电频谱带宽和高功率,这就需要使用碟形天线将发射能量集中到一个窄波束内。这种天线由一个玻璃纤维外壳保护。

Depending on the geographical position and orientation of the ship relative to the satellite, parts of the ship's superstructure or other large objects may obstruct the "view" of the dish antenna to the satellite.

根据船舶相对于卫星的地理位置和方向,船舶上层建筑的一部分或其他大型物体可能会阻碍碟形天线与卫星的"视线"。

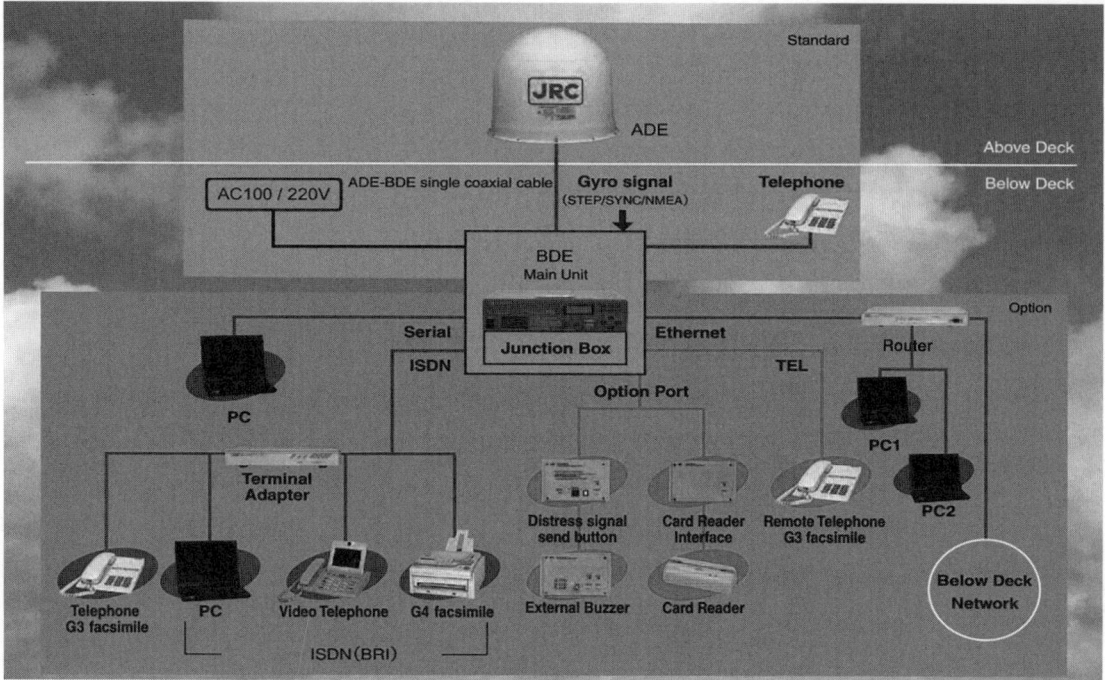

Figure 3.2 INMARSAT-F77 Equipment
图 3.2 INMARSAT-F77 设备

3.3 INMARSAT-C INMARSAT-C 船站

INMARSAT-C MESs are small, lightweight terminals designed for two-way message communication. INMARSAT-C MESs cannot be used for radiotelephone communications. They operate at 600 bit/s and provide access to the international telex/telex networks, E-mail services and computer databases. This low powered terminal with its omni-directional antenna and light weight is a practical solution for installation on the smallest vessels, thereby bringing benefits of satellite communications within the reach of all mariners. INMARSAT-C is mandatory for most vessels equipping themselves to sail in Sea Area A3.

INMARSAT-C MES 是为双向电文通信设计的小型轻量级终端。INMARSAT-C MES 不能用于无线电话通信。它们的工作频率为 600 bit/s,可接入国际电传/电报网络、电子邮件业务和计算机数据库。这种低功耗终端配有全向天线,重量轻,是安装在最小船舶上的实用解决方案,从而使所有海员都能享受到卫星通信的便利。INMARSAT-C 是大多数在 A3 海区航行的船舶必须配备的设备。

INMARSAT-C MESs can also fulfill a potentially vital role as a fixed or portable transmitter/receiver for use on board ship or in survival craft. The omni-directional antenna characteristics are particularly valuable for a vessel in distress as the MES continues to operate even when the vessel is listing severely. A distress message generator is included in the terminal software for storage of basic essential vessel information and automatic transmission of a distress alert. All modern INMARSAT-C

equipment nowadays features built-in GPS. That will ensure accurate location information to be sent to an RCC if a distress alert is ever transmitted.

INMARSAT-C MES 还可作为固定或便携式发射机/接收机在船上或救生艇上发挥潜在的重要作用。MES 的全向天线特性对于遇险船舶尤为重要,因为即使船舶严重倾斜,MES 仍能继续工作。终端软件中包含一个遇险电文生成器,用于存储基本的重要船舶信息和自动发送遇险报警。如今,所有现代化的 INMARSAT-C 设备都配备了内置 GPS。这将确保在发送遇险报警时向 RCC 发送准确的位置信息。

3.3.1　INMARSAT-C Services INMARSAT-C 业务

The INMARSAT-C services can be used for various of communication purpose as follows.

Telex	Messages can be sent to and from any telex terminal connected to the national and international telex network.
E-mail	E-mail can be sent to and from any computer terminal that is connected to the national and international PSDNs and PSTNs.
Ship-to-shore fax	Messages can be sent from the ship to a fax terminal connected to the national and international telephone networks. Fax messages cannot be sent in the shore-to-ship direction.
Ship-to-ship	Data can be sent between INMARSAT-B/C/F and INMARSAT-C terminals on other ships within the four ocean regions.
Distress and safety	Distress priority messages can be sent and routed automatically to the nearest MRCC, which will take the necessary action to inform rescue services and other ships and aircraft in the ship's vicinity.
EGC	All maritime INMARSAT-C MESs must have EGC receive facilities, enabling the reception of broadcasts to selected ships, or areas.
SafetyNET	Authorities can send MSI to ships within selected geographical areas.
FleetNET	Information can be transmitted to a selected group of ships rather like collective call sign messages.

INMARSAT-C 业务可用于以下各种通信目的。

电传	电文可在任何与国内和国际电传网络连接的电传终端之间发送。
电子邮件	电子邮件可收发自任何与国内和国际 PSDN 和 PSTN 相连的计算机终端。
船对岸传真	电文可从船上发送到与国内和国际电话网络连接的传真终端。传真电文不能从岸上发送到船上。
船对船	在四大洋区内,INMARSAT-B/C/F 终端和其他船舶上的 INMARSAT-C 终端之间可以发送数据。

遇险和安全	遇险优先等级电文可自动发送和转发到最近的 MRCC，MRCC 将采取必要行动，通知救援业务部门以及遇险船舶附近的其他船舶和飞机。
EGC	所有海事 INMARSAT-C MES 都必须具备 EGC 接收设施，以便接收发送到选定船舶或区域的广播。
安全网	机构可向选定地理区域内的船舶发送 MSI。
船队网	信息可以像群呼电文一样传送给选定的一组船舶。

Note：It is mandatory for all marine INMARSAT-C LESs to offer the minimum services of store and forward telex, distress alerting, distress priority messages and EGC SafetyNET.

注：所有 INMARSAT-C LES 必须提供最低限度存储和转发电传、遇险报警、遇险优先电文和 EGC 安全网服务。

3.3.2　INMARSAT-C LES Access Codes INMARSAT-C LES 接入码

INMARSAT-C LES access codes are shown in Table 3.7.

INMARSAT-C LES 接入码见表 3.7。

Table 3.7　INMARSAT-C LES Access Codes

表 3.7　INMARSAT-C LES 接入码

Land Earth Station Operator 陆地地球站运营商	Country 国家	AOR-E	AOR-W	IOR	POR
Bezeq	Israel 以色列	127		327	
Embratel	Brazil 巴西	114			
FT	France 法国	121	021	321	221
KDDI	Japan 日本	103	003	303	203
MCN	China 中国			311	211
Morsviazsputnik	Russia 俄罗斯	117		317	
OTESTAT	Greece 希腊	120		305	
Polish Telecom	Poland 波兰	116		316	

Continued　续表

Land Earth Station Operator 陆地地球站运营商	Country 国家	AOR-E	AOR-W	IOR	POR
Singapore Telecom	Singapore 新加坡			328	210
Stratos Mobile Networks	UK/New Zealand 英国/新西兰	102	002	302	202
	Netherlands/Australia 荷兰/澳大利亚	112	012	312	212
Italia Telecom	Italy 意大利	105		335	
Telenor	Norway 挪威	104	004	304	204
	USA 美国	101	001	301	201
Türk Telekom	Turkey 土耳其	110		310	
VISHIPEL	Vietnam 越南			330	
VSNL	India 印度			306	

3.3.3　INMARSAT-C Special Access Codes INMARSAT-C 专用接入码

The INMARSAT-C system supports a 2-digit code service, which can be used to access urgent, safety and other regularly used services/facilities ashore.

INMARSAT-C 系统支持两位代码业务,可用于访问岸上的紧急、安全和其他常用业务/设施。

Those available include:

- · 00 Automatically connected calls;
- · 31 Maritime enquiries;
- · 32 Request for medical advice;
- · 33 Request for technical assistance;
- · 37 Advice of time and charges for a call;
- · 38 Request for medical assistance;

- 39 Request for maritime assistance;

- 41 OBS messages (i.e. meteorological messages);

- 42 Sending weather danger and navigational reports to shore authorities;

- 43 Position reports to shore authorities, e.g. the Automated Mutual-Assistance Vessel Rescue System (AMVER), the Modernised Australian Ship Tracking and Reporting System (MASTREP), etc.

其中包括:

- 00 自动连接电话;

- 31 海事查询;

- 32 请求医疗建议;

- 33 请求技术援助;

- 37 通话时间和费用通知;

- 38 请求医疗援助;

- 39 请求海事援助;

- 41 OBS 信息(如气象电文);

- 42 向海岸机构发送气象危险和航行报告;

- 43 向岸上机构报告位置,如自动船舶救生互助系统 (AMVER)、现代化澳大利亚船舶跟踪和报告系统 (MASTREP) 等。

3.3.4 **INMARSAT-C Distress Alerting INMARSAT-C 遇险报警**

When using the INMARSAT-C system for distress alerting, ensure that the automatic scan facility is set to scan only the ocean region within which you are logged on.

在使用 INMARSAT-C 系统进行遇险报警时,请确保自动扫描设备设置为只扫描使用者登录时所在的洋区。

There are two methods of sending distress alerts in the INMARSAT-C system:

a.by using the remote distress alert button(s); or

b.by keying the information into the MES terminal using the edit facilities and then using the distress alert button(s).

INMARSAT-C 系统有两种发送遇险报警的方法:

a.使用遥控遇险报警按钮;或

b.使用编辑工具将信息输入 MES 终端,然后使用遇险报警按钮。

3.3.4.1 Using the Remote Distress Alert Button(s) on the MES 使用 MES 上的遥控遇险报警按钮

If the remote distress alert buttons are fitted to the MES and there is insufficient time to use the MES keyboard, an alert may be initiated in this manner. It is important to understand that the vessel's position information stored may be out of date unless recently updated. In the interests of safety of life at sea, operators are advised to keep the MES logged on, with up-to-date positional information in the store at all times.

如果在 MES 上安装了遥控遇险报警按钮,并且没有足够的时间使用 MES 键盘,则可以通过按动遥控报警按钮的方式发出报警。必须了解,除非最近更新过,否则所存储的船舶位置信息可能已经过时。为了确保海上人命安全,操作员应始终保持 MES 处于登录状态,并将最新的位置信息存储在其中。

The method is as follows:

a.Press the remote distress alert button(s) until there is an indication that the MES is in the distress alert mode. This condition should remain until an acknowledgement is received from the LES and then the nearest MRCC.

b.If no acknowledgement is received from both the LES and MRCC within 5 min, repeat the distress alert.

c.If possible, send updated information about the ship's distress situation using the edit facilities indicated below.

具体方法如下:

a.按遥控遇险报警按钮,直到出现 MES 处于遇险报警模式的指示。在收到 LES 和最近的 MRCC 的确认之前,应保持这种状态。

b.如果在 5 min 内未收到 LES 和 MRCC 的确认,则重复发出遇险报警。

c.如果可能,请使用下面的编辑工具发送有关船舶遇险情况的最新信息。

3.3.4.2 Using the Edit Facilities on the MES Terminal 使用 MES 终端的编辑工具

This method enables the operator to key in up-to-date information. However, owing to a system definition change, this system will eventually be discontinued.

通过这种方法,操作员可以键入最新信息。不过,由于系统定义发生变化,该系统最终将被停用。

The method is as follows:

a.Select the distress alert menus according to the manufacturer's operating instructions.

b.When requested, complete the following information:

· MES IMN: MES enters this automatically.

· LES required：Select the nearest LES within the ocean region to own ship's position.

· Position：Enter latitude and longitude manually via keyboard, or automatically from electronic navigator such as GPS.

· Date and time of last position update：Enter time manually or automatically from electronic navigator (all time to be quoted in UTC). Position status should read satisfactorily.

· Nature of distress：Select one of the following, unspecified, listing, fire/explosion, sinking, flooding, disabled and adrift, collision, abandoning ship, grounding, assistance required, piracy/armed robbery.

· Ship's course (0°-359°)：This may be entered manually or automatically.

· Ship's speed (knots)：This may be entered manually or automatically.

c.Press the appropriate key(s) to send the alert.

d.If an acknowledgement is not received from both the LES and MRCC within 5 min, repeat the distress alert.

具体方法如下：

a.根据制造商的操作说明选择遇险报警菜单。

b.如有要求,请填写以下信息：

· MES 识别码：MES 自动输入该码。

· 所需的 LES：在洋区内选择离本船最近的 LES。

· 位置：通过键盘手动输入经纬度,或从 GPS 等电子导航仪自动获取。

· 最后一次位置更新的日期和时间：手动输入时间或由电子导航仪自动输入时间(所有时间均以 UTC 表示)。位置状态的读数应令人满意。

· 遇险的性质：请在下列选项中选择一项:未指定、倾斜、火灾/爆炸、沉没、进水、失控漂流、碰撞、弃船、搁浅、所需援助、海盗/持械抢劫。

· 船舶航向(0°~359°)：可手动或自动输入。

· 船速(节)：可手动或自动输入。

c.按相应的键发送报警。

d.如果在 5 min 内未收到 LES 和 MRCC 的确认,则重复发出遇险报警。

3.3.4.3 INMARSAT-C Distress Priority Message INMARSAT-C 遇险优先等级电文

A distress priority message should be typed into the MES using the edit facilities. The message will be routed automatically to the nearest MRCC by the selected LES.

遇险优先等级电文应使用电文编辑工具录入 MES。电文将由选定的 LES 自动转发给最近

的 MRCC。

The method is as follows:

a.Ensure that the MES is logged on and tuned to the common channel of the NCS appropriate to the ocean region in which the vessel is sailing.

b.Prepare the distress message using the word processing facilities of the terminal.

c.Give details of the kind of assistance required, although this may be implied by the nature of distress.

d.Select distress priority.

e.Key in the code for the nearest LES to ship's own position. This LES will route the distress message to the nearest MRCC.

f.Press the appropriate key(s) for sending the message.

g.Wait for an acknowledgement from the LES.

具体方法如下:

a.确保 MES 处于登录状态,并调谐到适合船舶航行洋区的 NCS 公共频道。

b.使用终端的文字处理功能准备遇险电文。

c.详细说明所需的援助类型,即便这可能根据遇险性质推测出来。

d.选择遇险优先级。

e.键入距离本船位置最近的 LES 的代码。该 LES 将把遇险电文发送到最近的 MRCC。

f.按相应的键发送电文。

g.等待 LES 的确认。

3.3.5　INMARSAT-C Logging on/off INMARSAT-C 入网/退网

Follow the manufacturer's instructions on how to log on to the NCS in the current ocean region. This enables messages to be sent and received at any time. As vessels move out of the service area of one ocean region, they must log on to the ocean region that they are entering. Vessels will be able to communicate only through LESs within the ocean region within which they are logged on.

按照制造商的说明,在当前洋区登录 NCS。这样就可以随时收发电文。当船舶驶出一个洋区的覆盖范围时,必须在所进入的洋区登录入网。船舶只能通过其登录的洋区内的 LES 进行通信。

Note:When vessels wish to switch off an INMARSAT-C MES for any prolonged period of time, it is important to log off first. This will stop the NCS in that region from sending further messages until the MES is logged on again. If this is not done, any LES with traffic for that vessel will continue to try to contact the MES. After repeated unsuccessful attempts, the LES may reject the message and the ship may never receive it. Furthermore, certain LESs may charge the sender for use of satellite airtime even though the message is not received.

注：当船舶希望长时间关闭 INMARSAT-C MES 时，重要的是需要先退网。这将阻止该区域的 NCS 发送更多电文，直到 MES 再次登录。如果没有退网，任何与这条船通信的 LES 都会继续尝试与 MES 联系。在多次重复发送失败后，LES 可能会拒绝电文，船舶也可能永远收不到电文。此外，即使 MES 没有收到电文，某些 LES 也可能会向发送方收取卫星通话时间的费用。

It should be noted that certain INMARSAT-C terminals perform automatic logging functions and operators may not require manual intervention.

应该注意的是，某些 INMARSAT-C 终端具有自动记录功能，操作员可能不需要进行人工干预。

3.3.6 INMARSAT-C Equipment INMARSAT-C 设备

The typical INMARSAT-C MES has a small omni-directional antenna, which can be easily mounted on a vehicle or vessel. The omni-directional antenna characteristics are particularly valuable for a vessel in distress (as the MES continues to operate even when the vessel is listing severely).

典型的 INMARSAT-C MES 有一个小型全向天线，可以方便地安装在车辆或船舶上。全向天线的特性在船舶遇险时尤为重要（因为即使船舶严重倾斜，MES 仍能继续工作）。

An INMARSAT-C SES system consists of an antenna, an electronic unit, a message processor, a visual display unit, a keyboard and a printer(see Figure 3.3). The message processor usually contains a floppy disk drive for storing transmitted and received messages.

INMARSAT-C SES 系统由天线、电子设备、电文处理器、显示设备、键盘和打印机组成（见图 3.3）。电文处理器通常包含一个软盘驱动器，用于存储发送和接收的电文。

Transmitted messages may be prepared by keyboard entry into the text editor, or transferred from any other administrative computer in use aboard the vessel. It is possible to connect other input/output devices to the system. INMARSAT-C equipment carried on board most is often interfaced with GPS satellite navigation equipment to provide current position information in the event of distress.

传送的电文可通过键盘输入文本编辑器编写，或从船上使用的任何其他管理计算机传输。该系统还可以连接其他输入/输出设备。大多数船舶上携带的 INMARSAT-C 设备通常与 GPS 卫星导航设备连接，以便在遇险时提供当前位置信息。

A remote alarm is provided in the ship's wheelhouse to immediately alert the watchkeeper to the reception of any distress or urgent messages broadcast by Enhanced Group Calling. Facilities are also provided for initiating a distress alert from a remote location, such as the Master's office or (original) radio room. These facilities are known as Remote Distress Initiation Devices (RDIDs).

船舶驾驶室内设有远程报警器,可立即提醒值班员接收由增强型群呼系统广播的任何遇险或紧急电文。此外,还提供了从船长办公室或(原)电报间等远程位置发出遇险报警的设施。这些设施被称为远程遇险报警设备(RDID)。

INMARSAT-C has an advantage over INMARSAT-B/F77 in that it requires a narrower bandwidth of radio spectrum to enable communications. As a consequence, relatively low power is necessary to communicate with the satellites and only a small, lightweight, omni-directional (radiating equally in all directions) antenna is required.

与 INMARSAT-B/F77 相比,INMARSAT-C 的优势在于它只需要较窄的无线电频谱带宽就可进行通信。因此,与卫星通信所需的功率相对较低,而且只需要一个小型、轻便、全向(向所有方向均等辐射)天线。

The omni-directional characteristics of the antenna mean that it requires no moving parts and can transmit and receive messages even when the vessel is pitching and rolling heavily. Stabilization against yawing and course changes is not necessary.

天线的全向特性意味着天线不需要移动部件,即使在船舶剧烈倾斜和摇晃时也能收发电文。无须针对偏航和航向变化进行稳定。

The compact size of the antenna makes it simple to locate in a position where its view of the satellite will be unobstructed by parts of the ship's superstructure. However, any object within 1 m of the antenna which cause a shadow sector of greater than 2 degrees will seriously degrade the performance of the equipment.

天线的紧凑尺寸使得它很容易定位在一个位置,在那里它的卫星视野将不受船舶上层建筑的阻碍。不过,天线周围 1 m 内的任何物体如果造成超过 2°的阴影区,都会严重降低设备的性能。

Obstacles which appear in the fore and aft directions down to 5 degrees below horizontal, in the port and starboard directions, down to 15 degrees below horizontal must be taken into account.

必须考虑到在水平面以下 5°的前后方向和在水平面以下 15°的左右方向上出现的障碍物。

3.3.7 INMARSAT EGC INMARSAT 增强群呼

The INMARSAT system provides a service known as Enhanced Group Calling (EGC), which provides the broadcast of information to selected ships in an ocean region(see Figure 3.4). SafetyNET II is an enhancement to the current SafetyNET system. SafetyNET II provides an interactive web portal or application programing interface (API) for information providers to create their MSI messages and deliver them over the INMARSAT EGC system including INMARSAT-C, Mini-C, and Fleet Safety.

INMARSAT 系统提供一种称为"增强群呼(EGC)"的业务,向某一洋区的选定船舶广播信息(见图 3.4)。安全网 II 是当前安全网系统的增强版。安全网 II 提供了一个交互式门户网站或应用程序接口(API),供信息提供者创建 MSI 电文,并通过 INMARSAT EGC 系统(包括INMARSAT-C、Mini-C 和 Fleet Safety)传送这些电文。

EME

Antenna

IME

Electronic Unit

Displayer and Keyboard

Printer

Distress Button and Beeper

DTE : DCE

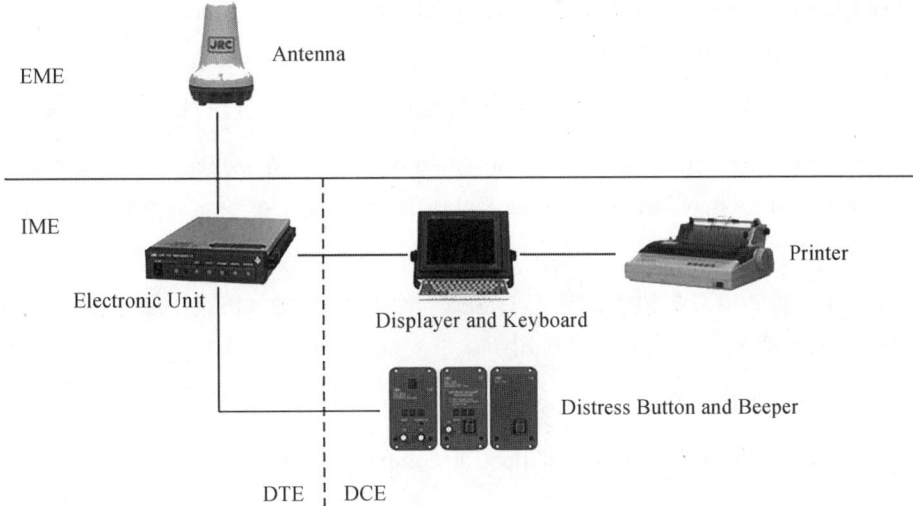

Figure 3.3 INMARSAT-C Equipment

图 3.3 INMARSAT-C 设备

3.3.7.1 Types of EGC Service Available EGC 业务类型

Two types of EGC messages are available：

· SafetyNET；and

· FleetNET.

EGC 电文有两种类型可用：

· 安全网；以及

· 船队网。

SafetyNET allows information providers authorized by the IMO to broadcast shore-to-ship Maritime Safety Information.

安全网允许经 IMO 授权的信息提供者广播岸对船海上安全信息。

Authorized information providers include：

· Hydrographic offices，for navigational warnings；

· Meteorological offices，for weather warnings and forecasts；and

· Rescue Coordination Centers，for shore-to-ship distress alert relays，search and rescue communications and other urgent information.

经授权的信息提供者包括：

· 航道局，用于航海警告；

· 气象局，用于天气报警和预报；以及

· 搜救协调中心，用于岸对船遇险报警转发、搜救通信和其他紧急信息。

The IMO has selected INMARSAT's SafetyNET as one of the primary means of promulgating Maritime Safety Information for the GMDSS.

IMO 已选择 INMARSAT 的安全网作为发布 GMDSS 海上安全信息的主要手段之一。

FleetNET allows registered information providers to broadcast messages to selected groups of SESs. The selected SESs may belong to a particular fleet or flag, or be a registered subscriber to a commercial service.

船队网允许注册的信息提供者向选定的 SES 群组广播电文。被选中的 SES 可能属于某个船队或船旗国,也可能是商业业务的注册用户。

Registered users of FleetNET may include:

· Shipowners, for the broadcast of fleet or company information;

· News subscription's services, for the broadcast of news bulletins; and

· Governments, for the broadcast of messages to a particular country's ships.

船队网的注册用户包括:

· 船东,用于播放船队或公司信息;

· 新闻订阅机构,用于播放新闻简报;以及

· 政府,用于向特定国家的船舶广播电文。

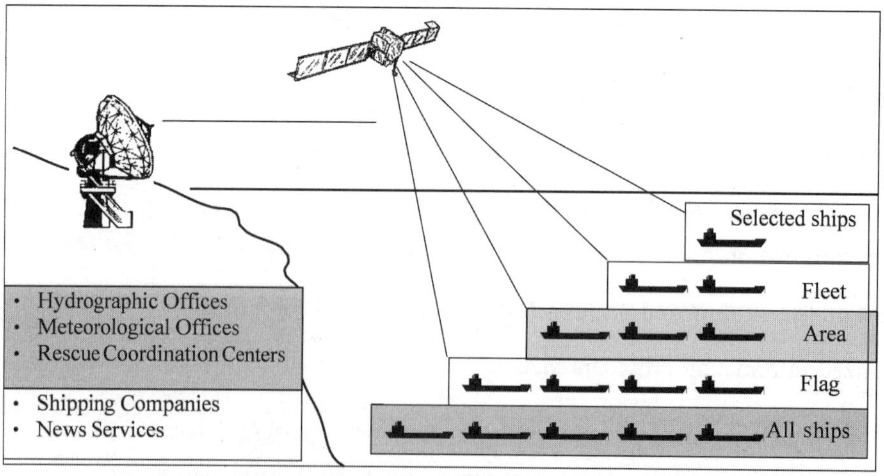

Figure 3.4   Basic Concept of the INMARSAT Enhanced Group Call System
(the shaded area indicates functions of the SafetyNET service)
图 3.4   INMARSAT 增强群呼系统的基本概念(阴影部分表示安全网业务的功能)

3.3.7.2   Shipboard Equipment 船载设备

All INMARSAT-C SES equipment currently available has an integral EGC facility. Some SES equipment can receive both incoming routine mail messages and EGC messages simultaneously. This equipment is termed a Class 3 SES. When engaged on these tasks the receiver is tuned to a

LES channel and not to the NCS common channel on which EGC broadcasts are made. During these brief periods an incoming EGC message will not be received. However, once the routine mail message is completed, the SES receiver will automatically re-tune to the NCS common channel and be free to receive any repeat of the EGC message.

目前所有的 INMARSAT-C SES 设备都有完整的 EGC 设施。有些 SES 设备可同时用于接收常规邮件电文和 EGC 电文。这种设备被称为 3 类 SES。在执行这些任务时,接收机会被调谐到 LES 频道,而不是被调谐到用来进行 EGC 广播的 NCS 的公共频道。在这些短暂的时间内,接收机将无法收到 EGC 电文。不过,一旦常规邮件电文接收完毕,SES 接收机将自动重新调谐到 NCS 公共频道,并可自由接收任何重复的 EGC 电文。

An EGC receiver is defined as a single-channel receiver with a dedicated message processor. LESs of Class 2 and 3 provide an EGC capability in addition to To-Ship and From-Ship messaging capabilities; Class 0 SESs are self-contained EGC receivers(see Figure 3.5).

EGC 接收机是指带有专用电文处理器的单通道接收机。2 类和 3 类 SES 除了提供 "发给船" 和 "船发送" 电文传送功能外,还提供 EGC 功能;0 类 SES 是独立的 EGC 接收机(见图 3.5)。

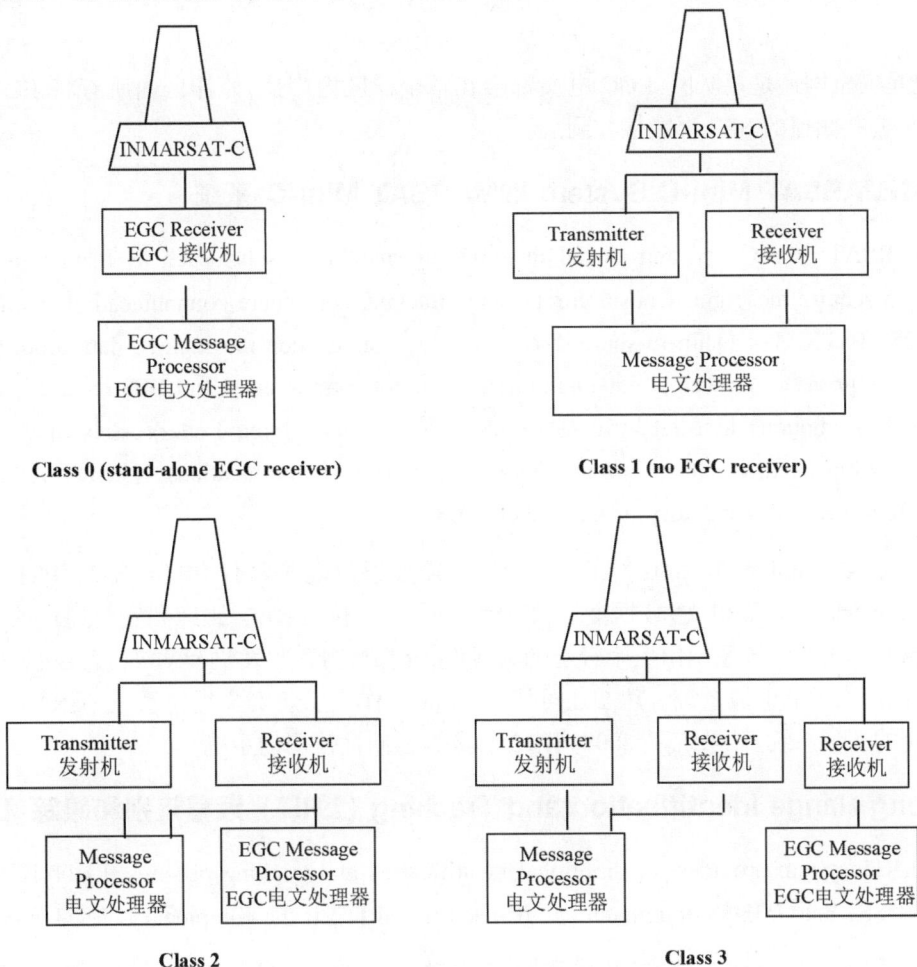

Class 0 (stand-alone EGC receiver)

Class 1 (no EGC receiver)

Class 2

Class 3

Figure 3.5　Classes of INMARSAT-C LESs

图 3.5　INMARSAT-C LES 的类别

Note: Most of the existing models of INMARSAT-C and Mini-C maritime terminals on the market are Class 2 SESs.

注：市场上现有的 INMARSAT-C 型和 Mini-C 型海事终端大多为 2 类 SES。

Ships selecting this option should ensure that their owners and agents are aware of the identity number of the terminal not dedicated to EGC reception, as any routine mail message addressed to the EGC dedicated terminal cannot be delivered. Dedication to EGC reception will not affect a terminal's capacity to transmit a distress alert.

选择此选项的船舶应确保其船东和代理知道非专用于接收 EGC 电文的终端的识别码，因为任何发给 EGC 专用终端的常规邮件都无法送达。专用于接收 EGC 电文的终端不会影响其发送遇险报警的能力。

3.3.7.3 Broadcasts of EGC Messages 广播 EGC 电文

An EGC message, whether SafetyNET or FleetNET, is broadcast over an entire ocean region and is received by all SES in that region which have their EGC facility tuned to the NCS common channel.

无论是安全网还是船队网，EGC 电文都会在整个洋区内广播，该洋区内所有将 EGC 设备调至 NCS 公共频道的 SES 都能接收到。

3.3.8 INMARSAT Mini-C System INMARSAT Mini-C 系统

INMARSAT Mini-C was introduced in 2002 for smaller vessels, such as fishing or leisure craft, which require messaging, position reporting, tracking and secure communications via E-mail, telex, X-25, PSTN, fax (ship-to-shore direction only), short code messaging, data reporting and polling. It comprises a lightweight antenna unit containing the transceiver and GPS receiver, and has low power consumption, assisted by a solar cell battery system if required. Vessels may also use Mini-C as a Ship Security Alert System (SSAS) and/or a communications system for the LRIT system, which became mandatory in December 2008.

INMARSAT Mini-C 于 2002 年推出，适用于需要通过电子邮件、电传、X-25、PSTN、传真（仅限船对岸方向）、短码电文、数据报告和轮询进行电文、位置报告、跟踪和安全通信的小型船舶，如渔船或休闲艇。该系统由一个轻巧的天线设备组成，内含收发机和 GPS 接收机，功耗低，必要时可使用太阳能电池系统。船舶还可使用 Mini-C 作为船舶安全报警系统（SSAS）和/或 LRIT 系统的通信系统，该系统于 2008 年 12 月成为强制性使用的系统。

3.3.9 Long Range Identification and Tracking (LRIT) 远程识别和跟踪(LRIT)

The LRIT system provides for the global identification and tracking of ships. LRIT is not part of the GMDSS, but GMDSS equipment can be used for LRIT, if the equipment is LRIT compliant.

LRIT 系统可在全球范围内识别和跟踪船舶。LRIT 不是 GMDSS 的一部分，但如果 GMDSS 设备符合 LRIT 的标准，GMDSS 可用于远程识别和跟踪系统。

The obligations of ships to transmit LRIT information and the rights and obligations of SOLAS Contracting Governments and of Search and Rescue Services to receive LRIT information are established in Chapter Ⅴ of the 1974 SOLAS Convention, Regulation 19-1.

1974 年《国际海上人命安全公约》第五章第 19-1 条规定了船舶发送 LRIT 信息的义务以及 SOLAS 缔约国政府和搜救业务机构接收 LRIT 信息的权利和义务。

The system requires vessels to automatically transmit their identity, position and date/time at 6 hourly intervals through a Communication Service Provider (CSP). The data is then sent to an LRIT Data Center (DC) which is linked to the International Data Exchange (IDE). The Data Distribution Plan (DDP) is used to verify the requests for information.

该系统要求船舶通过通信业务提供商(CSP)每 6 小时自动发送一次其身份、位置和日期/时间。数据随后被发送到与国际数据交换中心(IDE)相连的 LRIT 数据中心(DC)。数据分发计划(DDP)用于核实信息请求。

LRIT came into force on 1 January 2008, with compliance by 30 June 2009.

LRIT 于 2008 年 1 月 1 日生效,要求在 2009 年 6 月 30 日前遵照执行。

LRIT is a maritime domain awareness (MDA) initiative to allow member States to receive position reports from vessels operating under their flag, vessels seeking entry to a port within their territory, or vessels operating in proximity to the State's coastline.

LRIT 是一项海区感知(MDA)举措,允许成员国接收悬挂其国旗的船舶、试图进入其境内港口的船舶或在其海岸线附近作业的船舶的位置报告。

The LRIT regulation applies to the following ships engaged on international voyages:

· All passenger ships including high speed craft;

· Cargo ships, including high speed craft of 300 gross tonnage and above; and

· Mobile offshore drilling units.

LRIT 规定适用于以下从事国际航行的船舶:

· 所有客船,包括高速船;

· 货船,包括总吨位 300 及以上的高速船;以及

· 移动式近海钻井设备。

Ships operating exclusively in Sea Area A1, and fitted with an Automatic Identification System (AIS) are exempt, while ships operating in Sea Area A2 which are not fitted with INMARSAT-C GMDSS are required to fit a dedicated LRIT terminal. Ships operating into Sea Area A4 require a dedicated LRIT terminal that operates in conjunction with an approved Low Earth Orbit (LEO) communication service provider.

仅在 A1 海区运营并装有自动识别系统(AIS)的船舶可免于安装 LRIT 终端,而在 A2 海区运营且未安装 INMARSAT-C GMDSS 的船舶则必须安装专用的 LRIT 终端。在 A4 海区运

营的船舶需要安装专用的 LRIT 终端,该终端与经批准的低轨道通信业务提供商共同运行。

Ship LRIT equipment must be capable of being configured to transmit the following minimum information contained in an Automatic Position Report（APR）:

· The identity of the ship;

· The position of the ship; and

· The date and time of the position.

船舶上配置的 LRIT 设备所发送的自动位置报告（APR）应至少包含以下信息:

· 船舶的识别码;

· 船舶的位置;以及

· 船舶在该位置的日期和时间。

In addition, ship LRIT equipment must be able to respond to poll requests for an on-demand position report and be able immediately to respond to instructions to modify the APR interval to a maximum frequency of once every 15 min. APRs will be transmitted as a minimum four times per day（every 6 h）to a National Data Center or a Cooperative or Regional Data Center nominated by the Maritime Administration/Flag Register（the "Flag"）.

此外,船舶 LRIT 设备必须能够响应位置报告的轮询请求,并能够立即响应将 APR 间隔修改为最多每 15 min 一次的指令。每天至少向国家数据中心或海事局/船旗注册局（"船旗"）指定的合作或区域数据中心发送 4 次(每 6 h 一次) APR。

3.3.10 Ship Security Alert System（SSAS）船舶保安报警系统（SSAS）

The amendments to 1974 SOLAS Convention, Chapter XI-2, adding a new Regulation 6, require the installation of a new Ship Security Alert System（SSAS）onboard ships to which 1974 SOLAS Convention applies.

1974 年《国际海上人命安全公约》第 XI-2 章修正案增加了新的第 6 条,要求在适用 1974 年《国际海上人命安全公约》的船舶上安装新的船舶保安报警系统（SSAS）。

The purpose of the SSAS is to alert the ship's Flag State competent authority and also the company security officer of the relevant shipping line to the fact that the security of the ship is under threat or has been compromised by terrorists. There is a minimum of two activation points for the SSAS that initiates the transmission of the alert. It is for the Master to decide which crew members need to be aware of the location of the activation points. Once activated, a covert alert will be made to the relevant competent authority by short message service（SMS）or E-mail via INMARSAT Mini-C, and each Flag State must have procedures in place to ensure quick and effective receipt and handling of the alert. The alert will continue until it is deactivated or reset.

SSAS 的目的是提醒船舶船旗国主管机关和相关航运公司的保安员,船舶的安全正受到威胁或已经受到恐怖分子的破坏。SSAS 至少有两个启动点,用于启动报警的发送。由船长决定

哪些船员需要知道启动点的位置。一旦启动,将通过 INMARSAT Mini-C 以短信或电子邮件的方式向相关主管机关发出秘密报警,各船旗国必须制定程序,确保迅速有效地接收和处理报警。报警将一直持续到被解除或重置为止。

Periodic testing of the SSAS (once a year as a minimum) to test the communication process is advisable, it is important to contact those who will be involved in the test in advance to ensure that no unnecessary response activity is implemented.

为了测试通信过程,建议定期测试 SSAS(至少每年一次),重要的是要提前联系将参与测试的人员,以确保不会对此应答。

3.4 INMARSAT Traffic Accounting and Billing INMARSAT 通信计费与账单

A ship making a call via the INMARSAT system involves several different elements. Depending on the nature of the call, these elements can include the satellite link to a selected CES (known as the "Space Segment"), the CES, and the terrestrial lines.

船舶通过 INMARSAT 系统进行呼叫涉及几个不同的要素。根据呼叫的性质,这些要素可包括所选 CES 的卫星链路(称为"空间段")、CES 和地面线路。

The cost depends on many different factors, including: when, how, and by which CES the call is made.

费用取决于许多不同的因素,包括:何时、如何以及由哪个 CES 进行呼叫。

The minimum chargeable duration applicable—whether 3 min, 1 min, 6 s, or 1 s. Only "connect" time is chargeable, and not "holding" time. For example, in a telex call, the only time chargeable is from receiving the answerback of the called subscriber until the end of communications. The ship is not charged for the time the system takes to connect the call.

适用的最短收费时间为 3 min、1 min、6 s 或 1 s。只有"接通"时间才收费,"保持"时间不收费。例如,在电传呼叫中,只有从收到被叫用户的回话到通信结束这一段时间才收费。系统接通电话的时间不计费。

An automatic call is normally cheaper than an operator-assisted call.

自动呼叫通常比接线员协助呼叫便宜。

In the ship-to-shore direction, off-peak rates are generally available in periods of reduced traffic for calls made on a telephony channel (telephone voice, hand data and facsimile calls), but generally off-peak rates are not available for telex calls.

在船对岸之间的通话中,使用电话信道(电话语音、手持数据和传真通话)进行的通话,在通话量减少时一般可享受非峰时费率,但电传通话一般不享受非峰时费率。

There are no charges to the mariner for receipt of SafetyNET messages. Message transmission charges are set by National Telecommunication Administrations and the CES offering EGC services.

MSI to be broadcast through the International SafetyNET service is transmitted to the CES via telex, data-link or an INMARSAT-B or INMARSAT-C transmission, for which the normal charges will apply.

海员接收安全网电文无须付费。电文传输费由国家电信管理局和提供 EGC 业务的 CES 确定。通过国际安全网业务广播的 MSI 将通过电传、数据链路或 INMARSAT-B/INMARSAT-C 发送到 CES,这将适用正常收费。

Some CESs use special "nominal" currencies, such as the Gold Franc (GF), and the Special Drawing Right (SDR). A CES calculates the traffic invoices for a ship using one of these nominal currencies, and then converts the charge to an agreed currency, in order to invoice the Accounting Authority (AA). The conversion rate from the nominal currency (GF or SDR) to the agreed currency depends on the current exchange rate.

有些 CES 使用特殊的"名义"货币,如金法郎(GF)和特别提款权(SDR)。CES 使用这些名义货币中的一种计算船舶的通信费用,然后将费用转换为商定的货币,以便向会计局(AA)开具发票。从名义货币(GF 或 SDR)到商定货币的兑换率取决于当前汇率。

As a guide only, the SDR rate (rounded to the nearest cent) was: 1 SDR=US $ 1.36.

作为参考,SDR 汇率(四舍五入到最接近的美分)为:1 SDR=1.36 美元。

The SDR is always at a fixed rate against the GF of: 1 SDR=3.061 GF.

SDR 对金法郎的汇率始终是固定的:1 SDR=3.061 GF。

As a result, the GF exchange rate (rounded to the nearest cent) was: 1 GF=US $ 0.44.

因此,金法郎汇率(四舍五入到最接近的美分)为:1 金法郎=0.44 美元。

There are still some explanations about the unit used in the INMARSAT system. In computer to computer (data) communications, ASCII (American Standard Code for Information Interchange) is generally used to represent letters, numbers, and special characters. Each character is represented by 8 digital bits which is known as 1 byte.

关于 INMARSAT 系统中使用的单位还有一些解释。在计算机与计算机之间的(数据)通信中,通常使用 ASCII(美国信息交换标准码)来表示字母、数字和特殊字符。每个字符由 8 个比特表示,即 1 个字节。

1 character=8 bits=1 byte

1 个字符=8 个比特=1 个字节

1 kilobit (kbit)=1024 bits=128 characters=25 words (approximately)

1 个千比特(kbit)=1024 个比特=128 个字符=25 个字(大约)

1 A4 page full of text=2500 characters=20 kbits (approximately)

1 A4 页文字=2500 个字符=20 个千比特(大约)

In telex communications, ITA2 (International Telegraph Alphabet 2) is generally used. Each ITA2 code consists of 5 data bits, plus 1 start bit, and 1.5 stop bits (7.5 bits in all). At the standard rate of 50 bits/s, this makes the speed of telex communications 400 characters per minutes.

在电传通信中,通常使用 ITA2(国际电报字母 2)。每个 ITA2 编码包括 5 个数据比特、1 个起始比特和 1.5 个停止比特(共 7.5 个比特)。按照 50 比特/秒的标准速率计算,电传通信速度为每分钟 400 个字符。

3.5 COSPAS-SARSAT System COSPAS-SARSAT 系统

3.5.1 Introduction 简介

The COSPAS-SARSAT System provides distress alert and location information to search and rescue services for aviation, maritime, and land users in distress, with no discrimination and free of charge for the persons in distress. This objective is accomplished through the use of satellite systems, which relay or process the transmissions of distress radio beacons operating on 121.5 MHz or 406 MHz. The carriage of a float-free satellite EPIRB operating on the 406 MHz in the COSPAS-SARSAT system is required on all SOLAS ships.

COSPAS-SARSAT 系统为航空、航海和陆地的遇险用户的搜索和救援业务提供遇险报警和位置信息,对遇险者一视同仁并免费。这一目标是通过使用卫星系统来实现的,卫星系统转发或处理在 121.5 MHz 或 406 MHz 频率上运行的遇险无线电信标的传输。所有 SOLAS 船舶都必须在 COSPAS-SARSAT 系统中携带一个 406 MHz 的自浮式卫星 EPIRB。

On 1 July 1988, the four partner States providing the space segment signed the International COSPAS-SARSAT Programme Agreement, which ensures the continuity of the system and its availability to all States on a non-discriminatory basis. In January 1992, the Government of the Russian Federation assumed responsibility for the obligations of the Union of Soviet Socialist Republics.

1988 年 7 月 1 日,提供空间段的四个合作国家签署了《国际 COSPAS-SARSAT 方案协定》,该协定确保了该系统的连续性,并在不歧视的基础上向所有国家提供服务。1992 年 1 月,俄罗斯联邦政府承担了苏联的义务。

3.5.2 System Overview 系统概述

Figure 3.6 shows the COSPAS-SARSAT system, which comprises of:

- A space segment operating in Low Earth Orbit (LEO), Geostationary Orbit (GEO) and Medium Earth Orbit (MEO);

- A ground segment consisting of satellite receiving stations, known as Local User Terminals (LUTs), and data distribution centers, known as Mission Control Centers (MCCs); and;

- Emergency radio beacons operating at 406 MHz, the characteristics of which comply with

appropriate provisions of the International Telecommunication Union（ITU）and COSPAS-SARSAT specifications.

图 3.6 显示了 COSPAS-SARSAT 系统,该系统包括:

· 在低轨道(LEO)、地球静止轨道(GEO)和中轨道(MEO)运行的空间段;

· 由卫星接收站(即本地用户终端 LUT)和数据分发中心(即任务控制中心 MCC)组成的地面段;以及

· 工作频率为 406 MHz 的紧急无线电信标,其特性符合国际电信联盟(ITU)的有关规定和 COSPAS-SARSAT 的规格。

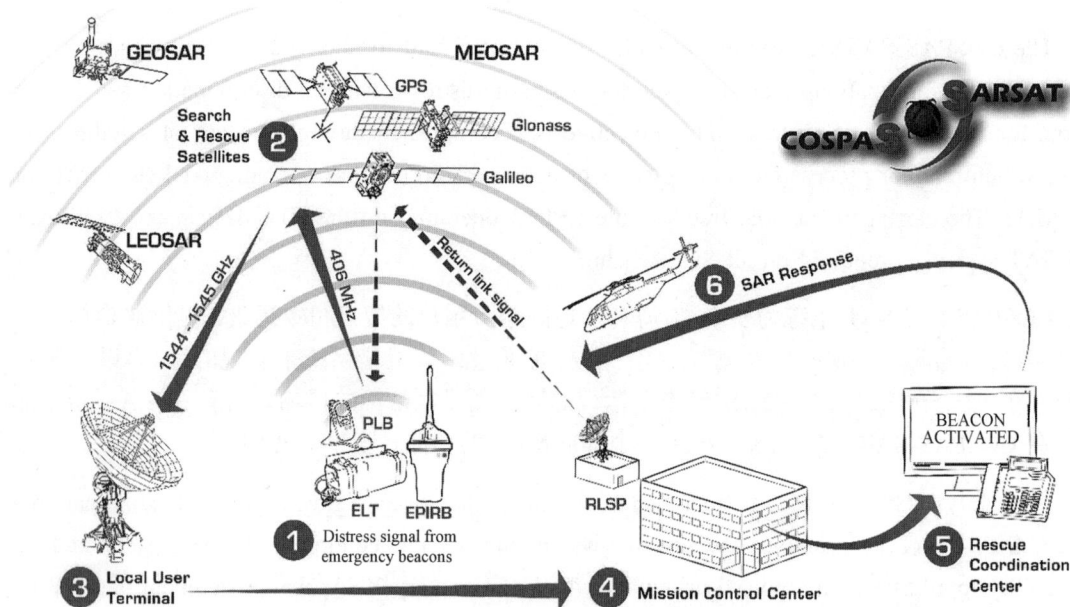

Figure 3.6   COSPAS-SARSAT System
图 3.6   COSPAS-SARSAT 系统

There are three kinds of beacons being used nowadays. ELTs are used primarily on aircraft, EPIRBs on maritime vessels and PLBs by individuals on land. ELTs, EPIRBs, and PLBs may operate on the 406 MHz frequencies with 121.5 MHz used for homing. The 406 MHz beacons transmit a digital code that contains information about the type of beacon. Each 406 MHz beacon in the world has a unique identifier. The unique identifier allows for additional information, the registration data, to be linked to each beacon.

目前使用的信标有三种。ELT 主要用于飞机,EPIRB 用于海上船舶,PLB 用于陆地上的个人。ELT、EPIRB 和 PLB 可以在 406 MHz 频率上工作,同时也使用 121.5 MHz 进行定位。406 MHz 信标可发送包含信标类型信息的数字代码。世界上每个 406 MHz 信标都有一个唯一的标识符。有了这个唯一的标识符,就可以将其他信息,即注册数据,与每个信标联系起来。

From 1 February 2009, satellite detection of 121.5 MHz and 243 MHz distress beacons was

discontinued. Only 406 MHz distress beacon transmissions are detected by satellite, and the 121.5 MHz signal used only for aircraft homing on the 406 MHz beacon.

a.After the satellite receives a beacon signal, it relays the signal to earth stations referred to as Local User Terminals (LUTs).

b.The LUT processes the data, computes the location of the distress beacon using Doppler processing, and transmits an alert message to its respective Mission Control Center (MCC) via a data communication network.

c.The MCC performs matching and merging of alert messages with other received messages, geographically sorts the data, and transmits a distress message to another MCC, an appropriate SAR authority such as a national RCC or a foreign SAR Point of Contact (SPOC).

d.The RCC investigates the beacon alert and launches assets to find the parties in distress when necessary.

自 2009 年 2 月 1 日起,卫星不再探测 121.5 MHz 和 243 MHz 的遇险信标。卫星只能探测到 406 MHz 的遇险信标发射,121.5 MHz 信号仅用于飞机对 406 MHz 信标的定位。

a.卫星接收到信标信号后,会将信号转发给被称为本地用户终端(LUT)的地球站。

b.LUT 处理数据,利用多普勒处理技术计算遇险信标的位置,并通过数据通信网络向各自的任务控制中心(MCC)发送报警电文。

c.MCC 将报警电文与其他接收到的电文进行匹配和合并,对数据进行地理分类,并向另一个 MCC、适当的搜救机构,如本国的 RCC 或国外搜救联络点 (SPOC)发送遇险电文。

d.RCC 对信标报警进行调查,并在必要时启动搜寻遇险船舶程序。

3.5.3　Modes of Operation 运行模式

The COSPAS-SARSAT system provides two modes for the detection of beacon signals—the real time mode and the global coverage mode.

COSPAS-SARSAT 系统提供两种信标信号探测模式:实时模式和全球覆盖模式。

3.5.3.1　Real Time Mode 实时模式

In this mode, a repeater on board the satellite relays the signals transmitted from 121.5 MHz or 406 MHz EPIRBs directly to ground, where it is received and processed by a LUT. If both a beacon and a LUT are simultaneously within view of a satellite, the EPIRB transmissions can be processed immediately.

在这种模式下,卫星上的中继器将 121.5 MHz 或 406 MHz EPIRB 发射的信号直接转发到地面,由 LUT 接收和处理。如果信标和 LUT 同时出现在卫星视野内,则 EPIRB 发射的信号可立即得到处理。

A satellite covers an area within approximately 2000 km either side of its track over the ground. If a LUT is not within view of a satellite, the information from the EPIRB which is relayed to earth

is lost. This fact limits the detection and location of EPIRBs operating in the real time mode to particular geographical areas surrounding a LUT.

卫星覆盖的区域大约在其地面轨道两侧 2000 km 的范围内。如果 LUT 不在卫星的视野内,EPIRB 转发给地球的信息就会丢失。这种情况将以实时模式运行的 EPIRB 的探测和定位限制在 LUT 周围的特定地理区域内。

3.5.3.2 Global Coverage Mode 全球覆盖模式

In this mode, signals from an activated 406 MHz EPIRB are frequency and time—tagged and stored in the satellite's memory. As the satellite's path brings it into view of a LUT, information, including the beacon unique identifier, frequency of detection and time of detection, is continuously relayed down to the LUT.

在这种模式下,激活的 406 MHz EPIRB 发出的信号被频率和时间标记并存储在卫星存储器中。当卫星运行路径进入 LUT 的视野时,包括信标唯一标识符、探测频率和探测时间在内的信息就会不断向下转发到 LUT。

The global coverage mode is so described because it does not suffer the geographical limitations of the real time mode and allows detection and location anywhere on the earth's surface. It is this fact that makes 406 MHz EPIRBs acceptable for the GMDSS.

全球覆盖模式,因其没有实时模式的地理限制,可以在地球表面的任何地方进行探测和定位。因此 406 MHz EPIRB 可以用于 GMDSS。

3.5.4 COSPAS-SARSAT Space Segment COSPAS-SARSAT 空间段

The COSPAS-SARSAT space segment includes satellites in LEO and GEO. Satellites in LEO and their corresponding ground receiving stations are known as the LEOSAR system, while satellites in GEO and their corresponding ground receiving stations constitute the GEOSAR system.

COSPAS-SARSAT 空间段包括低轨道和地球静止轨道上的卫星。低轨道上的卫星及其相应的地面接收站被称为 LEOSAR 系统,而地球静止轨道上的卫星及其相应的地面接收站则构成 GEOSAR 系统。

3.5.4.1 LEOSAR Space Segment LEOSAR 空间段

The nominal LEOSAR system configuration comprises four satellites, two COSPAS and two SARSAT. Russia supplies two COSPAS satellites placed in near-polar orbits from 700 to 1000 km altitude and equipped with SAR instrumentation at 121.5 MHz and 406 MHz. The USA supplies two NOAA meteorological satellites of the SARSAT system placed in sun-synchronous, near-polar orbits at about 850 km altitude, and equipped with SAR instrumentation at 121.5 MHz and 406 MHz supplied by Canada and France.

LEOSAR 系统的名义配置包括四颗卫星:两颗 COSPAS 卫星和两颗 SARSAT 卫星。俄罗斯提供两颗 COSPAS 卫星,置于 700～1000 km 高度的近极轨道上,配备 121.5 MHz 和 406 MHz 搜救设备。美国提供两颗 SARSAT 系统 NOAA 气象卫星,置于高度约为 850 km 的太阳同步近极轨道上,配备有加拿大和法国提供的 121.5 MHz 和 406 MHz 搜救设备。

Each satellite makes a complete orbit of the earth around the poles in about 100 min, traveling at a velocity of 7 km per second. The satellite views a "swath" of the earth over 6000 km wide as it circles the globe, giving an instantaneous "field of view" about the size of a continent. When viewed from the earth, the satellite crosses the sky in about 15 min, depending on the maximum elevation angle of the particular pass. The satellites low-altitude results in a low uplink power requirement, a pronounced Doppler shift, and short intervals between successive passes. The near-polar orbit results in complete world coverage over a period of time.

每颗卫星以每秒 7 km 的速度绕地球两极运行一圈,耗时约 100 min。卫星在环绕地球时可看到 6000 多千米宽的地球"掠影",瞬时 "视场"大约相当于一个大陆的大小。从地球上看,卫星穿越天空的时间约为 15 min,具体时间取决于特定经过的最大仰角。卫星高度低,因此对上行链路功率的要求低,多普勒频移明显,连续通过的时间间隔短。近极地轨道可在一段时间内完全覆盖全球。

3.5.4.2　GEOSAR Space Segment GEOSAR 空间段

The GEOSAR space segment is composed of geostationary satellites with the capability to relay the transmissions of COSPAS-SARSAT 406 MHz beacons. Geostationary satellites orbit at an altitude of 36000 km, with an orbit period of 24 h, thus appearing fixed relative to the earth, at approximately 0 degrees latitude (i.e., over the equator).

GEOSAR 空间段由地球同步静止卫星组成,具有转发 COSPAS-SARSAT 406 MHz 信标的能力。地球同步静止卫星的轨道高度为 36000 km,轨道周期为 24 h,因此相对于地球而言似乎是固定的,大约位于 0 度纬度(即赤道上空)。

A single geostationary satellite provides GEOSAR uplink coverage of about one third of the globe, except for polar regions. Therefore, five geostationary satellites equally spaced in longitude can provide continuous coverage of all areas of the globe between approximately 70° North and 70° South.

除极区外,一颗地球同步静止卫星的上行链路可覆盖全球约三分之一的地区。因此,五颗经度间隔相等的地球同步静止卫星可以连续覆盖北纬 70 度和南纬 70 度之间的所有地区。

When the two systems are combined, COSPAS-SARSAT is able to provide a robust capability by providing：

· Global LEOSAR coverage；

· Near-instantaneous GEOSAR coverage；

· Independent LEOSAR Doppler positioning；

· High probability of detection/location with the LEOSAR system anywhere on land or at sea, even in situations where obstacles block the beacon transmission to a GEOSAR satellite; and

- High system capacity.

当这两个系统结合在一起时,COSPAS-SARSAT 就能提供以下强大的功能:

- LEOSAR 全球覆盖范围;

- 近乎实时的 GEOSAR 覆盖范围;

- 独立的 LEOSAR 多普勒定位;

- 利用 LEOSAR 系统在陆地或海上任何地方进行探测/定位的概率很高,即使在信标向 GEOSAR 卫星发射信号时受到障碍物阻挡的情况下也是如此;以及

- 系统容量大。

The satellites in the two types of orbit are considered complementary. While the geostationary satellites offer near-instantaneous detection of 406 MHz distress beacons, they do not provide Doppler locating capabilities and their field of view is limited to the area between 70°N and 70°S.

这两种轨道上的卫星被认为是互补的。虽然地球同步静止卫星可以近乎瞬时地探测到 406 MHz 的遇险信标,但它们不提供多普勒定位功能,而且其视场仅限于北纬 70°和南纬 70°之间的区域。

The LEO satellites provide global coverage and Doppler locating capabilities but have an inherent delay given their orbital characteristics and field of view.

低轨道卫星提供全球覆盖和多普勒定位功能,但由于其轨道特性和视场,存在固有的延迟。

3.5.4.3 MEOSAR System MEOSAR 系统

Global Navigation Satellite System (GNSS) satellites orbit the earth at an altitude between 19000 and 23000 km, a range considered as Medium Earth Orbit. Hence this component of COSPAS-SARSAT is known as the Medium Earth Orbit Search and Rescue System, or MEOSAR. It will complement the existing LEOSAR and GEOSAR systems.

全球导航卫星系统(GNSS)卫星绕地球运行的高度在 19000～23000 km,这一范围被视为中轨道。因此,COSPAS-SARSAT 的这一部分被称为中轨道搜救系统,或 MEOSAR。它将补充现有的 LEOSAR 和 GEOSAR 系统。

The current LEOSAR and GEOSAR systems that detect and locate distress beacons have shortcomings that MEOSAR system will overcome. The GEOSAR system constantly covers the entire earth except the high-latitude (i.e., polar) regions. While the GEOSAR system can nearly instantaneously receive beacons' distress messages across most of the globe, it cannot locate a beacon unless the location is encoded in the beacon's message from a local navigation (GNSS) receiver. The LEOSAR system can locate a beacon without location information being transmitted in the beacon message (or can confirm the location even if position information is transmitted in the beacon message), but the LEOSAR satellites have a view of only a small part of the earth at any given time, which at times creates a delay in the distress signal reaching a ground station. While LEOSAR and GEOSAR still provide valuable search-and-rescue capabilities, MEOSAR is a revolution in technology.

目前用于探测和定位遇险信标的 LEOSAR 和 GEOSAR 系统存在缺陷,MEOSAR 系统将克服这些缺陷。GEOSAR 系统持续覆盖整个地球,但高纬度(即极区)除外。虽然 GEOSAR 系统几乎可以实时接收到全球大部分地区的信标遇险电文,但它无法确定信标的位置,除非本地导航(GNSS)接收机将信标位置编码进信标发射的信息内。LEOSAR 系统可以在信标电文中不发射位置信息的情况下确定信标的位置(或者即使在信标电文中发射了位置信息也能确认位置),但 LEOSAR 卫星在任何特定时间都只能看到地球的一小部分,这有时会造成遇险信号到达地球站的延迟。尽管 LEOSAR 和 GEOSAR 仍能提供有价值的搜救功能,但 MEOSAR 则是一场技术革命。

Once fully operational, the MEOSAR system will offer the advantages of both the LEOSAR and GEOSAR systems without their limitations by providing transmission of the distress message and independent location of the beacon, with near-real-time worldwide coverage. The MEOSAR system will facilitate other planned enhancements for COSPAS-SARSAT beacons, such as a return-link-service (RLS) transmission to a distress beacon that will provide, for example, the user with a confirmation that the distress message has been received.

一旦全面运行,MEOSAR 系统将兼具 LEOSAR 和 GEOSAR 系统的优点,而没有局限性。它能提供遇险电文的发射和信标的独立定位,覆盖全球范围且近乎实时。MEOSAR 系统将促进 COSPAS-SARSAT 信标的既定的计划增强功能,如向遇险信标发送返回链路业务(RLS),向用户提供遇险电文已收到的确认电文等。

The large number of MEOSAR satellites that will be in orbit when the system is fully operational will allow each distress message to be relayed at the same time by several satellites to several ground antennas, improving the likelihood of quick detection and improving the accuracy of the location determination.

当该系统全面运行时,将有大量的 MEOSAR 卫星在轨道上,这将使每条遇险电文能同时由几颗卫星转发到几个地面天线,从而提高快速探测的可能性,并提高定位的准确性。

At the beginning of 2013, COSPAS-SARSAT entered a Demonstration and Evaluation (D&E) phase for the MEOSAR system to show that MEOSAR performance met expectations, and that distress alerts received by SAR authorities from the MEOSAR system have the required reliability and accuracy.

2013 年年初,COSPAS-SARSAT 进入了 MEOSAR 系统的演示和评估(D&E)阶段,以表明 MEOSAR 的性能符合预期,搜救机构从 MEOSAR 系统收到的遇险报警具有所需的可靠性和准确性。

The MEOSAR early operational capability (EOC), where distress alerts provided by the MEOSAR system are provided to SAR authorities for operational use, began in December 2016. As of 1 May 2023, twenty-nine MEO earth stations (Local User Terminals known as MEOLUTs), capable of simultaneously tracking up to 400 satellites, were commissioned for MEO search-and-rescue satellite payloads, and at least 18 more MEOLUTs (with multiple antennas each) are planned between 2023 and 2025.

MEOSAR 早期业务能力(EOC)于 2016 年 12 月开始,将 MEOSAR 系统的遇险报警提供给搜救机构供搜救使用。截至 2023 年 5 月 1 日,29 个 MEO 地球站(称为 MEOLUT 的本地用户终端),能够同时跟踪多达 400 颗卫星,被委托用于 MEO 搜救卫星有效载荷,并且计划在 2023 年和 2025 年之间至少增加 18 个 MEOLUT (每个 MEOLUT 都有多个天线)。

In November 2022, the "Declaration of Intent Between the Cooperating Agencies of the International COSPAS-SARSAT Programme and the Maritime Safety Administration of the People's Republic of China for Cooperation on the COSPAS-SARSAT MEOSAR Satellite System" was signed, associating the six SAR/BDS (BeiDou) payloads to the System as the fourth MEOSAR constellation (in addition to Galileo, GLONASS and GPS).

2022 年 11 月,"国际 COSPAS-SARSAT 项目合作机构与中华人民共和国海事局关于 CO-SPAS-SARSAT MEOSAR 卫星系统合作意向声明"的协议签署。六个 SAR/BDS(北斗)有效载荷与该系统相关联,成为第四 MEOSAR 星座 (此外还有伽利略,GLONASS 和 GPS)。

3.5.5 New Developments 最新进展

3.5.5.1 Space Segment 空间段

The parties to the COSPAS-SARSAT agreement continue to plan for the long-term operation of the LEOSAR space segment and the longer-term operation of the GEOSAR system.

COSPAS-SARSAT 协定方继续规划 LEOSAR 空间段的长期运行和 GEOSAR 系统的长期运行。

Future space segment plans include the study of placing search and rescue instruments in a Medium Earth Orbit (MEO) onboard global navigation satellite systems such as the United States Global Positioning System (GPS), Russian GLONASS, the proposed European Galileo system and Chinese Beidou system. Search and rescue instruments in that orbit could significantly enhance current operations.

未来的空间段计划包括研究将搜救设备置于中轨道(MEO)上的全球导航卫星系统,如美国全球定位系统(GPS)、俄罗斯全球导航卫星系统(GLONASS)和欧洲伽利略系统以及中国的北斗卫星系统。该轨道上的搜救设备可以大大增强目前的系统运行。

3.5.5.2 Distress Beacons 遇险信标

In order to make effective use of search and rescue instruments in Geostationary Orbits, new 406 MHz distress beacons have been introduced with the capability to accept position information from internal or external navigation devices such as GPS receivers. This has the potential to provide near-instantaneous alerting and locating via the GEOSAR system.

为了有效利用地球静止轨道上的搜救设备,新的 406 MHz 遇险信标已经被采用,它能够接受来自内部或外部导航设备(如 GPS 接收机)的位置信息。这有可能通过 GEOSAR 系统提供近乎实时的报警和定位。

A GPS equipped beacon has a location accuracy of 120 m and location is provided by geostationary satellites within minutes. Non-GPS beacons have a location accuracy of 5 km. The satellite system takes 90 min on average to calculate the initial position from a beacon which is not GPS equipment, but it may take up to 5 h depending on the conditions.

配备 GPS 的信标的定位精度为 120 m, 地球同步静止卫星可在几分钟内提供定位。没有配备 GPS 的信标的定位精度为 5 km。卫星系统计算没有配备 GPS 设备信标的初始位置平均需要 90 min, 但根据具体情况, 可能需要长达 5 h。

Maritime Mobile Services
海上移动业务

Chapter 4

4.1　General Introduction　概述

The term "maritime" or "marine" in this section refers to MF/HF/VHF communication systems, which are used for distress alerting, SAR coordinating communications, on-scene communications and general radiocommunications, to carry out radiotelephone, radiotelex and Digital Selective Calling (DSC) services.

本节中的"海事"或"海上"一词是指 MF/HF/VHF 通信系统,用于遇险报警、搜救协调通信、现场通信和常规无线电通信,以提供无线电话、无线电传和数字选择性呼叫(DSC)业务。

The system consists of the following three subsystems:

MF communication subsystem, which is used for medium-range service;

HF communication subsystem, which is used for long-range service; and

VHF communication subsystem, which is used for short-range service.

该系统由以下三个子系统组成:

MF 通信子系统,用于中程业务;

HF 通信子系统,用于远程业务;以及

VHF 通信子系统,用于短程业务。

4.1.1　Frequency and Coverage　频率和覆盖范围

The number of times that the alternating current in a radio wave performs its complete cycle per second is known as its frequency. The international unit of measurement of frequency is the

hertz（abbreviated-Hz）.

无线电波中的交流电每秒完成一个完整周期的次数称为频率。频率的国际计量单位是赫兹(缩写为 Hz)。

The wavelength of a radio wave is the distance between two successive positive peaks of two cycles. Wavelength is inversely proportional to frequency, i.e. as the frequency of a radio wave increases, the wavelength decreases, and vice-versa.

无线电波的波长是两个周期内连续两个正峰值之间的距离。波长与频率成反比,即无线电波的频率越高,波长越短,反之亦然。

The wavelength of a radio wave is determined by the formula:

wavelength（m）= velocity（m）per second（s）divided by frequency in hertz（Hz）.

无线电波的波长由公式确定:

波长(米)= 波速(米每秒)除以频率(赫兹)。

The velocity of a radio wave is a constant 300000000 m per second.

无线电波的速度是常数,每秒 300000000 m。

4.1.1.1　Units of Frequency 频率单位

Units of frequency are:

频率单位为:

The kilohertz（kHz）= 1000 hertz

The megahertz（MHz）= 1000000 hertz

The gigahertz（GHz）= 1000000000 hertz

4.1.1.2　Sub-division of the Radio Frequency Spectrum 无线电频谱的细分

Table 4.1 shows the ITU radio Frequency Bands used in GMDSS.

表 4.1 列出了 GMDSS 使用的国际电联无线电频段。

Table 4.1　ITU Radio Frequency Bands in GMDSS

表 4.1　GMDSS 中的国际电联无线电频段

Medium Frequencies 中频	MF	300 to 3000 kHz
High Frequencies 高频	HF	3 to 30 MHz
Very High Frequencies 甚高频	VHF	30 to 300 MHz

Continued　续表

Ultra High Frequencies 超高频	UHF	300 to 3000 MHz
Super High Frequencies 极高频	SHF	3 to 30 GHz

4.1.1.3　Radio Coverage 无线电覆盖范围

Short-range Services（up to 40 n mile）短程业务（最多 40 n mile）

VHF provides a short-range service on the band between 156 MHz and 174 MHz，where：

· 156. 525 MHz（Channel 70）for distress alerts and safety calls by DSC；

· 156. 8 MHz（Channel 16）for distress and safety traffic by radiotelephony，including SAR coordinating functions and on-scene communications.

VHF 在 156 MHz 和 174 MHz 之间的频段提供短程业务：

· 156.525 MHz（70 频道），用于通过 DSC 发出遇险报警和安全呼叫；

· 156.8 MHz（16 频道），用于通过无线电话进行遇险和安全通信，包括搜救协调功能和现场通信。

Medium-range Services（up to 200 n mile）中程业务（最多 200 n mile）

A medium-range service is mainly provided on frequencies in the 2 MHz band. In the ship-to-shore，ship-to-ship and shore-to-ship directions，2187. 5 kHz will be used for distress alerts and safety calls by DSC and 2182 kHz will be used for distress and safety traffic by radiotelephony，including SAR coordinating functions and on-scene communications. 2174. 5 kHz will be used for distress and safety traffic by radiotelex（NBDP）.

中程业务主要通过 2 MHz 频段提供。在船对岸、船对船和岸对船方向，2187.5 kHz 用于 DSC 遇险报警和安全呼叫，2182 kHz 用于无线电话遇险和安全通信，包括搜救协调功能和现场通信。2174.5 kHz 将用于无线电传（NBDP）的遇险和安全通信。

Frequencies near 500 kHz are used in the shore-to-ship direction. For instance，the frequency 518 kHz is being used to transmit navigational and meteorological warnings in the NAVTEX system.

500 kHz 附近的频率用于岸对船方向。例如，在 NAVTEX 系统中，518 kHz 的频率用于发送航行和气象警告。

Long-range Services（150 to more than 900 nm）远程业务（150 n mile 至 900 n mile 以上）

Use of HF provides a long-range service in both the ship-to-shore and shore-to-ship directions. In areas covered by INMARSAT it can be used as an alternative to satellite communications and outside these areas it provides the only long-range communication capability. Frequencies have been designated in the 4, 6, 8, 12 and 16（MHz）bands for HF service.

HF 的使用可提供船对岸和岸对船方向的远程业务。在 INMARSAT 覆盖的地区,HF 可作为卫星通信的替代,而在这些地区之外,HF 则是唯一的远程通信手段。HF 业务指定使用 4、6、8、12 和 16(MHz)频段。

Coast stations, participating in the HF distress and safety watchkeeping network, need to choose from five available frequency bands to relay an alert. The choice depends on the position of the ship in distress, the geographical area to be alerted and the current propagation characteristics. It is envisaged that ships equipped with the HF option will maintain a watch on the 8 MHz alerting frequency and one of the other dedicated HF frequencies. The latter will be the frequency most appropriate to the area in which the ship is sailing.

参与 HF 遇险和安全值守网络的海岸电台需要从五个可用频段中选择一个来转发报警。这取决于遇险船舶的位置、需要发出报警的地理区域以及当前的传播特性。配备 HF 设备的船舶将使用 8 MHz 报警频率和其他专用 HF 频率之一进行值守。后者将是最适合船舶所航行区域的频率。

4.1.2 Modes of Communications 通信模式

Marine radio equipment uses various modes of emission for different functions. These modes can be summarized as follows:

- Radiotelephone—the most common mode of operation. In this mode, voice signals are transmitted over a radio link using various forms of modulation.
- Narrow Band Direct Printing（NBDP）telegraphy—telex signals are transmitted over radio.
- Digital Selective Calling（DSC）—a paging system that uses data signals to automate the transmission of distress, urgency or safety calls via MF, HF or VHF radio.

海上无线电设备使用不同的发射模式来实现不同的功能。这些模式可归纳如下:

- 无线电话——最常见的操作模式。在这种模式下,语音信号通过各种调制方式在无线电链路上传输。
- 窄带直接印字(NBDP)电报——通过无线电传输电传信号。
- 数字选择性呼叫（DSC）——一种寻呼系统,使用数字信号通过 MF、HF 或 VHF 无线电自动发送遇险、紧急或安全呼叫。

4.2 Digital Selective Calling 数字选择性呼叫

A Digital Selective Calling (DSC) message is a brief burst of digitized information transmitted from one station to alert another station or stations. It indicates to the receiving station(s) who is calling and the purpose of the call.

数字选择性呼叫（DSC)电文是一个台为提醒另一个或多个台而发送的一段简短的数字化信息。它向接收台表明呼叫发起者和呼叫目的。

The digital techniques used in DSC systems provide higher resistance to interference and fading than radiotelephone transmissions on the same frequency. For these reasons, DSC usually provides a greater transmission range than voice modes of operation.

DSC 系统使用的数字技术比相同频率的无线电话传输具有更强的抗干扰和抗衰减能力。因此，与语音操作模式相比，DSC 的传输范围通常更大。

4.2.1 DSC Shipborne Equipment DSC 船载设备

DSC is used as a means of establishing initial contact between stations. Following an alert by DSC message, communications must be established between the transmitting station and the receiving station(s) by either radiotelephony or NBDP.

DSC 是一种在台与台之间建立初始通信的手段。通过 DSC 电文发出报警后，必须通过无线电话或 NBDP 在发射台和接收台之间建立通信。

The DSC signal processing functions are carried out by a DSC modem (modulator demodulator) or DSC controller. To enable the transmission and reception of DSC messages, the controller is electrically connected to an associated transmitter and watchkeeping receiver. Some manufacturers produce integrated DSC watchkeeping receivers and controllers in one chassis.

DSC 信号处理功能由 DSC 调制解调器或 DSC 控制器执行。为了能够发送和接收 DSC 电文，控制器与相关的发射机和值守机相连接。一些制造商将 DSC 值守机和控制器集成在一个机箱中。

If transmission of a DSC alert is required, an operator can encode the DSC controller with information identifying the station (or stations) with whom communication is desired and the purpose of the call. On command, this information is fed to the transmitter for broadcasting.

如果需要发送 DSC 报警，操作员可以向 DSC 控制器输入信息，以确定希望与之通信的电台(或多个电台)以及呼叫的目的。根据指令，这些信息将被发送到发射机进行广播。

Most DSC systems also control the frequency of the associated MF/HF transmitter, automatically changing it to the DSC distress frequency when a distress message is sent from the controller.

大多数 DSC 系统还能控制相关 MF/HF 发射机的频率，在控制器发送遇险电文时自动将其更改为 DSC 遇险频率。

All controllers feature a "DISTRESS" button, that automatically sends a distress alert using pre-programmed information.

所有控制器都有一个"遇险"按钮,可使用预先编程的信息自动发送遇险报警。

The DSC controller can be connected to the ship navigation equipment (GPS, etc.) to automatically update the location and time information.

DSC 控制器可与船舶导航设备(GPS 等)连接,自动更新位置和时间信息。

When not transmitting, the DSC controller is connected to the DSC watchkeeping receiver. All DSC calls on the frequency to which the receiver is tuned are examined by the controller and, if found to be addressed to that ship, the operator is alerted by audible and visual alarms. The contents of the DSC message are available to the operator on an alphanumeric display screen. If a printer is connected, the operator can also see the contents of the DSC messages on the printer.

不发射时,DSC 控制器与 DSC 值守机相连。控制器会检查接收机调谐频率上的所有 DSC 呼叫,如果发现呼叫对象是本船,则会发出声光警报提醒操作员。操作员可在字母数字显示屏上看到 DSC 电文的内容。如果连接了打印机,操作员还可在打印机上看到 DSC 电文的内容。

4.2.2　DSC Frequencies DSC 频率

The DSC distress and safety frequencies are listed below.

DSC 遇险和安全频率如下。

MF/HF DSC distress and safety frequencies (in kHz): 2187.5, 4207.5, 6312.0, 8414.5, 12577.0, 16804.5.

MF/HF DSC 遇险和安全频率(单位: kHz): 2187.5, 4207.5, 6312.0, 8414.5, 12577.0, 16804.5。

VHF DSC distress and safety channel: VHF marine Channel 70 (156.525 MHz).

VHF DSC 遇险和安全频道:VHF 海上 70 频道(156.525 MHz)。

Frequencies shown in Table 4.2 are used for international DSC ship and coast station calling.

表 4.2 所示频率用于国际 DSC 船舶和海岸电台呼叫。

Table 4.2   International DSC Ship and Coast Station Calling Frequencies

表 4.2   国际 DSC 船舶和海岸电台呼叫频率

Frequency band 频段	Use 用途	Ship transmit（kHz） 船舶发射(kHz)	Shore transmit（kHz） 岸上发射(kHz)
MF Ⅰ	International calling 国际呼叫	458.5	455.5
	Inter-ship calling 船舶间呼叫	2177.0	—
MF Ⅱ	International calling 国际呼叫	2189.5	2177.0
4 MHz	International calling 国际呼叫	4208.0	4219.5
		4208.5	4220.0
		4209.0	4220.5
6 MHz	International calling 国际呼叫	6312.5	6331.0
		6313.0	6331.5
		6313.5	6332.0
8 MHz	International calling 国际呼叫	8415.0	8436.5
		8415.5	8437.0
		8416.0	8437.5
12 MHz	International calling 国际呼叫	12577.5	12657.0
		12578.0	12657.5
		12578.5	12658.0
16 MHz	International calling 国际呼叫	16805.0	16903.0
		16805.5	16903.5
		16806.0	16904.0
18 MHz	International calling 国际呼叫	18898.5	19703.5
		18899.0	19704.0
		18899.5	19704.5
22 MHz	International calling 国际呼叫	22374.5	22444.0
		22375.0	22444.5
		22375.5	22445.0
25 MHz	International calling 国际呼叫	25208.5	26121.0
		25209.0	26121.5
		25209.5	26122.0
VHF	Distress and international calling 遇险呼叫和国际呼叫	Channel 70 70 频道	Channel 70 70 频道

4.2.3　**Call Formats 呼叫格式**

The DSC call sequence is undertaken in 9 steps：

a.Dot pattern；

b.Phasing sequence；

c.Format specifier；

d.Address（the stations being called，a specific station or ALL ships）；

e.Category（the priority of the call）；

f.Self-identification；

g.Messages；

h.End of Sequence（EOS）；

i.Error Check Character（ECC）.

DSC 呼叫顺序分为 9 个步骤：

a.点阵；

b.定相序列；

c.格式符；

d.地址(被呼台、特定台或所有台)；

e.类别(呼叫优先级)；

f.自识别；

g.电文；

h.序列结束(EOS)；

i.差错校验符（ECC）。

4.2.4　**Maritime Mobile Service Identity（MMSI）海上移动业务 识别码(MMSI)**

Each ship and coast station fitted with DSC is allocated a unique 9-digit identification number，known as a Maritime Mobile Service Identity（MMSI）. The MMSI is permanently programmed into the DSC equipment，and is sent automatically with each transmission.

每艘装有 DSC 的船舶和海岸电台都有一个独一无二的 9 位识别码,即海上移动业务识别码（MMSI）。MMSI 已永久性地编入 DSC 设备中,并在每次发射时自动发送。

MMSIs are allocated on an international basis，with the first three digits representing the na-tionality of the administration responsible for the ship. These three digits are known as the Maritime

Identification Digits (MID). The Chinese MID is 412 and 413. A typical Chinese MMSI would be 412001000.

MMSI 是在世界范围内分配的,前三位数字代表负责船舶的主管机关的国籍。这三位数字称为海上识别数字(MID)。中国的 MID 为 412 和 413。典型的中国 MMSI 为 412001000。

MMSIs allocated to a coast radio station always commence with two leading zeros. For example, the MMSI of the Shanghai Radio Station is 004122100.

分配给海岸电台的 MMSI 总是以两个零开头。例如,上海海岸电台的 MMSI 为 004122100。

Group MMSI numbers begin with a single 0 before the MID.

MMSI 组呼码在 MID 前加上一个 0。

Group MMSIs can be manually programmed into a DSC-equipped radio by the user at will (unlike the self-ID). Any number with a leading zero can be used as a Group MMSI, and they do not need to be registered, but the entity deciding on a Group MMSI should use the MID of the host country. Safety and Urgency calls ("Announcements") can be sent to a Group MMSI. Each vessel desiring to be part of a group would enter the same Group MMSI into their DSC equipment, which usually can be named for convenience by the user.

MMSI 组呼码可由用户根据意愿手动编程到配备 DSC 的无线电中(与自识别码不同)。任何以零开头的数字都可用作 MMSI 组呼码,而且无须注册,但决定 MMSI 组呼码的公司或者单位应使用所在国的 MID。可以用 MMSI 组呼码发送安全和紧急呼叫("公告")。每艘希望入组的船舶都要在其 DSC 设备中输入相同的 MMSI 组呼码,用户通常可以为其命名以方便使用。

4.2.5 Distress Alert Attempts and Cancellation of an Inadvertent DSC Distress Alert 遇险报警尝试和取消误发射的 DSC 遇险报警

At MF and HF, Distress Alert Attempts may be transmitted either as single frequency or multi-frequency call attempts but, at VHF, only single frequency call attempt is used.

在 MF 和 HF,遇险报警尝试可作为单频或多频呼叫尝试发送,但在 VHF,只使用单频呼叫尝试。

4.2.5.1 Single Frequency Call Attempt 单频呼叫尝试

In new equipment the uninterrupted burst of five 7.2 s alerting sequence comprising the Distress Alert Attempt will be immediately followed by an "expansion sequence" which will repeat the position with increased precision. Older equipment will probably not receive the "expansion sequence", but the distress alert will be received as usual. The single frequency call attempt is sent once, followed by an interval of a few minutes before trying again on another frequency if desired. If the operator does not make any further adjustments to the DSC controller, the alert will be automatically repeated on the same frequency after 3-4 min.

在新设备中,包括遇险报警尝试的 5 个 7.2 s 的不间断报警序列发送之后会立即出现一个

"扩展序列",以更高的精度重复该位置。老式设备可能收不到"扩展序列",但遇险报警会照常收到。单频呼叫尝试发送一次后,间隔几分钟后再试一次(如果需要的话,可使用另一个频率)。如果操作员未对 DSC 控制器进行任何进一步调整,报警将在 3～4 min 后自动在同一频率上重复发送。

On receiving a DSC distress alert on MF/HF, coast stations must send a DSC Distress Acknowledgement on the same frequency between 1 and 2 min after reception (VHF DSC Distress Acknowledgements are sent as soon as possible). Thus, an interval of 3 min would be appropriate before manually repeating a single frequency distress alert on MF or HF. VHF Distress Alert Attempts may be sent simultaneously with MF or HF Distress Alert Attempts at any time.

在接收到 MF/HF 的 DSC 遇险报警后,海岸电台必须在接收后 1～2 min 在同一频率上发送 DSC 遇险确认(VHF DSC 遇险确认会尽快发送)。因此,在手动重复 MF 或 HF 单频遇险报警之前,最好间隔 3 min。VHF 遇险报警尝试可随时与 MF 或 HF 遇险报警尝试同时发送。

4.2.5.2　Multi-Frequency Call Attempt 多频呼叫尝试

This is only permitted if the ship can comply with one of the following two conditions:

a.The calls can be transmitted within 1 min or less;

b.a continuous watch for acknowledgements can be kept on all frequencies except for the transmit frequency in use.

船舶只有在符合以下两个条件之一的情况下,才允许这样做:

a.通话可在 1 min 或更短时间内发射;

b.除使用中的发射频率外,可在所有频率上持续守听确认应答。

The frequencies selected should always include the 2 MHz and 8 MHz bands plus at least one other. The individual distress alerting sequences used for multi-frequency Distress Alert Attempts take 9 s to transmit as each one comprises the 7.2 s alerting sequence followed by the 1.8 s "expansion sequence".

所选频率应始终包括 2 MHz 和 8 MHz 频段,外加至少一个其他频段。多频率遇险报警尝试所使用的单个遇险报警序列的传输时间为 9 s,因为每个序列包括 7.2 s 的报警序列和 1.8 s 的"扩展序列"。

The "multi-frequency" concept does not apply to VHF transmissions, since there is only one VHF channel available. The VHF DSC equipment returns to watchkeeping mode immediately after transmission. Consequently, VHF DSC Distress Alert Attempts may be sent simultaneously with MF/HF Distress Alert Attempts as mentioned above.

"多频"概念不适用于 VHF 发射,因为只有一个 VHF 频道可用。VHF DSC 设备在发射后会立即返回值守模式。因此,VHF DSC 遇险报警尝试可与上述 MF/HF 遇险报警尝试同时发送。

The purpose of VHF and MF is essentially to attract the attention of other ships in the vicinity,

and this is why all DSC receivers must be kept operational at all times, and in all Sea Areas, for distress and safety watchkeeping purposes.

VHF 和 MF 的主要目的是吸引附近其他船舶的注意,这也是所有海区的所有 DSC 接收机必须始终保持工作状态的原因,以便进行遇险和安全值守。

4.2.5.3 Cancellation of an Inadvertent DSC Distress Alert 取消误发射的 DSC 遇险报警

To cancel the distress alert using the following voice-only procedure:

a.Immediately cancel the distress alert over the telephony distress traffic channel associated with each DSC channel on which the "distress alert" was transmitted.

b.Monitor the radiotelephony distress traffic channel associated with the DSC channel on which the distress was transmitted and respond to any communications concerning that distress alert as appropriate.

c.Separate notification of the accidental transmission and its cancellation should be sent to the relevant RCC, e.g. by INMARSAT-C.

使用语音取消遇险报警程序如下:

a.立即通过与发射"遇险报警"的各 DSC 频道相关的电话遇险通信频道取消遇险报警。

b.监控与发射遇险信号的 DSC 频道相关的无线电遇险通信频道,并酌情应答与该遇险报警相关的任何通信。

c.应将误报警发送和取消发送的通知单独发送给相关的 RCC,例如通过 INMARSAT-C。

There is no penalty if accidental DSC distress alerts are cancelled by this procedure.

如果通过此程序取消了 DSC 误报警,则不会受到任何处罚。

4.2.6 Testing of DSC Equipment and Watchkeeping DSC 设备的测试和值守

A test is considered successful when a DSC call to another station is followed by an acknowledgement received from that other station.

如果在向另一个台发出 DSC 呼叫后收到了该台的确认,则认为测试成功。

To simplify operation of the equipment, "Test Call" and "Test Call Acknowledgement" sequences have been developed.

为简化操作,DSC 设备具有"测试呼叫"和"测试呼叫确认"序列。

These calls are given the "Safety" category and may be used on VHF, MF and HF equipment.

这些呼叫属于"安全"类别,可在 VHF、MF 和 HF 设备上使用。

The calls are transmitted on the DSC Distress and Safety frequencies, avoiding use of 2 MHz as far as possible.

呼叫可以通过 DSC 遇险和安全频率发送,尽量避免使用 2 MHz。

The Test Call contains the Format Specifier "Individual", Category "Safety", First Telecommand "Test" and EOS symbol "RQ".

测试呼叫包含格式规范"单呼"、类别"安全"、第一遥控指令"测试"和 EOS 标志"RQ"。

These can be entered manually, but some equipment enters them automatically when "External Test" (or something similar) is selected from a menu. All the operator then has to do is to enter the MMSI of the station to be called and select the frequency.

这些信息可以手动输入,但有些设备会在从菜单中选择"外部测试"(或类似功能)时自动输入。操作员只需输入要呼叫的电台的 MMSI 并选择频率即可。

After receiving a Test Call, suitably equipped coast stations will send an automatic DSC Test Call Acknowledgement. When selecting a suitable coast station, it is necessary to firstly ascertain that it keeps watch on the required frequency—not all GMDSS stations scan all 6 MF/HF frequencies. Also, the frequency should be checked to ensure that the Test Call is not initiated if other signals are in progress. Future MF/HF DSC controllers will be designed to block transmission of Routine Calls and Test Calls if the frequency is occupied (pre-existing equipment only does this for Routine Calls on VHF).

在收到测试呼叫后,装备合适的海岸电台将自动发送 DSC 测试呼叫确认。在选择合适的海岸电台时,首先要确定该电台是否在所需频率上值守——并非所有 GMDSS 电台都会扫描全部 6 个 MF/HF 频率。此外,还应检查频率,以确保在其他信号正在进行发送时不启动测试呼叫。未来的 MF/HF DSC 控制器将设计成在频率被占用时阻止常规呼叫和测试呼叫的发射(现有设备仅在 VHF 上的常规呼叫有此功能)。

The Test Call and Test Call Acknowledgement can also be exchanged between ships, but in practice, a coast station would normally be preferred.

测试呼叫和测试呼叫确认也可以在船舶之间进行,但在实际操作中,通常还是选择海岸电台。

In accordance with COMSAR/Circ.35, issued by MSC 78, the ITU indicated that excessive Test Calls on DSC distress and safety frequencies were overloading the system to the point where interference to distress and safety calls had become a cause for concern. In view of managing and reducing the number of Test Calls on MF/HF DSC distress and safety frequencies, it was agreed that live testing on DSC should be limited to once a week.

根据 MSC 78 发布的 COMSAR/Circ.35,国际电联指出,DSC 遇险和安全频率上过多的测试呼叫使系统超载,以至于其对遇险和安全呼叫的干扰令人担忧。为了管理和减少 MF/HF DSC 遇险和安全频率上的测试呼叫数量,国际电联同意 DSC 发射测试应限制在每周一次。

Although transmission of the special "Test" format by a DSC-equipped VHF radio on Channel 70 is now permitted, it will only be practicable with ship and shore-based radio equipment meeting the requirements of Recommendation ITU-R M.493-11, or version higher. Regular use of DSC VHF

Channel 70 on a routine basis to make contact with another vessel or a coast station will confirm the VHF DSC equipment is operating correctly.

虽然现在允许装有 DSC 的 VHF 无线电在 70 频道上发射特殊的"测试"格式,但只有符合 ITU-R M.493-11 建议或更高版本要求的船舶和岸基无线电设备才可用。按惯性定期使用 VHF DSC 70 频道与另一艘船或海岸电台联系,可确认 VHF DSC 设备运行正常。

When it is necessary to make a test however, the call should be transmitted only to a specifically selected station, which may then also acknowledge the Test Call. Normally there would be no further communication between the two stations involved.

然而,当需要进行测试时,呼叫只能发送到一个特定选择的电台,该台也可以确认测试呼叫。通常情况下,两个相关台之间不会有进一步的通信。

On VHF, if no suitable stations are within range, it may be convenient to test the DSC by calling own ship's duplicate unit, preferably using low power (1 W).

在 VHF 上,如果范围内没有合适的电台,可以通过呼叫自己船上的同类设备来测试 DSC,最好使用低功率(1 W)。

4.3 NBDP Equipment and Systems NBDP 设备和系统

4.3.1 Overview 概述

NBDP (or "radiotelex") is a method of sending telex information over a radio channel. The system employs special error detection and correction methods to counter the effects of interference or fading over the radio circuit.

NBDP(或"无线电报")是一种通过无线电频道发送电报信息的方法。该系统采用特殊的检错和纠错方法来抵消无线电线路上的干扰或衰减的影响。

4.3.2 Identification Number and Answerback 选呼码和应答码

All NBDP equipment is programmed with a unique identification or "selcall" (selective calling) number, which works in the same fashion as the DSC MMSI number.

所有 NBDP 设备都有一个独特的选呼(选择性呼叫)码,其工作方式与 DSC MMSI 号码相同。

The selcall number used is either a 5-digit number, or (in the case of GMDSS ships) the ship's MMSI, followed by a plus (+) sign.

选呼码是一个五位数,或者(对于 GMDSS 船舶)船舶的 MMSI,后面跟一个加号 (+)。

Selcall numbers for coast stations are usually a 4-digit number, followed by a plus (+) sign.

海岸电台的选呼码通常是一个四位数,后面跟一个加号 (+)。

If an NBDP station is interrogated（requested for its identification）by the use of the "Who Are You"（WRU）command, it will send an "Answerback"—comprising its selcall number and other information（usually the name of the ship or coast station in abbreviated form）.

如果使用"你是谁"（WRU）命令对 NBDP 台进行询问（要求确认其身份），该台将发送"应答码"，应答码包括选呼码和其他信息（通常是船名或海岸电台名称的缩写）。

Answerback may also be sent by the use of the "Here is" command.

应答码也可以使用"这里是"命令发送回电。

4.3.3   System Codes 系统代码

The marine radiotelex code consists of the normal 26 letters of the alphabet, numerals 0 to 9, punctuation marks, symbols for carriage return, line feed, letter shift, figure shift, "Here is", "Who are you?", plus three special characters known as RQ, A（alpha）and B（beta）. The three special characters are used to control the direction of the radio circuit（similar to the action of the "press to talk" button in a radiotelephone system）and for the correction of errors.

海事无线电传代码由 26 个普通字母、数字 0 至 9、标点符号、回车、换行、字母移位、数字移位、"这里是"、"你是谁?"符号以及三个特殊字符 RQ、A 和 B 组成。这三个特殊字符用于控制无线电线路的方向(类似于无线电话系统中"按键通话"按钮的作用)和纠错。

4.3.4   Transmission of Information 信息发射

Each character of the marine radiotelex code is represented by a combination of three "lows" and four "highs"—or three "marks" and four "spaces". A mark or space is represented by a different audio tone. These tones are generated by the NBDP equipment, passed to the radio transmitter where they are modulated into a radio signal for transmission. At the receiving station, the tones are de-modulated by the radio receiver and passed to the NBDP equipment for processing and display on a monitor or a printer.

海事无线电传代码的每个字符由三个"低音"和四个"高音"或三个"传号"和四个"空号"组合而成。一个传号或空号由不同的音频音调表示。这些音调由 NBDP 设备产生,然后传送到无线电发射机,在那里被调制成无线电信号进行发射。在接收台,这些音调由无线电接收机解调,然后传给 NBDP 设备进行处理,并显示在显示器或打印机上。

4.3.5   Modes of Transmission 发射模式

The following sections describe the various modes of transmission offered by the NBDP system.

下文将介绍 NBDP 系统提供的各种发射模式。

4.3.5.1   Automatic Re-transmission Request（ARQ）Mode 自动请求重复（ARQ）模式

This mode offers full error correction capabilities, and is useable even in very poor radio conditions. In this mode, only two stations can communicate with each other at any one time, as the

sending and receiving stations are synchronized (electronically locked) together. The originating station is called the MASTER, whilst the called or receiving station is called the SLAVE. The MASTER station remains the MASTER throughout the entire contact, no matter which station is transmitting at any one time, as the MASTER controls the timing of the whole system.

这种模式具有全面的纠错功能,即使在无线电条件很差的情况下也可以使用。在这种模式下,由于发送台和接收台同步(电子锁定),因此任何时候都只能有两个台相互通信。发送台称为主台,被叫台或接收台称为副台。由于主台控制着整个系统的定时,因此在整个联络过程中,无论任何时候哪个台在发送信息,主台始终是主台。

The MASTER station transmits three characters in 210 milliseconds (ms), then switches to receive for 240 ms. During the receive period, the MASTER station looks for a logic reply from the SLAVE to indicate that the three characters have been received correctly.

主台在 210 毫秒(ms)内发送三个字符,然后在 240 ms 内转为接收。在接收期间,主台会查看副台的逻辑回复,以表明已正确接收到三个字符。

If the correct reply is received the MASTER station then proceeds with the next three characters. However, if there has been an error in the reception at either end due to interference or fading, the last three characters are repeated for a total of 32 transmissions, at which point radio contact is automatically broken off. The MASTER station will then attempt to re-establish contact and, if successful, it will continue the communication from the point where it was broken off.

如果收到正确的回复,主台将继续发送下三个字符。但是,如果由于干扰或衰减导致两端接收错误,则会重复最后三个字符,总共发送 32 次,此时无线电连接会自动中断。主台随后将尝试重新建立连接,如果成功,将从中断处继续通信。

Both MASTER and SLAVE stations only acknowledge receipt of the correct logic signal consisting of the 3/4 ratio. All other signals are treated as errors and not printed. Therefore, interference and fading should not cause misprints, but only a slowing down of the traffic flow between the two stations.

主台和副台只确认收到由四个空号、三个传号固定组成的正确逻辑信号。所有其他信号均被视为错误信号,不予打印。因此,干扰和衰减不会导致打印错误,只会减慢两个台之间的通信。

On completion of the traffic in one direction, an automatic changeover takes place by the sending (MASTER) station transmitting "+?". When this is acknowledged by the receiving (SLAVE) station, a change of direction of traffic takes place, and the SLAVE station is now the sending station (but not the MASTER station).

单向传输完成后,发送台(主台)发送 "+?" 会自动换流。当接收台(副台)确认后,通信方向发生改变,副台现在是发送台(但不是主台)。

In the event of a loss of signal for 15 s, the MASTER station will then resume command and start calling the SLAVE station, as it did at the start of the contact (this is referred to as "re-phasing"). When contact is re-established, the flow of traffic will continue, so that if the SLAVE station was the transmitting station at the time of loss of signal, then the SLAVE station will resume sending traffic from exactly where it left off, and the MASTER station automatically returns to the receiving situation.

如果信号丢失 15 s,主台将恢复指令并开始呼叫副台,就像初始建立连接一样(这被称为"重新定相")。重新建立连接后,通信将继续进行,因此,如果信号丢失时副台是发送台,那么副台将从其离开时的位置继续发射信息,而主台则自动返回到接收状态。

The system also offers a selective calling capability similar to DSC, using the vessel's selcall number.

该系统还使用船舶的选呼码提供类似于 DSC 的选择性呼叫功能。

ARQ operation requires that both stations have their transmitters active, in order to exchange acknowledgment signals (unlike FEC operation).

ARQ 操作要求两个台的发射机都处于激活状态,以便交换确认信号(与 FEC 操作不同)。

Some Commonly Used Manual Commands:

AMV+	For AMVER reports.
DIRTLX…+	Insert the Telex country code and Telex number without any spaces. This is a real time connection.
HELP+	The ship station needs to immediately receive a list of available facilities within the system.
MAN or OPR+	For operator or manual assistance.
MED+	For urgent medical messages.
MSG+	For retrieving traffic from a coast station.
NAV+	The ship station needs to immediately receive navigation warnings.
OBS+	Ship's weather report, which is automatically routed to local meteorological office. Indicates FREQ+ instructions accepted by computer.
POS+	Indicates that the following message contains the ship's position.
TLX…+	Store and Forward Mode, insert telex number of subscriber.
URG+	The ship station needs to be connected immediately to a manual assistance operator and an audible alarm may be activated. This code should only be used in case of emergency.
WX+	The ship station needs to immediately receive weather information.

一些常用手动命令:

AMV+	用于 AMVER 报告。

DIRTLX……+	输入 Telex 国家代码和 Telex 用户号码,不留空格。这是实时连接。
HELP+	船舶电台需要立即收到系统内可用设施的列表。
MAN 或 OPR+	用于操作员或人工辅助。
MED+	用于紧急医疗电文。
MSG+	用于从海岸电台检索通信。
NAV+	船舶电台需要立即接收航行警告。
OBS+	船舶天气报告,自动发送至当地气象局。表示计算机接受的 FREQ+指令。
POS+	表示以下电文包含船位。
TLX……+	存储和转发模式,插入用户的电传号码。
URG+	需要立即将船舶电台连接到人工辅助操作员,并可能启动声音报警。该代码只能在紧急情况下使用。
WX+	船舶电台需要立即接收天气信息。

4.3.5.2　Forward Error Correction（FEC）Mode 前向纠错（FEC）模式

This is a broadcast（or one way）mode of operation. One sending station may transmit a message to an unlimited number of receiving stations.

这是一种广播(或单向)运行模式。一个发送台可以向数量不限的接收台发送电文。

The transmitting station sends each character twice, the first transmission of a specific character is followed by the transmission of four other characters, after which the re-transmission of the first character takes place, thereby allowing for time diversity reception. Receiving stations compare the two characters, and if both are the same, print the character.

发送台将每个字符发送两次,第一次发送一个特定字符后,再发送另外四个字符,然后重新发送第一个字符,这样就可以实现时间分集接收。接收台比较两个字符,如果两个字符相同,则打印该字符。

If interference or fading have caused mutilation of one of the characters, the system prints it as ＊. As the system does not require any acknowledgments by receiving stations, their transmitters are switched off. Please note that the asterisk（＊）is not a telex character（refer to Recommendation ITU-T F.1 in the ITU Maritime Manual）, but is generated internally and not transmitted.

如果干扰或衰减导致其中一个字符残缺,系统会将其打印为"＊"。由于系统不需要接收台的任何确认,因此它们的发射机将被关闭。请注意,星号（＊）并非电传字符(请参阅《ITU海事手册》中的 ITU-T F.1 建议),而是在内部生成的,不会传输。

4.3.5.3　Selective Forward Error Correction（SELFEC）Mode 选择性前向纠错（SELFEC）模式

This is a variation of the FEC mode. In SELFEC, the transmitting station only sends to a specified ship or ships, which are addressed by their selcall number. This system is used to send messages to particular ships that cannot use their transmitters（the ship may be in port loading hazardous cargoes, etc.）.

这是 FEC 模式的一种变体。在 SELFEC 模式下,发射台只向指定的一艘或多艘船舶发送信息,这些船舶通过其自选呼码寻址。该系统用于向无法使用发射机的特定船舶发送信息(船舶可能正在港口装载危险货物等)。

4.3.5.4　GMDSS Applications GMDSS 的应用

NBDP is used for the broadcast of Maritime Safety Information（MSI）on various MF and HF frequencies, and for communications following a DSC distress alert. FEC mode is used for both these applications, as they each require the broadcast of data to a large number of ship stations. ARQ and SELFEC modes are mainly used in commercial communications.

NBDP 用于在各种 MF 和 HF 频率上广播海上安全信息（MSI）,以及 DSC 遇险报警后的通信。这两种应用都使用 FEC 模式,因为它们都需要向大量船舶电台广播数据。ARQ 和 SELFEC 模式主要用于商业通信。

4.3.6　NBDP Equipment NBDP 设备

NBDP equipment consists of a modem（modulator, demodulator）, a computer type monitor, a keyboard and a printer.

NBDP 设备由一个调制解调器(调制器、解调器)、一个计算机显示器、一个键盘和一台打印机组成。

The modem is connected to the radio equipment in much the same way as a DSC controller, excepting that NBDP systems do not use dedicated watchkeeping receivers—they use the receiver built into the vessel's MF/HF transceiver. Some NBDP systems offer control of the transceiver's frequency selection, which allows the system to scan a number of coast station channels for any selcalls and（the subsequent）commercial traffic.

调制解调器与无线电设备的连接方式与 DSC 控制器大致相同,但 NBDP 系统不使用专用的值守机,而是使用船舶 MF/HF 收发机内置的接收机。一些 NBDP 系统可控制收发机的频率选择,从而使系统能够扫描多个海岸电台频道,以查看是否有任何自呼叫和(随后的)商业通信。

4.3.7 Frequencies Used in NBDP NBDP 使用的频率

Table 4.3 shows the frequencies used in NBDP communications.

表 4.3 列出了 NBDP 通信中使用的频率。

Table 4.3　Frequencies Used in NBDP
表 4.3　NBDP 中使用的频率

Frequency 频率	Use 用途
490 kHz	Used exclusively for the transmission by coast stations of meteorological and navigational warnings, and urgent information to ships, by means of telex. Broadcasts on this frequency will normally be in a local language. 专门用于海岸电台通过电传向船舶发送气象和航行警告以及紧急信息。 该频率的广播通常使用当地语言
518 kHz	In the MF maritime mobile service, used exclusively for the transmission by coast stations of meteorological and navigational warnings, and urgent information to ships, by telex (the international navigational telex, or NAVTEX system). 在 MF 海上移动业务中,专门用于海岸电台通过电传(国际航行电传,或 NAVTEX 系统)向船舶发送气象和航行警告以及紧急信息
2174.5 kHz	Exclusively reserved for distress and safety traffic using telex in the MF band. It should be used for ship-to-ship on-scene communications in FEC mode. 专门用于在 MF 波段使用电传进行遇险和安全通信。 它应在 FEC 模式下用于船对船现场通信
4209.5 kHz	In the HF maritime mobile service, used exclusively for the transmission by coast stations of meteorological and navigational warnings, and urgent information to ships, by NAVTEX type transmission. 在 HF 海上移动业务中,海岸电台通过 NAVTEX 类型的发射,专门用于向船舶发送气象和航行警告以及紧急信息
4177.5 kHz; 6268 kHz; 8376.5 kHz; 12520 kHz; 16695 kHz	In the HF maritime mobile bands, these frequencies are reserved exclusively for distress and safety using telex. 在 HF 海上移动波段中,这些频率专门留给遇险和安全电传使用
4210 kHz; 6314 kHz; 8416.5 kHz; 12579 kHz; 16806.5 kHz; 22376 kHz; 26100.5 kHz	In the HF maritime mobile bands, these frequencies are reserved exclusively for the transmission by coast stations of Maritime Safety Information (MSI) by telex in FEC mode. 在 HF 海上移动波段中,这些频率专门用于海岸电台以 FEC 模式通过电传发射海上安全信息(MSI)

4.4　Radiotelephony (RT) 无线电话(RT)

Maritime radiotelephony refers to radiotelephone communication, when using MF, HF, VHF frequency bands, between ship and ship, ship and shore station, or ship and shore-based subscriber through coast station.

海上无线电话是指使用 MF、HF、VHF 波段,在船与船、船与岸基站或船与岸上用户之间通过海岸电台进行的无线电话通信。

The procedures detailed in the following sections are applicable to radiotelephone stations, except in cases of distress, urgency or safety, to which special provisions of the ITU Radio Regulations are applicable. The service of ship radiotelephone stations shall be performed or controlled by an operator holding an appropriate radio operation certificate recognized by a competent administration.

以下各节详述的程序适用于无线电话电台,但遇险、紧急或安全情况除外。国际电联《无线电规则》的特殊规定适用于这些情况。船舶无线电话电台的业务应由持有主管机关认可的无线电操作证书的持证人员操作或控制。

A call sign is a unique alphanumeric identity that belongs to the vessel and acts in the same way as the registration number of a car. The call sign enables two vessels with the same vessel name to be identified separately. The call sign is also useful when the actual vessel name is difficult to understand. It can be used in an identification procedure via all means of communications.

呼号是属于船舶的唯一字母数字标识,其作用与汽车登记号相同。使用呼号可以分别识别具有相同船名的两艘船舶。当实际船名难以理解时,呼号也很有用。它可以通过各种通信手段用于识别程序。

These call signs are issued by the appropriate authorities in the country of registration of the vessel and can be referenced back to a database of information about the vessel and its owners etc.

这些呼号由船舶注册国的有关机构签发,并可追溯到船舶及其所有人等信息的数据库。

If a vessel does not have its own call sign, the vessel owner must apply for a call sign at the appropriate authorities before any new communication equipment can be used on a vessel.

如果船舶没有自己的呼号,船东必须向有关机构申请呼号,然后才能在船上使用新的通信设备。

Each call sign begins with the call sign alphanumeric prefix that indicates nationality, e.g. prefixes allocated to Chinese ships are BAA to BZZ. The prefix is usually followed by 2 or 3 alphanumeric characters.

每个呼号以表示国籍的呼号字母数字前缀开头,例如分配给中国船舶的前缀为 BAA 至 BZZ。前缀后通常有 2 或 3 个字母数字字符。

Also, Coast Radio Stations using terrestrial communications have their own call signs and can be contacted from any vessel's radio station.

此外,使用地面通信的海岸无线电台有自己的呼号,可以通过任何船舶的无线电台与之联系。

4.4.1　Use of Frequencies 频率的使用

4.4.1.1　Bands between 1605 kHz and 4000 kHz 1605 kHz 和 4000 kHz 之间的频段

Unless otherwise specified in the present ITU Radio Regulations notably the use of different modes of emissions on specified distress frequencies, the class of emission to be used in the bands between 1605 kHz and 4000kHz shall be J3E.

除非国际电联《无线电规则》对特定遇险频率上使用不同发射模式另有规定,否则在 1605 kHz 至 4000 kHz 频段内使用的发射类别应为 J3E。

The frequency 2182 kHz is an international distress frequency for radiotelephony. The class of emission to be used for radiotelephony on the frequency 2182 kHz shall be J3E or H3E.

2182 kHz 是国际无线电话遇险频率。在 2182 kHz 频率上用于无线电话的发射类别应为 J3E 或 H3E。

The frequency 2182 kHz may also be used for call and reply by coast stations to announce the transmission, on another frequency, of traffic lists.

2182 kHz 频率还可用于海岸电台的呼叫和应答,以在另一个频率上发布通话表。

In addition, an administration may assign to its stations other frequencies for call and reply.

此外,主管机关还可以为其电台分配其他频率,用于呼叫和应答。

To facilitate the use of the frequency 2182 kHz for distress purposes, all transmissions on 2182 kHz shall be kept to a minimum. Before transmitting on the carrier frequency 2182 kHz, a station shall listen on this frequency for a reasonable period to make sure that no distress traffic is being sent; this provision does not however apply to stations in distress.

为便于使用 2182 kHz 频率进行遇险,应尽量减少 2182 kHz 频率上的所有发射。在使用载波频率 2182 kHz 发射之前,电台应在该频率上监听一段合理的时间,以确保没有正在发送遇险信息;但这一规定不适用于遇险电台。

Coast stations which use 2182 kHz for calling shall be able to use at least one other frequency in the authorized bands between 1605 kHz and 2850 kHz. Coast stations authorized to use radiotelephony on one or more frequencies other than 2182 kHz in the authorized bands between 1605 kHz and 2850 kHz shall use class J3E emissions on those frequencies.

使用 2182 kHz 呼叫的海岸电台应能使用 1605 kHz 和 2850 kHz 之间授权频段中的至少一个其他频率。经授权在 1605 kHz 和 2850 kHz 之间的授权频段内使用 2182 kHz 以外的一个或多个频率进行无线电通话的海岸电台,应在这些频率上使用 J3E 发射。

4.4.1.2　Bands between 4000 kHz and 27500 kHz 4000 kHz 和 27500 kHz 之间的频段

The class of emission to be used for RT transmissions in the bands between 4000 kHz and 27500 kHz shall be J3E. Ship RT stations employing J3E emission in the bands between 4000 kHz and 27500 kHz shall at no time use peak envelope power in excess of 1.5 kW per channel.

在 4000 kHz 至 27500 kHz 频段内的无线电话发射使用的发射类别应为 J3E。在 4000 kHz 至 27500 kHz 频段内使用 J3E 发射的船用无线电话电台,在任何时候每个信道使用的峰值包络功率均不得超过 1.5 kW。

Distress and safety frequencies are listed below.

遇险和安全频率如下。

4125 kHz 421

6215 kHz 606

8291 kHz 833

12290 kHz 1221

16420 kHz 1621

Ship stations should listen on the frequency to ensure no distress traffic is being sent before transmitting on the carrier frequencies.

船舶电台在使用载波频率发射信号之前,应监听该频率,确保没有遇险信息发送。

4.4.1.3   156 MHz and 174 MHz 156 MHz 和 174 MHz

The class of emission used for RT on VHF bands must be G3E. The carrier power of ship station VHF transmitters shall not exceed 25 W.

用于 VHF 波段无线电话的发射类型必须为 G3E。船舶电台 VHF 发射机的载波功率不得超过 25 W。

The marine frequency band for VHF radiocommunication, extending between 156 MHz and 174 MHz, contains 57 individual VHF Channel (channels) numbered consecutively from VHF Channel 1 to VHF Channel 28 and from VHF Channel 60 to VHF Channel 88.

用于 VHF 无线电通信的海上频段在 156 MHz 和 174 MHz 之间,包含 57 个 VHF 频道,从 VHF 1 频道到 VHF 28 频道以及从 VHF 60 频道到 VHF 88 频道连续编号。

Channel 16 (156. 8 MHz) is the international channel for distress traffic and for calling on RT in the authorized maritime mobile service VHF bands. VHF Channel 16 may also be used：

· by coast and ship stations for call and reply；

· by coast stations to announce the transmission of traffic lists and important maritime information on another channel.

16 频道(156.8 MHz)是国际频道,用于遇险通信和在授权的海事移动业务 VHF 频段内进行无线电话呼叫。以下情况也可使用 VHF 16 频道：

· 由海岸电台和船舶电台进行呼叫和回复;

· 由海岸电台在另一频道上发布通话表和重要海事信息。

To assist in the reception of distress calls and distress traffic, all transmissions on VHF Channel 16 shall be kept to a minimum and shall not exceed 1 min. Also, before transmitting, a station should listen on VHF Channel 16 for a short period to ensure that no distress traffic is being transmitted on this channel. This provision does not apply to stations in distress.

为更好接收遇险呼叫和遇险通信,VHF 16 频道上的所有发射应保持在最低限度,且不得超过 1 min。此外,在发射前,电台应在 VHF 16 频道上短暂监听,以确保该频道上没有遇险通信。本规定不适用于遇险电台。

· Ship stations should where practicably maintain watch on VHF Channel 16 when within the service area of a coast station providing international maritime mobile RT service in the band 156-174 MHz.

· Channel 06 may be employed for communications between ship stations and aircraft stations engaged in coordinated SAR operations and ship stations should avoid harmful interference on this channel.

· Channel 13 is designated worldwide as a navigation safety communication channel primarily for inter-ship navigation safety communications.

· Channels 15 and 17 may be used for on board communications provided the radiated power does not exceed 1 W (low power setting) and such communications are permitted in the waters of the coastal state in which the ship is operating.

· Channel 70 is used for Digital Selective Calling for Distress, Safety.

· Channels 75 and 76 should be restricted to navigation related communications and as these channels are located in the band either side of Channel 16. Measures should be taken to minimize the risk of harmful interference on that channel such as using low power (1 W). At WRC-12, it was agreed that these channels shall also be used to enhance the satellite detection of AIS transmissions from ships. New AIS Class-A and Class-B "SO" transceivers fitted with this capability, will automatically transmit a special AIS Message 27 which can be detected by satellite, alternatively on Channels 75 and 76 (at 12.5 W) every 3 min, when outside VHF coverage of a terrestrial AIS base station. These transmissions are not expected to cause interference to Channel 16.

· The frequencies of 161.965 MHz and 162.025 MHz are known as AIS 1 and AIS 2 and are used exclusively for AIS.

· 在 156~174 MHz 频段提供国际海上移动无线电话业务的海岸电台业务区内,船舶电台应在可行的情况下保持 VHF 16 频道守听。

· 06 频道可用于参与协调搜救行动的船舶电台和航空电台之间的通信,船舶电台应避免对该信道造成有害干扰。

· 13 频道被指定为全球航行安全通信频道,主要用于船舶之间的航行安全通信。

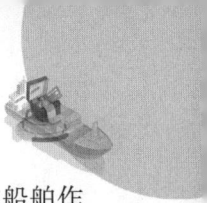

- 15 和 17 频道可用于船上通信,但辐射功率不得超过 1 W(低功率设置),且在船舶作业的沿海国水域内允许进行此类通信。

- 70 频道用于遇险、安全的数字选择性呼叫。

- 75 和 76 频道应仅限于与航行有关的通信,因为这些频道位于 16 频道两侧的频段内。应采取措施尽量减少该频道受到有害干扰的风险,如使用低功率(1 W)。在世界无线电大会第十二届会议上,各方同意这些频道也应用于加强卫星对船舶 AIS 发射信号的探测。新的 AIS A 级和 B 级"SO"收发机配备了这一功能,当处于地面 AIS 基站 VHF 覆盖范围之外时,将每隔 3 min 在 75 和 76 频道(12.5 W)上自动发送可被卫星探测到的特殊 AIS 电文"27"。预计这些发射不会对 16 频道造成干扰。

- 161.965 MHz 和 162.025 MHz 频率被称为 AIS 1 和 AIS 2,专门用于 AIS。

Each country determines their own individual channel allocations, based on the ITU guidelines. The band is extensively used by ship, coastal and port operation stations worldwide.

每个国家根据国际电联的指导方针确定各自的频道分配。该频段被世界各地的船舶电台、海岸电台和港口电台广泛使用。

AIS Frequencies AIS 频率

AIS is used for the exchange of data in ship-to-ship communications and also in communication with shore-based facilities. The purpose of AIS is to help identify vessels, assist in target tracking, simplify information exchange (e.g. reduce verbal reporting), and provide additional information to assist situation awareness. AIS may be used together with VHF voice communications. AIS was designated two VHF frequencies: 161.975 MHz (Channel 87B) and 162.025 MHz (Channel 88B) by the International Telecommunications Union World Radio Conference in 1997.

AIS 用于船对船通信以及与岸基设施通信中的数据交换。AIS 的目的是帮助识别船舶,协助目标跟踪,简化信息交换(例如减少口头报告),以及提供额外信息以帮助了解情况。AIS 可与 VHF 语音通信一起使用。AIS 被指定了两个 VHF 频率:1997 年,国际电信联盟世界无线电大会指定了 161.975 MHz(87B 频道)和 162.025 MHz(88B 频道)。

Port Operation Service 港口作业业务

Communications in the port operation service shall be restricted to those relating to operational handling, the movement and the safety of ships, and, in emergency, to the safety of persons.

港口作业业务中的通信应仅限于与港口作业、船舶航行和安全有关的通信,以及在紧急情况下与人员安全有关的通信。

Messages of a public correspondence nature are excluded from this service. When VHF Channel 16 is being used for distress, urgency, or safety communications, ships wishing to use the port operations service may establish contact on VHF Channel 12, or another port operation channel indicated in heavy type in the ITU List of Coast Stations and Special Service Stations.

该业务不包括公共通信性质的电文。当 VHF 16 频道用于遇险、紧急或安全通信时,希望

使用港口作业业务的船舶可与 VHF12 频道或国际电联《海岸电台和特别业务电台表》中用粗体字标明的其他港口作业频道建立联系。

Ship Movement Service 船舶航行业务

Communications in the ship movement service shall be restricted to those relating to the movement of ships. Messages of a public correspondence nature are excluded from this service. Ships wishing to use the port operation service or ship movement service should call on the appropriate working channel for that service, indicated in heavy type in the ITU List of Coast Stations and Special Service Stations.

船舶航行业务中的通信应仅限于与船舶航行有关的通信。公共通信性质不在此业务范围内。希望使用港口作业业务或船舶航行业务的船舶,应呼叫国际电联《海岸电台和特别业务电台表中》用粗体字标明的该业务的适当工作频道。

When contact on Channel 16 VHF has been established between a coast station in the port operations service and a ship station, the ship station should indicate the particular service required, for example, navigational information, docking instructions, etc. The port station shall then indicate the channel to be used for exchange of traffic by reference (preferably) to its channel designator.

当港口作业业务中的海岸电台与船舶电台之间通过 VHF 16 频道建立联系时,船舶电台应说明所需的特定业务,例如航行信息、停靠指示等。然后,港口电台应参照(最好是)其信道代号,指明用于交换信息的信道。

However, a brief exchange of traffic (not to exceed 1 min) concerning the safety of navigation need not be transmitted on a working frequency when all ships within range must receive the transmission. Stations hearing a transmission concerning the safety of navigation shall listen to the message until they are satisfied that the message is of no concern to them. They shall not make any transmission likely to interfere with the message.

但是,当范围内的所有船舶都必须接收有关航行安全的信息时,则不必在工作频率上进行简短的信息交换(不超过 1 min)。各电台在听到有关航行安全的信息时,应仔细聆听该信息,直到确信该信息与自己无关为止。它们不得进行任何可能干扰信息的传送。

4.4.2 RT Tests 无线电话测试

When a ship station have to send signals for testing or adjustments that are liable to interfere with the working of neighboring coast stations, the consent of these stations shall be obtained before such signals are sent. When it is necessary for a station to make test transmissions, the use of artificial antennas and reduced power should be employed wherever practicable.

当船舶电台需要发送信号进行测试或调整,而这些信号可能会干扰邻近海岸电台的工作时,应在发送这些信号前征得这些海岸电台的同意。当船舶电台必须进行测试发射时,应尽可能使用人工天线并降低功率。

The number and duration of any test signals shall be kept to a minimum, particularly on the frequencies to the maritime mobile and maritime mobile-satellite services for distress and safety purposes. Testing on the distress and safety calling frequencies should be avoided, but where this is unavoidable, it should be indicated that these are test transmissions.

任何测试信号的数量和持续时间应保持在最低限度,特别是在用于遇险和安全目的的海上移动和海上移动卫星业务频率上。应避免在遇险和安全呼叫频率上进行测试,但在不可避免的情况下,应说明这些是测试信号。

Before transmitting any test signals, stations should listen on the frequency concerned to ensure that no other transmissions are in progress. Test signals must include the call sign or other identification of the station emitting the test signals, and must be spoken slowly and distinctly.

在发射任何测试信号之前,电台应监听有关频率,以确保没有其他发射正在进行。测试信号必须包括发射测试信号的台站的呼号或其他标识,并且必须缓慢而清晰地说出。

Any emission causing harmful interference to any of the frequencies to the maritime mobile and maritime mobile-satellite services for distress and safety purposes is prohibited.

任何对用于遇险和安全目的的海上移动和海上移动卫星业务的任何频率造成有害干扰的发射都应该被禁止。

Maritime Safety Information in the GMDSS
GMDSS 中的海上安全信息

Chapter 5

5.1 General Introduction 概述

It is obviously important to broadcast Maritime Safety Information (MSI) to the ships at sea. It is defined in general terms as "navigational and meteorological forecasts, and other urgent safety-related messages". The categories of MSI under the GMDSS have expanded considerably, in keeping with the requirements of world shipping and the capabilities of new technology. The new developments have offered the greatest potential benefit and improvement in safety services for all vessels.

向海上船舶广播海上安全信息(MSI)显然非常重要。海上安全信息的一般定义是"航行和气象预报,以及其他与安全有关的紧急信息"。GMDSS 下的 MSI 类别已大大扩展,以符合世界航运的要求和新技术的能力。新的技术发展为所有船舶的安全服务提供了最大的潜在利益和改进。

There are seven basic categories of MSI within the GMDSS:

· Navigational warnings;

· Meteorological warnings;

· Ice reports;

· Search and rescue information;

· Meteorological forecasts;

· Pilot service messages;

· Electronic navigational systems update messages.

GMDSS 的 MSI 有七个基本类别:

· 航行警告;

- 气象警告；

- 冰况报告；

- 搜救信息；

- 气象预报；

- 引航服务电文；

- 电子导航系统更新电文。

Prior to the GMDSS, in order to receive all necessary messages in the above categories, operators would require the broadcast times and frequencies of the numerous radio stations and take time to copy each relevant broadcast. Under the GMDSS, a vessel anywhere in the world should be able to receive all types of information by just flipping the switch of two small receivers.

在 GMDSS 出现之前,为了接收上述各类必要的电文,操作员需要知道众多广播电台的广播时间和频率,并花时间复制每一个相关的广播。在 GMDSS 下,世界上任何地方的船舶只需打开两个小型接收机的开关,就能接收所有类型的信息。

The MSI service is an internationally coordinated network of broadcasts of Maritime Safety Information from different information providers, such as:

- National Hydrographic Offices, for navigational warnings and electronic chart correction;

- National Meteorological Offices, for weather warnings and forecasts;

- Rescue Coordination Centers, for shore-to-ship distress alerts, and other urgent information;

- International Ice Patrol, for North Atlantic Ice hazards.

MSI 业务是一个国际协调网络,由不同的信息提供者广播海上安全信息,比如:

- 国家航道局,用于航行警告和电子海图校正;

- 国家气象局,提供气象警告和预报;

- 搜救协调中心,提供岸对船遇险报警和其他紧急信息;

- 国际冰况巡查组织,负责对北大西洋冰况预报。

Only information providers approved by the IMO, the IHO or the WMO are given the authorization to make SafetyNET broadcasts.

只有经国际海事组织、国际水道测量组织或世界气象组织批准的信息提供者才有权进行安全网广播。

5.1.1　Means of Broadcasting MSI MSI 的广播方式

The GMDSS supports two independent systems for broadcasting MSI.

GMDSS 支持两个独立的 MSI 广播系统。

The International NAVTEX Service, whereby the Information Provider forwards the MSI for a given area to a 518 kHz MF NAVTEX transmitter; note that reception of NAVTEX MSI is limited by the range of the MF transmitter to the coastal area immediately around the transmitter.

国际 NAVTEX 业务,即信息提供者将特定区域的 MSI 转发到 518 kHz 的中频 NAVTEX 发射机上;请注意,NAVTEX MSI 的接收受限于中频发射机在发射机周围沿海地区的发射范围。

The International SafetyNET Service, whereby the Information Provider forwards the MSI for a given area to an INMARSAT Land Earth Station (LES), for broadcasting via the satellite network over an entire INMARSAT ocean region; consequently, vessels can receive SafetyNET MSI anywhere in that ocean region, irrespective of their distance from the LES/Information Provider.

国际安全网业务,即信息提供者将特定区域的 MSI 转发到 INMARSAT 陆地地球站 (LES),通过卫星网络向整个 INMARSAT 覆盖的洋区广播;因此,船舶可以在洋区的任何地方接收安全网 MSI,而不论其与陆地地球站/信息提供者的距离有多远。

MSI for a given area is generally broadcast over either NAVTEX or SafetyNET (except for some exceptional circumstances where a message may be broadcast using both services); vessels equipped with both a NAVTEX receiver and SafetyNET receiver should select the appropriate receiver to receive MSI for the area in which the vessel is operating. Where a coastal area is not covered by the International NAVTEX service, for example around Australia, MSI for that area will be broadcast on SafetyNET.

特定区域的 MSI 一般通过 NAVTEX 或安全网进行广播(某些特殊情况除外,即电文可同时通过两种业务进行广播);同时配备 NAVTEX 接收机和安全网接收机的船舶应选择适当的接收机,以接收船舶所在区域的 MSI。在国际 NAVTEX 业务未覆盖的沿海地区,例如澳大利亚周边地区,该地区的 MSI 将通过安全网进行广播。

The MSI service is shown in Figure 5.1.

MSI 业务如图 5.1 所示。

There are supplementary methods of broadcasting information in connection with the safety of life at sea.

a. Radio facsimile including weather maps, ice charts and other information of importance to mariners.

b. Radio weather services and navigational warnings broadcasted by some coast stations via HF telex and VHF/MF/HF radiotelephone.

还有一些与海上人命安全有关的补充信息广播方式。

a. 无线电传真,包括天气图、冰面图和其他对航海者十分重要的信息。

b. 一些海岸电台通过高频电传和甚高频/中频/高频无线电话广播无线电气象业务和航行警告。

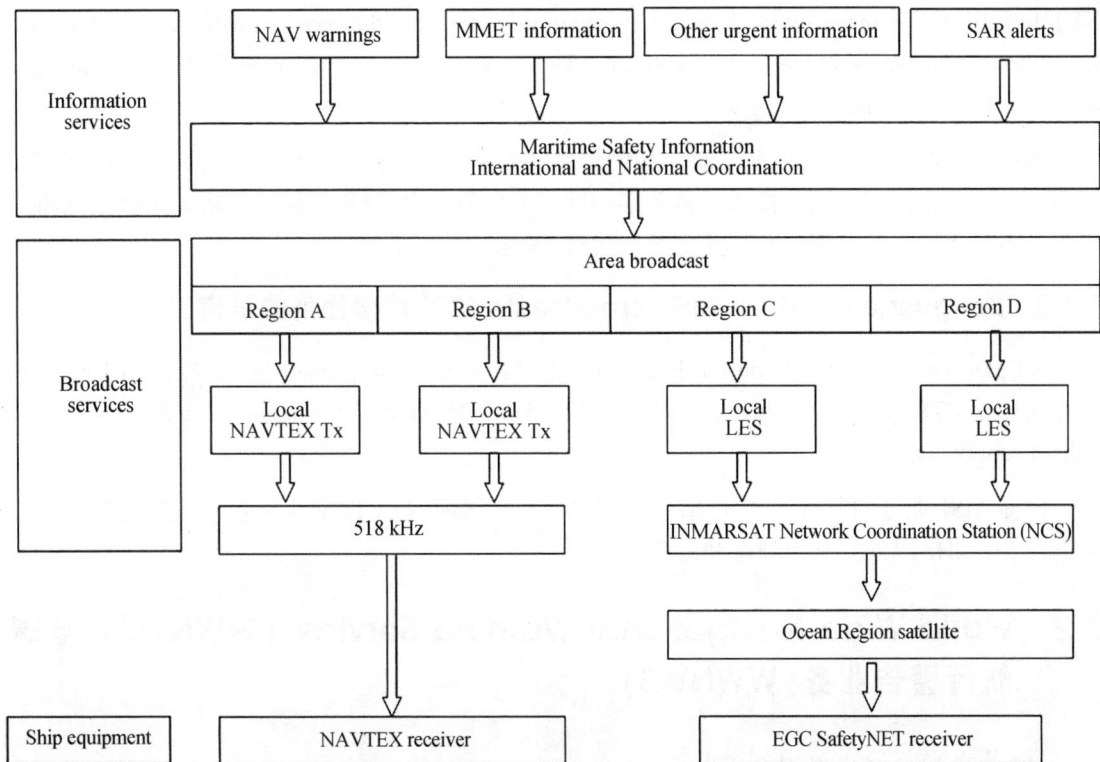

Figure 5.1　The MSI Service

图 5.1　MSI 业务

5.1.2　Scheduled and Unscheduled MSI Broadcasts 定时和非定时 MSI 广播

To ensure that the user knows when to receive MSI for a given area and subject, many MSI broadcasts are scheduled, under IMO coordination, to a particular time, LES, and satellite. For example, all navigational warnings and meteorological forecasts are scheduled broadcasts (and given safety priority, which does not produce an alarm at the terminal when received), while meteorological warnings and distress alerts are unscheduled broadcasts (and given urgent or distress priority, which produces an alarm at the terminal).

为确保用户知道何时可接收到特定区域和内容的 MSI,许多 MSI 广播在 IMO 的协调下,按特定时间、LES 和卫星进行排定。例如,所有航行警告和气象预报都是定时广播(被赋予安全优先权,在接收时不会在终端产生警告),而气象警告和遇险报警则是非定时广播(被赋予紧急或遇险优先权,在接收时会在终端产生警告)。

To be sure of receiving a scheduled MSI broadcast, the receiver must be tuned to the appropriate channel/satellite at the specified time, and programmed to receive information for the area concerned.

要确保接收到定时的 MSI 广播,接收机必须在指定时间调谐到相应的频道/卫星,并设置为接收相关地区的信息。

A smaller number of MSI messages are transmitted as unscheduled broadcasts, for example urgent navigational warnings, severe weather warnings, and distress alert relays. Unscheduled Safety-

NET broadcasts are made over all satellites covering an area, so the receiver will not miss the message, no matter what satellite it is logged-into. The user is advised of the receipt of an unscheduled broadcast by the terminal giving an alarm.

较少数量的 MSI 电文以非定时广播的形式发送,例如紧急航行警告、恶劣天气警告和遇险报警转发。非定时安全网广播通过覆盖某一区域的所有卫星进行,因此接收机无论登录到哪个卫星都不会错过电文。用户收到非定时广播时,终端会发出警告。

5.1.3 Language Used for MSI Broadcasts MSI 广播使用的语言

All MSI broadcasts made on the International MSI service are printed in the English language. National NAVTEX service uses frequencies other than 518 kHz and languages as decided by the Administration concerned.

国际 MSI 业务的所有 MSI 广播均以英文发布。国内 NAVTEX 业务主要使用主管机关确定的除 518 kHz 以外的其他频率和语言。

5.2 World-Wide Navigational Warning Service(WWNWS)全球航行警告业务(WWNWS)

The WWNWS is concerned with:

a.Long-range(NAVAREA)warnings, usually of a long-term nature, primarily concerned with routing and passage Changes through main shipping lanes;

b. Coastal warnings, usually dealing with short-term, short-range information and sent by NAVTEX, MF RT, or VHF; and

c.Local warnings, mainly dealing with inshore waters and usually broadcast on VHF only.

全球航行警告业务包括:

a.远程(NAVAREA)警告,通常具有长期性,主要涉及主要航道的航线和通航变更;

b.沿海警告,通常涉及短期、短程信息,由 NAVTEX、MF 无线电话或 VHF 发送;以及

c.本地警告,主要涉及近岸水域,通常只通过 VHF 广播。

The WWNWS provides for the coordinated transmission of radio navigational warnings globally by dividing the world into 21 geographical areas known as NAVAREAs, each area is identified by a Roman numeral. To provide adequate notification to ships, at least two daily transmissions are deemed necessary. Thus, arrangements for this are built into transmission schedules for each NAVAREA broadcast. Messages are numbered consecutively throughout the year for each area.

WWNWS 将全球划分为 21 个地理区域(NAVAREA),每个区域用一个罗马数字标识,从而在全球范围内协调发送无线电航行警告。为了向船舶提供充分的通知,每天至少需要发送两次警告。因此,每个 NAVAREA 广播的时间表中都有这方面的安排。每个区域的电文全年连续编号。

Within the WWNWS, provision is made to meet national Maritime Safety Information needs by having local control and coordination for navigational warnings concerning local and coastal areas. The use of the English language for all broadcasts is mandatory, but provision exists for transmitting second-language broadcasts. Although the broadcasting and coordinating arrangements for NAVAREA and NAVTEX warnings are significantly different, the contents of both message classes are similar. The subject matter of such warnings includes the following:

a.Reports of defective lights, fog signals, buoys, etc., in main shipping lanes;

b.The presence of dangerous wrecks in or near main shipping lanes and, if relevant, their marking;

c.The establishment of major new aids to navigation or significant changes to existing ones;

d.The presence of unwieldy tows in congested waters;

e.Drifting mines;

f.Areas in which SAR and anti-pollution operations are in progress or ongoing (for avoidance of such areas);

g.Notification from MRCCs or Maritime Rescue Sub-Centers (MRSCs) of a ship or aircraft in distress, overdue or missing in open seas;

h.The presence of newly discovered wrecks or natural hazards, liable to cause danger to shipping and, if relevant, their marking;

i.Unexpected suspension or alteration to established shipping routes;

j.The existence of cable-laying or underwater operations either in progress or ongoing, such as towage of submerged objects (manned or unmanned), for whatever reason, and other underwater operations that potentially are a danger in or near shipping lanes;

k.Information concerning new offshore structures in or near shipping lanes;

l.Failure or changes to important radio navigational aids; and

m.Information relating to safety of shipping by special operations over wide areas.

在 WWNWS 内部,通过对当地和沿海地区的航行警告进行地方控制和协调,以满足国家的海上安全信息服务需求。所有的广播都必须使用英语,但也有转播第二语言广播的规定。尽管 NAVAREA 和 NAVTEX 警告的广播和协调安排有很大不同,但两类电文的内容是相似的。这类警告的主题包括以下内容:

a.主要航道上的灯光、雾号、浮标等出现故障的报告;

b.主要航道内或附近是否有危险沉船,如果有,是否对其进行标记;

c.建立新的大型导航设备或对现有设备进行重大改动;

d.在拥挤的水域出现难以控制的拖船;

e.漂浮的水雷;

f.正在进行搜救和防污作业的区域(以避开这些区域);

g.MRCC 或海上救援分中心（MRSC）发出的船舶或飞机遇险、在公海逾期未归或失踪的通知；

h.新发现的可能对航运造成危险的沉船或自然灾害，以及相关标识；

i.既定航线意外中止或改变；

j.正在进行的缆线铺设或水下作业，如水下物体拖拽（有人或无人），无论出于何种原因，以及其他可能对航道内或航道附近造成危险的水下作业；

k.有关航道内或航道附近新建近海建筑的信息；

l.重要的无线电导航设备发生故障或变化；以及

m.有关在开阔区域开展特别行动以确保航运安全的信息。

Like NAVAREAs, METAREAs are geographically defined sea regions used for coordinating the transmission of meteorological information to mariners on international voyages. These 21 defined regions are identical to the 21 NAVAREAs and are identified by the same Roman numerals.

与 NAVAREA 一样，气象区域（METAREA）也是按地理位置界定的海区，用于协调向国际航行的海员发送气象信息。这 21 个定义区域与 21 个 NAVAREA 相同，并用相同的罗马数字标识。

The World Meteorological Organization（WMO）website provides detailed information about each METAREA.

世界气象组织（WMO）网站提供有关每个 METAREA 的详细信息。

5.3 NAVTEX System NAVTEX 系统

5.3.1 System Overview 系统概述

The NAVTEX system provides the automatic dissemination of local Maritime Safety Information（MSI）by Narrow Band Direct Printing（NBDP）telegraphy operating in the Forward Error Correction（FEC）broadcast mode. Depending on the geographical features of its area of responsibility（in main, the length of coastline）, the NAVTEX system may be chosen by Administrations as an alternative to providing such information by the INMARSAT-C EGC service.

NAVTEX 系统通过在前向纠错（FEC）广播模式下运行的窄带直接印字（NBDP）电报自动广播本地海上安全信息（MSI）。根据其责任区的地理特征（主要是海岸线的长度），各国政府可选择 NAVTEX 系统来替代 INMARSAT-C EGC 业务提供这类信息。

The system provides navigational safety information, weather warnings and forecasts relevant to vessels within specified coastal areas. Range is generally within 300-400 n mile.

该系统为特定沿海地区的船舶提供航行安全信息、天气警告和预报。范围一般在 300~400 n mile。

The establishment of each transmitter has been internationally coordinated, and the radius of coverage of the signals from each transmitter is designed to be 400 n mile; the station identifiers of the transmitters in the coordinated zone are represented by a single letter of the alphabet(B1). Transmitters in the zone are generally selected from the letters A−Z in accordance with the principle of sequencing from west to east and from north to south, but the station labels of the 24 stations in the zone shall not be duplicated, and the station labels of similar transmitters in similar regions shall be coordinated to avoid overlapping of the coverage of the transmitted signals.

每个发射台的确立经国际协调,各发射台信号的覆盖半径设计为 400 n mile;协调区内各发射台识别以一个英文字母(B1)表示。区内发射台一般按自西向东和自北向南排序的原则,在英文字母 A~Z 中选用,但本区内 24 个台的标识不得重复,相近区域相近发射台的台标应协调使用以避免发射信号覆盖重叠。

5.3.2　Frequencies Used 使用的频率

Broadcasts of MSI by land stations operating in the NAVTEX service are made on the (MF) frequency of 518 kHz. A second NAVTEX (MF) frequency of 490 kHz is available for national language broadcast. The (HF) frequency of 4209.5 kHz is also allocated for nation NAVTEX transmissions. There is also provision for transmissions on other nationally assigned frequencies for national transmissions, which is also in language other than English. Some of these are on 424 kHz (refer to ALRS for details).

在 NAVTEX 业务中运行的陆地电台通过 518 kHz(中频)频率广播 MSI。第二个 NAVTEX(中频)频率为 490 kHz,用于国内语言广播。4209.5 kHz(高频)频率也分配给国内 NAVTEX 广播。此外,还规定在国家分配的其他频率上进行国内广播,这些广播也可以使用英语以外的语言,其中一些使用 424 kHz 频率(详见《无线电信号表》)。

5.3.3　Subject Indicator Characters 信息类型标识

Each class of NAVTEX message carries a different subject indicator character allowing a shipboard operator to program a NAVTEX receiver to reject certain classes of message that is not required.

每类 NAVTEX 电文都有不同的信息类型标识,允许船上操作员对 NAVTEX 接收机进行编程,以拒绝接收某些类别的电文。

Navigational warnings, meteorological warnings, and search and rescue information cannot be rejected by an operator.

操作员不能拒收航行警告、气象警告和搜救信息。

Subject indicator characters used in the NAVTEX system are:

A　　Navigational warning;

B　　Meteorological warning;

C　　Ice reports;

D　　Search and rescue information, and pirate attack warnings;

E   Meteorological forecasts；

F   Pilot service messages；

G   AIS；

H   LORAN messages；

I   Spare；

J   GNSS messages；

K   Other electronic navaid messages（messages concerning radio navigation services）；

L   Navigational warnings—additional to "A"；

V   Special services—allocation by the NAVTEX panel；

W   Special services—allocation by the NAVTEX panel；

X   Special services—allocation by the NAVTEX panel；

Y   Special services—allocation by the NAVTEX panel；

Z   No messages on hand.

NAVTEX 系统中使用的信息类型标识有：

A   航行警告；

B   气象警告；

C   冰况报告；

D   搜救信息和海盗袭击警告；

E   气象预报；

F   引航业务电文；

G   AIS；

H   LORAN 电文；

I   备用；

J   GNSS 电文；

K   其他电子导航电文（有关无线电导航业务的电文）；

L   航行警告——"A"的附加警告；

V   特殊业务——由 NAVTEX 小组分配；

W   特殊业务——由 NAVTEX 小组分配；

X   特殊业务——由 NAVTEX 小组分配；

Y   特殊业务——由 NAVTEX 小组分配；

Z　手头无信息。

Subject indicator characters A，B，D and L cannot be rejected by the receiver and will always be printed.

信息类型标识 A、B、D 和 L 不能被接收机拒收,将始终被打印。

5.3.4　Format of a NAVTEX Message NAVTEX 电文格式

The International NAVTEX service uses a single frequency with transmissions from nominated stations within each NAVAREA/METAREA being arranged on a time-sharing basis to reduce the risk of mutual interference. All necessary information is contained in each transmission. Similarly, broadcasts on other IMO coordinated frequencies are operated on a time-sharing basis.

国际 NAVTEX 业务使用单一频率,每个 NAVAREA/METAREA 内指定台站的发射以分时方式安排,以减少相互干扰的风险。每次发射都包含所有必要信息。同样,IMO 其他协调频率上的广播也以分时方式进行。

The power of each transmitter is regulated so as to reduce the risk of interference between transmitters with the same B1 character in different parts of the world.

每台发射机的功率都经过调节,以降低世界不同地区具有相同 B1 标识字符的发射机之间的干扰风险。

A dedicated NAVTEX receiver which has the ability to select messages to be printed, according to：

(a) A technical code (B1B2B3B4), which appears in the preamble of each message; and

(b) Whether or not the particular message has already been printed.

专用的 NAVTEX 接收机,可根据需要选择要打印的电文：

(a) 技术代码(B1B2B3B4),出现在每条电文的报头中;以及

(b) 该电文是否已被打印。

Certain essential classes of safety information such as navigational and meteorological warnings and search and rescue information are non-rejectable to ensure that ships using NAVTEX always receive the most vital information.

某些重要的安全信息,如航行和气象警告以及搜救信息是不可拒收的,以确保使用 NAVTEX 的船舶始终能收到最重要的信息。

NAVTEX coordinators exercise control of messages transmitted by each station according to the information contained in each message and the geographical coverage required. Thus a user may choose to accept messages either from the single transmitter which serves the sea area around his position, or from a number of transmitters as appropriate. Ideally, the user should select the station within whose coverage his vessel is currently operating and the station into whose coverage area his vessel will transit next. Figure 5.2 shows the format of NAVTEX message.

NAVTEX 协调国根据每条电文所包含的信息和所需的地理覆盖范围对每个发射台发送的电文进行控制。因此,用户可以选择接收业务于其所在位置周围海域的单个发射台发送的电文,也可以酌情接收多个发射台发送的电文。理想情况下,用户应选择其船舶目前正在其覆盖范围内运行的发射台,以及其船舶下一步将进入其覆盖范围的发射台。图 5.2 显示了 NAVTEX 电文的格式。

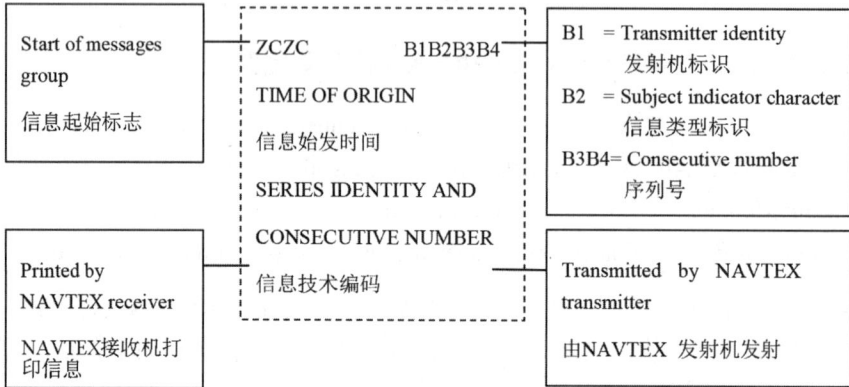

Figure 5.2　Format of NAVTEX Message
图 5.2　NAVTEX 电文的格式

5.3.5　Broadcast Schedules 广播时间表

As there is only one frequency presently used for NAVTEX transmissions, mutual interference between stations is avoided by a time-sharing arrangement. In general, each NAVTEX station in an area is allocated a designated 10 min period every 4 h to make its broadcasts.

由于目前只有一个频率用于 NAVTEX 发射,因此通过分时播发避免了各台之间的相互干扰。一般来说,一个区域内的每个 NAVTEX 广播台每 4 h 会在指定的 10 min 进行广播。

Details of NAVTEX stations and their allocated broadcasting times may be found in the List of Coast Stations and Special Service Stations published by the International Telecommunication Union (ITU) or the Admiralty List of Radio Signals. Generally, NAVTEX information is broadcast in the English language.

有关 NAVTEX 播发台及其分配广播时间的详细信息,请参阅国际电信联盟 (ITU) 发布的《海岸电台和特别业务电台表》或《无线电信号表》。一般来说,NAVTEX 信息以英语广播。

NAVTEX messages are given priorities of VITAL, IMPORTANT and ROUTINE.

· VITAL—transmitted on receipt (subject to not causing interference to other stations).

· Important—next available time slot.

· Routine—at the normal allocated time slot.

NAVTEX 电文的优先级分别为 "极其重要""重要"和"常规"。

· 极其重要——收到后立即播发(以不对其他电台造成干扰为前提)。

· 重要——下一个可用时段。

· 常规——在正常分配的时段。

Messages numbered 01 to 99 if previously received without too many errors will not be reprinted. SAR messages will have the number 00 and always be reprinted whether received previously or not. Most NAVTEX receivers also delete any messages between 60 and 72 h old.

编号为 01 至 99 的电文,如果之前接收时没有出现过多错误,则不会重新打印。SAR 电文的编号为 00,无论以前是否收到过,都会被重新打印。大多数 NAVTEX 接收机还会删除 60 至 72 h 前的电文。

5.3.6　Shipboard Equipment 船载设备

5.3.6.1　NAVTEX Receivers NAVTEX 接收机

To receive NAVTEX broadcasts, a ship must be equipped with a dedicated NAVTEX receiver tuned to 518 kHz. Once switched on and programmed, the receiver will provide fully automatic operation and broadcasts will not be missed even if the bridge watchkeeper is busy with other duties. Messages are received in printed form on a paper roll, and on recent models, displayed electronically with local storage.

要接收 NAVTEX 广播,船上必须配备调谐到 518 kHz 的专用 NAVTEX 接收机。一旦开启并设置好,接收机将自动运行,即使值班驾驶员忙于其他工作,也不会错过广播。接收到的电文可以打印在纸卷上,最新的型号还可以通过本地存储以电子方式显示。

A spare quantity of paper rolls must be kept on board, if the NAVTEX receiver requires it.

如果 NAVTEX 接收机需要纸卷,船上必须备有备用纸卷。

5.3.6.2　Station Identification 发射台识别

NAVTEX receivers allow the operator to select or reject individual stations by their identification code letter.

NAVTEX 接收机允许操作员根据识别字符选择或拒收个别发射台。

5.4　INMARSAT SafetyNET INMARSAT 安全网

5.4.1　General Information 一般信息

SafetyNET is an international automatic direct-printing satellite-based service for the promulgation of Maritime Safety Information (MSI), navigational and meteorological warnings, meteorological forecasts, Search and Rescue (SAR) information and other urgent safety-related messages to ships. It has been developed as a safety service of the INMARSAT-C Enhanced Group Call (EGC) system to provide a simple and automated means of receiving MSI on board ships at sea. The message-selection features of SafetyNET receivers enable mariners to receive safety information broadcasts that are tailored to their particular needs.

安全网是一种基于卫星的国际自动直接打印业务,用于向船舶发布海上安全信息(MSI)、航行和气象警告、气象预报、搜救(SAR)信息以及其他与安全有关的紧急电文。该系统是作为INMARSAT-C 增强群呼(EGC)系统的一项安全业务而开发的,为海上船舶接收 MSI 提供了一种简单而自动化的方式。安全网接收机的信息选择功能可使海员接收到适合其特定需求的安全信息广播。

SafetyNET fulfils an integral role in the GMDSS developed by the IMO and incorporated into the 1988 amendments to the International Convention for the Safety of Life at Sea (SOLAS), as amended, as a requirement for ships to which the Convention applies.

安全网在 IMO 开发的 GMDSS 中发挥着不可或缺的作用,该系统已被纳入 1988 年《国际海上人命安全公约》(SOLAS)修正案,并作为对适用该公约的船舶的必备要求。

Fleet SafetyNET is the digital satellite communications system comprising of a Fleet Broadband Ship Earth System, and type approved Maritime Safety Terminal (MST) for use within the GMDSS, enabling ships to meet the majority of the satellite communications requirements of the GMDSS including distress alerting, reception of Maritime Safety Information (MSI), voice distress and general communications.

船队安全网是数字卫星通信系统,由船队宽带船舶地球系统和 GMDSS 内使用的经型式认可的海上安全终端(MST)组成,使船舶能够满足 GMDSS 的大部分卫星通信要求,包括遇险报警、接收海上安全信息(MSI)、语音遇险和一般通信。

As a part of INMARSAT's GMDSS modernization programme, SafetyNET Ⅱ was developed by INMARSAT with the support from the wider maritime community in 2017. SafetyNET Ⅱ, introduced in NCSR 5/14/5, is an enhancement of the existing SafetyNET service, within the EGC system.

作为 INMARSAT GMDSS 现代化计划的一部分,2017 年 INMARSAT 在广大海事界的支持下开发安全网 Ⅱ。在 NCSR 5/14/5 中推出的安全网 Ⅱ 是 EGC 系统内现有安全网业务的增强版。

5.4.2　Coverage 覆盖范围

All navigable waters of the world between 76°N and 76°S are covered by satellites in the INMARSAT system. Each satellite transmits EGC messages on a designated channel; this channel is optimized to enable the signal to be received by type approved INMARSAT EGC terminals. Reception of EGC messages is normally not affected by the position of the ship within the satellite ocean region, atmospheric conditions or time of day.

INMARSAT 系统的卫星覆盖了北纬 76 度和南纬 76 度之间的所有可航行水域。每颗卫星都在一个指定的频道上发射 EGC 电文;该频道经过优化,可使经型式认可的 INMARSAT EGC 终端接收到信号。EGC 电文的接收通常不受卫星洋区内船舶位置、大气条件或时间的影响。

SafetyNET and SafetyNET Ⅱ messages are addressed to a geographical area. These area calls can be addressed to a fixed geographical area (NAVAREA/METAREA or coastal warning area) or to a user defined area selected by an MSI provider. Area calls will be received automatically by any INMARSAT EGC receiver within the area. To receive EGC coastal warnings, the INMARSAT

EGC receiver must be set up with appropriate NAVTEX B1 and B2 codes—where the B1 code is the designator of the defined area and the B2 code is the subject indicator character.

安全网和安全网 Ⅱ 电文是针对某一地理区域的。这些区域呼叫可以指向一个固定的地理区域(NAVAREA/METAREA 或沿海警告区域)或 MSI 信息提供者选择的用户自定义区域。区域内的任何 INMARSAT EGC 接收机都将自动接收区域呼叫。要接收 EGC 沿海警告,IN-MARSAT EGC 接收机必须设置适当的 NAVTEX B1 和 B2 代码,其中 B1 代码是所定义区域的播发台代号,B2 代码是信息类型标识字符。

5.4.3　Broadcasting of MSI 播发 MSI

For coastal warning areas messages, the MSI provider must ensure that the preamble includes the B1 code identifier allocated for the particular area, along with the appropriate B2 code subject indicator. The EGC receiver can be set to reject messages concerning certain optional subjects, which may not be required by the ship (e.g. LORAN messages may be rejected in a ship, which is not fitted with a LORAN receiver). Receivers also use the B2 code subject indicator to identify coastal warnings, which, because of their importance, may NOT be rejected.

对于沿海警告区域电文,MSI 提供者必须确保报头部分包括为播发台分配的 B1 标识字符和适当的表示信息类型的 B2 标识字符。EGC 接收机可设置为拒绝接收某些可选内容的电文,因为这些内容可能不是船舶所需要的(例如,没有安装 LORAN 接收机的船舶可能会拒绝接收 LORAN 电文)。接收机还使用 B2 标识字符来识别沿海警告,这些警告很重要,因此不会被拒收。

Reception of certain types of messages, such as shore-to-ship distress alerts, SAR information, meteorological warnings and forecasts and navigational warnings, addressed to a geographical area within which the EGC receiver is located, is mandatory and cannot be suppressed by ships in the affected area. These messages are identified by the C2 service codes: 00, 04, 14, 24, 31, 34 and 44.

接收某些类型的电文,如针对 EGC 接收机所在的地理区域的岸对船遇险报警、搜救信息、气象警告和预报以及航行警告是强制性的,不能被受影响区域的船舶禁止。这些电文的 C2 业务代码为:00、04、14、24、31、34 和 44。

When a message has been received error-free, a record is made of the message identification (the unique sequence number, the unique identifier and the service code) associated with that message. The unique sequence number is used to suppress the printing of repeated transmissions of the same message.

当接收到无误的电文时,与该电文相关的电文编码(唯一序列号、唯一标识符和业务代码)就会被记录。唯一序列号用于防止打印重复发送同一电文。

An EGC receiver is capable of storing at least 255 message identifications. These message identifications are stored with an indication of the number of hours that have elapsed since the last receipt of the message. Subsequent reception of the same message identification will reset this timer. After between 60 and 72 h, message identifications may be automatically erased. If the number of received message identifications exceeds the capacity of memory allocated, the oldest message identification will be erased.

EGC 接收机可存储至少 255 个电文标识。这些电文标识在存储时会显示自上次接收电文以来已过去的小时数。如果再次接收到相同的电文标识,则会重置计时器。60 至 72 h 后,信息标识可能会被自动清除。如果接收到的电文标识数量超过了内存容量,最早的电文标识将被清除。

In the case of a ship in distress, it is normal to create a circular user defined area (C2 service code 14), defined by the position of the casualty and a radius around the casualty to alert ships that may be able to render assistance. If no response is received from any ship at the first call, the area can be expanded in steps until an acknowledgement by one or more ships is received. In cases where the position of the distress is unknown, a shore-to-ship distress alert can be transmitted to all ships (C2 service code 00), in a given satellite ocean region. SAR coordination messages shall only be addressed to circular (C2 service code 14) or to rectangular (C2 service code 34) user defined areas.

在船舶遇险的情况下,通常会创建一个由用户定义的圆形区域(C2 业务代码 14),该区域由遇险者的位置和遇险者周围的半径定义,以提醒可能能够提供援助的船舶。如果第一次呼叫没有收到任何船舶的回应,则可逐步扩大该区域,直到收到一艘或多艘船舶的确认。在遇险位置不明的情况下,可向特定卫星海区的所有船舶(C2 业务代码 00)发送岸对船遇险报警。搜救协调电文只能发送到圆形(C2 业务代码 14)或矩形(C2 业务代码 34)用户定义区域。

5.4.4　Message Formatting and C Code for SafetyNET 电文格式和安全网的 C 代码

EGC messages include instructions to the LES for processing MSI in the form of a special address header that consists of five (or six) C codes as described in Table 5.1. In order for a message to be correctly processed, it shall always consist of data conforming to C codes "1" to "5". Additionally, C code "0" shall be used when required by the service provider.

EGC 电文包括到 LES 的指令,用于以表 5.1 中所述的五个(或六个)C 代码组成的特殊地址报头的形式来处理 MSI。为了使电文能被正确处理,它必须始终包含符合 C 代码"1"到"5"的数据。此外,在业务提供商要求时,应使用 C 代码"0"。

Example:

例如:

WWHK82 VHHH 181800

40:1:31:11:01:00

HONG KONG METEOROLOGICAL SERVICE PROVIDES THE FOLLOWING WARNING/INFORMATION FOR THE SOUTH CHINA SEA.

WARNINGS

NIL.

SYNOPSIS (181800UTC) AND 24-HOUR FORECAST

UNSETTLED WEATHER IS AFFECTING NORTHERN PART OF THE SOUTH CHINA SEA (SCS).

SIGNIFICANT SWELL/HIGH SEAS

NIL.

SEA FOG/REDUCED VISIBILITY

VISIBILITY DOWN TO 1000 M IN SQ SH AND TS.

Table 5.1　C Codes Used in EGC System
表 5.1　EGC 系统使用的 C 代码

C Codes C 代码					
C0 ocean region code（when required） 洋区码（如需要）	C1 Priority code 优先代码	C2 Service code 业务代码	C3 Address code 地址代码	C4 Repetition code 重复代码	C5 Presentation code 显示代码
1-digit code 1 位数字代码	1-digit code 1 位数字代码	2-digit code 2 位数字代码	2, 4, 10 or 12 alpha-numeric code 2、4、10 或 12 位字母数字代码	2-digit code 2 位数字代码	1-or 2-digit code 1 或 2 位数字代码
0：AOR-W 1：AOR-E 2：POR 3：IOR 9：All ocean regions 0：大西洋西区 1：大西洋东区 2：太平洋区 3：印度洋区 9：全部洋区	1：Safety 2：Urgency 3：Distress 1：安全 2：紧急 3：遇险	00：All ships（general call） 00：所有船舶（一般呼叫） 04：Navigational, meteorological or piracy warning or meteorological forecast to a rectangular area 04：矩形区域的航行、气象或海盗警告或气象预报 13：Navigational, meteorological, coastal or piracy warning or meteorological forecast to a coastal warning area 13：沿海警告区域的航行、气象、沿海或海盗警告或气象预报	2-digit 00（all ships） 2 位数 00（所有船舶） 12 alphanumeric rectangular area address D1D2N（S）D3D4D5E（W）D6D7D8D9D10 12 位字母数字矩形区域地址 D1D2N（S）D3D4D5E（W）D6D7D8D9D10 4 alphanumeric coastal warning area address X1X2B1B2 4 位字母数字沿海警告区域地址 X1X2B1B2	Category（a） （a）类 For EGC messages to be repeated a finite number of times EGC 电文的重复次数是有限的 Category（b） （b）类 For EGC messages to be repeated at specified intervals until cancelled by the MSI provider. 按指定时间间隔重复发送 EGC 电文，直至 MSI 提供者取消	Always 0 or 00 始终为 0 或 00

Continued 续表

		14: Shore-to-ship distress alert to a circular area 14:圆形区域的岸对船遇险报警	10 alphanumeric circular area address D1D2N(S) D3D4E(W)M1M2M 10位字母数字圆形区域地址 D1D2N(S) D3D4E(W)M1M2M		
		24:Navigational, meteorological or piracy warning or meteorological forecast to a circular area 24:圆形区域的航行、气象或海盗警告或气象预报	10 alphanumeric circular area address D1D2N(S)D3D4E(W) M1M2M3 10位字母数字圆形区域地址 D1D2N(S) D3D4E(W)M1M2M3	Category (a) (a)类 For EGC messages to be repeated a finite number of times EGC电文的重复次数是有限的	
		31:NAVAREA, METAREA, or piracy warning, or meteorological forecast to a NAVAREA/METAREA 31:NAVAREA/ METAREA 的 NAVAREA METAREA 警告,或海盗警告或气象预报	2-digit NAVAREA/ METAREA number 2位 NAVAREA/META REA 编号	Category (b) (b)类 For EGC messages to be repeated at specified intervals until cancelled by the MSI provider 按指定时间间隔重复发送 EGC 电文,直至 MSI 提供者取消	Always 0 or 00 始终为0 或 00
		34: SAR coordination to a rectangular area 34:搜救协调矩形区域	12 alphanumeric rectangular area address D1D2N(S) D3D4D5E (W)D6D7D8D9D10 12位字母数字矩形区域地址 D1D2N(S)D3 D4D5E(W)D6D7 D8D9D10		
		44: SAR coordination to a circular area 44:搜救协调圆形区域	10 alphanumeric circular area address D1D2N (S) D3D4E (W)M1M2M3 10位字母数字圆形区域地址 D1D2N (S) D3D4E (W)M1M2M3		

5.4.5　Requirements of the EGC Receiver EGC 接收机的要求

The basic requirements of the EGC receiver are that it should continuously receive the broadcast channel and process the messages being transmitted through the satellite. For this reason, MSI providers shall repeat their most important unscheduled messages 6 min after the first broadcast so that the terminal would receive EGC messages on the repeated broadcast.

EGC 接收机的基本要求是,它应持续接收广播频道,并处理通过卫星发送的电文。因此, MSI 提供者应在第一次广播后 6 min 重复发送最重要的非定时信息,以便终端接收重复广播的 EGC 电文。

Although the MES receives all SafetyNET messages on the broadcast channel, it may suppress some messages from being displayed or printed automatically. For example:

- All messages addressed to geographical areas (circular or rectangular) other than those including the ship's current position will be automatically suppressed;

- For coastal warnings only it may be programmed to suppress:

a.Messages containing B1 codes for coastal warning areas which have not been set up in the terminal;

b.Messages containing B2 codes for subject matter of no relevance to the ship(see Table 5.2).

虽然 MES 可以接收广播频道上的所有安全网电文,但它可能会拒绝某些电文的自动显示或打印。例如:

- 除包括船舶当前位置在内的地理区域(圆形或矩形)外,所有发送到其他地理区域的电文都将被自动屏蔽;

- 对于沿海警告,如下可将其编程为"拒收":

a.包含未在终端中设置的沿海警告区域 B1 代码的电文;

b.含有 B2 代码的电文,其内容与船舶无关(见表 5.2)。

The MES also suppresses the printing of messages previously received. It is not possible to reject mandatory "all ship" messages such as shore-to-ship distress alerts for the area within which the ship is located. When a distress or urgency message is received, an audio and visual alarm will be given.

MES 还会禁止打印之前收到的电文。无法拒收强制性的发给"所有船"的电文,如船舶所在区域的岸对船遇险报警。收到遇险或紧急电文时,将发出声光报警。

It is recommended that, in order to ensure that all necessary MSI is available before sailing, the EGC receiver should remain in operation while the ship is in port.

为了确保在开航前具备所有必要的 MSI,建议在船舶靠港时,EGC 接收机应保持工作状态。

Table 5.2 B2 Code Subject Indicators for Coastal Warnings

表 5.2 沿海警告信息类型识别字符 B2

B₂Code 代码	Subject 内容
A	Navigational warnings 航行警告
B	Meteorological warnings 气象警告
C	Ice reports 冰况报告
D	Search and rescue information, and acts of piracy warnings 搜救信息和海盗行为警告
E	Meteorological forecasts 气象预报
F	Pilot service messages 引航业务电文
G	AIS
H	LORAN messages LORAN 电文
I	Not used 未使用
J	SATNAV messages SATNAV 电文
K	Other electronic navaid messages 其他电子导航电文
L	Other navigational warnings—additional to B2 code A 其他航行警告——B2 代码 A 的附加警告
V W X Y	Special services allocation by the International SafetyNET Coordinating Panel 国际安全网协调小组分配的特别服务
Z	No messages on hand 手头没有电文

Where automatic updates are not available, provision is made for a visual indication if the ship's position has not been updated during the last 12 h. It is only possible to reset this indication by revalidating the ship's position. If the MES's position has not been updated for more than 12 h, ALL SafetyNET messages will be printed or stored in memory.

在无法自动更新的情况下,如果船位在过去 12 h 内没有更新,则会有视觉提示。只有通过重新验证船位才能重置该指示。如果 MES 的位置超过 12 h 未更新,所有安全网电文将被打印出来或存储在内存中。

5.4.6   **Introduction of SafetyNET Ⅱ** 安全网 Ⅱ 介绍

SafetyNET Ⅱ is an enhancement to the current SafetyNET system. SafetyNET Ⅱ provides an interactive web portal or application programing interface (API) for information providers to create their MSI messages and deliver them over the INMARSAT EGC system including INMARSAT-C, Mini-C, and Fleet Safety as illustrated by Figure 5.3.

安全网 Ⅱ 是当前安全网系统的增强版。如图 5.3 所示,安全网 Ⅱ 提供了一个交互式门户网站或应用程序接口(API),供信息提供者创建 MSI 电文,并通过 INMARSAT EGC 系统(包括 INMARSAT-C、Mini-C 和 Fleet Safety)发送这些电文。

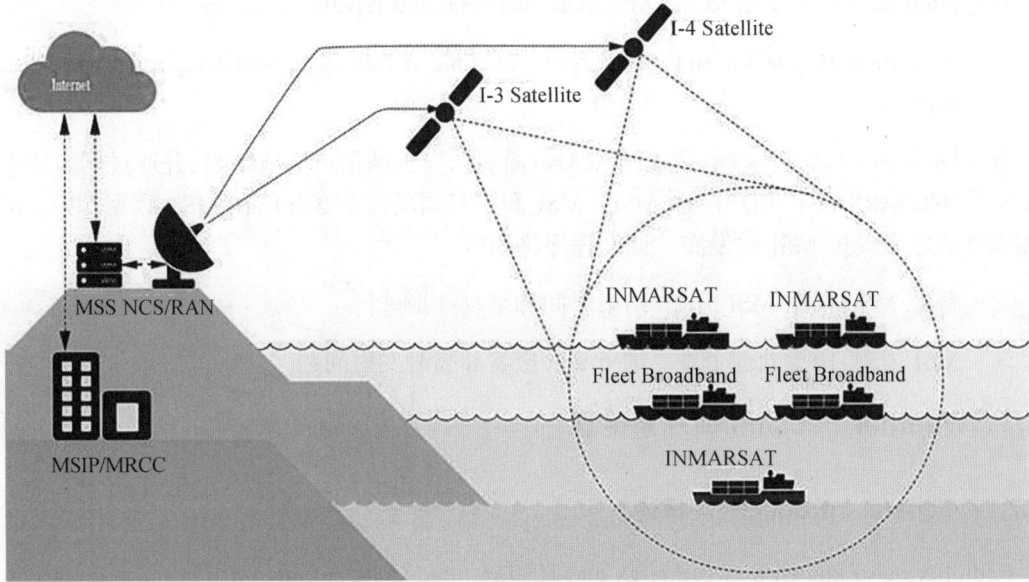

Figure 5.3   Overview SafetyNET Ⅱ
图 5.3   安全网 Ⅱ 概述

The Maritime Safety Server (MSS) is the core of SafetyNET Ⅱ. The MSS is owned and operated by INMARSAT as part of its commitment to maritime safety services and its public service agreement obligations. The MSS interfaces between the shore-based maritime safety infrastructure, e.g. MSIPs, and the seafarer, who uses a Maritime Safety Terminal (MST), via the Fleet Broadband system. Additionally, the MSS provides interconnectivity to the INMARSAT-C system for the purposes of sending and receiving Maritime Safety Information (MSI). The MSS offers high resilience through internal application redundancy and geographical redundancy.

海事安全服务器(MSS)是安全网Ⅱ 的核心。MSS 由 INMARSAT 拥有和运营,是其对海上安全服务的承诺和公共服务协议义务的一部分。MSS 是岸基海事安全基础设施(如 MSIP)与使用海上安全终端(MST)的海员之间通过船队宽带系统进行连接的接口。此外,MSS 还提供与 INMARSAT-C 系统的互联,以发送和接收海上安全信息(MSI)。MSS 通过内部应用冗余和地理冗余提供高弹性。

The MSIP is responsible for providing reliable communication links to the system's network

for efficient handling of shore-to-ship distress alert relays and distress traffic, preferably via dedicated communication links.

MSIP 负责为系统网络提供可靠的通信链路,最好是通过专用通信链路,以便有效处理岸对船遇险报警转发和遇险通信。

SafetyNET Ⅱ can broadcast MSI to Fleet SafetyNET users through the Radio Access Network (RAN), and to INMARSAT-C users through the Network Coordination Station (NCS). The MSI and all scheduling information are stored in the MSS database. The MSS uses a scheduler component to schedule the MSI promulgation. The scheduler will schedule:

· Each MSI according to the MSI start/end time and repetition scheme.

· MSI transmission for individual spots handling 6 min echo and temporary transmission problems.

安全网 Ⅱ 可以通过无线电接入网(RAN)向船队安全网用户广播 MSI,并通过网络协调站(NCS)向 INMARSAT-C 用户广播 MSI。MSI 和所有调度信息都存储在 MSS 数据库中。MSS 使用调度程序来安排 MSI 的发布。调度程序将调度:

· 每个 MSI,根据 MSI 开始/结束时间和重复计划进行。

· MSI 发射,用于处理个别点的 6 min 应答和临时发射问题。

5.4.7　Weather Facsimile 气象传真

5.4.7.1　General Introduction 概述

Radiofax, also known as weatherfax and HF fax (due to its common use in the short waves), is an analogue mode for transmitting images in grayscale. It is also related to slow-scan television (SSTV). The term weatherfax was coined after the technology that allows the transmission and reception of weather charts (surface analysis, forecasts, and others) from a transmission site (usually the meteorological office) to a remote site (where the actual users are).

无线电传真又称气象传真和高频传真(因其常用于短波),是一种模拟工作模式传输灰度图像。它也与慢扫描电视(SSTV)有关。气象传真一词是根据从发射台(通常是气象局)向远程电台(实际用户所在地)发送和接收气象图表(地面分析图、预报图和其他图)的技术而创造的。

Facsimile machines were used in the 1950s to transmit weather charts across the United States via land-lines first and then internationally via HF radio. Radio transmission of weather charts provides great flexibility to marine and aviation users, for they now have the latest weather information and forecasts at their disposal to use in the planning of voyages.

20 世纪 50 年代,传真设备首先通过陆地线路向全美发送天气图,然后通过高频无线电向全球发送天气图。无线电发送天气图为航海和航空用户提供了极大的灵活性,因为他们现在可以随时获得最新的天气信息和预报,用于制订航行计划。

Radiofax relies on facsimile technology, where printed information is scanned line by line and encoded into an electrical signal which can then be transmitted over land-line or via radio waves to great distances. Since the amount of information transmitted per unit time is directly proportional to the bandwidth available, the speed at which a weather chart can be transmitted varies depending on the quality of the media used for transmission.

无线电传真依靠传真技术,将印刷信息逐行扫描并编码成电信号,然后通过陆地线路或无线电波发送到很远的地方。由于单位时间内发送的信息量与可用带宽成正比,因此天气图的发送速度因发送介质的质量而异。

Today radiofax charts and images are available via FTP or HTTP downloads from sites in the Internet, such as the ones hosted by the National Oceanic and Atmospheric Administration (NOAA). Radiofax transmissions are also broadcast by NOAA from multiple sites in the USA at regular daily schedules. Radio weatherfax transmissions are particularly useful to shipping, where there are limited facilities for accessing the Internet.

如今,无线电传真海图和图像可通过 FTP 或 HTTP 从互联网网站下载,如美国国家海洋和大气管理局(NOAA)的网站。NOAA 还从美国的多个站点每天定时播发无线电传真。因为船舶上网设施有限,无线电气象传真对航运业特别有用。

5.4.7.2   Transmission Details 信息发送

Radiofax is transmitted in single sideband and uses frequency modulation. The signal shifts up or down a given amount to designate white or black pixels. A deviation less than that for a white or black pixel is taken to be a shade of grey. With correct tuning , the signal shares some characteristics with SSTV, with black at 1500 Hz and peak white at 2300 Hz. The official ITU radio emission designation is F3C.

无线电传真以单边带发送,使用频率调制。信号上下移动一定的幅度来定义白色或黑色像素。小于白色或黑色像素的偏差被视为灰色阴影。在正确调谐的情况下,信号与 SSTV 有某些相同之处,黑色为 1500 Hz,白色峰值为 2300 Hz。国际电信联盟的官方无线电发射代号为 F3C。

Usually, 120 lines per minute (LPM) are sent (For monochrome fax, possible values are: 60, 90, 100, 120, 180, 240. For colour fax, LPM can be: 120, 240). A value known as the index of cooperation (IOC) must also be known to decode a radio fax transmission—this governs the image resolution, and derives from early radio fax machines which used drum readers, and is the product of the total line length and the number of lines per unit length (known sometimes as the factor of cooperation), divided by π (3.1416). Usually the IOC is 576.

通常每分钟发送 120 行 (LPM)(对于单色传真,LPM 可能为 60、90、100、120、180、240;对于彩色传真,LPM 可以是 120、240)。要对无线电传真发送进行解码,还必须知道合作指数 (IOC) 的值——它决定了图像的分辨率,源于早期使用鼓式读取器的无线电传真机,是总行长与单位长度行数的乘积(有时称为合作系数)除以 π (3.1416)。通常 IOC 为 576。

5.4.7.3 Automatic Picture Transmission（APT）Format 自动图像发送（APT）格式

APT format permits unattended monitoring of services（see Table 5.3）. It is employed by most terrestrial weather facsimile stations as well as geostationary weather satellites.

- The start tone triggers the receiving system. It was originally meant to allow enough time for the drum of mechanical systems to get up to speed. It consists of rapid modulation of the video carrier，resulting in a characteristic rasp-like sound.

- The phasing signal，consisting of a periodic pulse，synchronizes the receiver so that the image will be centered on the paper.

- The stop tone marks the end of the transmission.

APT 格式允许对服务进行无人值守监听(见表 5.3)。大多数地面气象传真站和地球同步静止气象卫星都采用这种格式。

- 启动音触发接收系统。它的初衷是为机械系统的转鼓留出足够的启动时间。它由视频载波的快速调制组成,产生一种特有的沙沙声。

- 由周期性脉冲组成的相位信号使接收机同步,从而使图像在相纸上居中。

- 停止音标志着发送结束。

Table 5.3 Automatic Picture Transmission Format
表 5.3　自动图像发送格式

Signal 信号	Duration 持续时间	IOC576	IOC288	Remarks 备注
Start tone 启动音	5 s	300 Hz	675 Hz	200 Hz for colour fax modes 彩色传真模式为 200 赫兹
Phasing signal 相位信号	30 s			White line interrupted by a black pulse 白行被黑色脉冲打断
Image 图片	Variable 可变	1200 lines	600 lines	at 120 LPM 每分钟 120 行
Stop tone 停止音	5 s	450 Hz	450 Hz	
Black 黑色	10 s			

Table 5.4 gives an example of the details of weather facsimile broadcast station.
表 5.4 举例说明了气象传真广播站的详细情况。

Table 5.4 Information of RIO DE JANEIRO, BRAZIL for Weather Facsimile

表 5.4 巴西里约热内卢的天气传真信息

Call signs 呼号	Frequencies 频率	Time 时间	Emission 发射模式	Power 功率
PWZ–33	12665 kHz	ALL BROADCAST TIME 所有时间播发	J3C	1 kW
PWZ–33	16978 kHz	ALL BROADCAST TIME 所有时间播发	J3C	1 kW

Time 时间	Contents of Transmission 传输内容	RPM/IOC 每分钟转数/合作系数	Valid Time 有效时间	Map Area 图示区域
0745/1630	TEST CHART 测试图	120/576		
0750/1635	SURFACE ANALYSIS（Hpa） 地面分析图	120/576	00/12	A
0810/1655	WAVES SIG HEIGHT（m）AND DIR PROG 12/00Z+36HR 对 12 或 00 时(世界时)之后 36 小时的显著波高及其方向的预报	120/576	00/12	B
0830/1715	WIND AT 10 m（KTS）PROG 12/00Z +36 HR 对 12 或 00 时(世界时)之后 36 小时的 10 m 高度处的风波和风向的预报	120/576	00/12	C
0850/1735	SEA SURFACE TEMPERATURE 海表温度	120/576	12/00	D

The existing stations of weather fax are shown in Table 5.5.

现有气象传真站见表 5.5。

Table 5.5 Stations List of Weather Fax（Part）

表 5.5 气象传真站清单(部分)

Frequency（kHz） 频率（kHz）	Call sign 呼号	Station 台站	Country 国家
5100	AXM 32	Melbourne Meteo 墨尔本气象局	AUS 澳大利亚
11030	AXM 34	Melbourne Meteo 墨尔本气象局	AUS 澳大利亚
13920	AXM 35	Melbourne Meteo 墨尔本气象局	AUS 澳大利亚
20469	AXM 37	Melbourne Meteo 墨尔本气象局	AUS 澳大利亚

Continued 续表

Frequency（kHz） 频率(kHz)	Call sign 呼号	Station 台站	Country 国家
2754	CKN	CF Victoria 维多利亚 CF	CAN 加拿大
4268	CKN	CF Victoria 维多利亚 CF	CAN 加拿大
6456	CKN	CF Victoria 维多利亚 CF	CAN 加拿大
12753	CKN	CF Victoria 维多利亚 CF	CAN 加拿大
5526.5	BAF 6	Beijing Meteo 北京气象局	CHN 中国
8122	BAF 36	Beijing Meteo 北京气象局	CHN 中国
10117	BAF 4	Beijing Meteo 北京气象局	CHN 中国
14367	BAF 8	Beijing Meteo 北京气象局	CHN 中国
16026	BAF 9	Beijing Meteo 北京气象局	CHN 中国
18237	BAF 33	Beijing Meteo 北京气象局	CHN 中国
5100	BDF	Shanghai Meteo 上海气象局	CHN 中国
7420	BDF	Shanghai Meteo 上海气象局	CHN 中国
11420	BDF	Shanghai Meteo 上海气象局	CHN 中国
18940	BDF	Shanghai Meteo 上海气象局	CHN 中国
3365	JMJ	Tokyo Meteo 东京气象局	J 日本
3622.5	JMH	Tokyo Meteo 东京气象局	J 日本
5405	JMJ 2	Tokyo Meteo 东京气象局	J 日本

Continued   续表

Frequency（kHz） 频率(kHz)	Call sign 呼号	Station 台站	Country 国家
7305	JMH 2	Tokyo Meteo 东京气象局	J 日本
9438	JMJ 3	Tokyo Meteo 东京气象局	J 日本
9970	JMH 3	Tokyo Meteo 东京气象局	J 日本
13597	JMH 4	Tokyo Meteo 东京气象局	J 日本
14692.5	JMJ 4	Tokyo Meteo 东京气象局	J 日本
18220	JMH 5	Tokyo Meteo 东京气象局	J 日本
18441.2	JMJ 5	Tokyo Meteo 东京气象局	J 日本
23523	JMH 6	Tokyo Meteo 东京气象局	J 日本
4346	NMC	USCG San Francisco 旧金山美国海岸警卫队	USA 美国
8682	NMC	USCG San Francisco 旧金山美国海岸警卫队	USA 美国
12730	NMC	USCG San Francisco 旧金山美国海岸警卫队	USA 美国
17151.2	NMC	USCG San Francisco 旧金山美国海岸警卫队	USA 美国
22527	NMC	USCG San Francisco 旧金山美国海岸警卫队	USA 美国
6453	NPG	USN San Francisco 旧金山美国海军	USA 美国
9090	NPG	USN San Francisco 旧金山美国海军	USA 美国

Ship Reporting Systems
船舶报告系统

Chapter 6

6.1 General Introduction 概述

Ship Reporting Systems (SRSs) contribute to safety of life at sea, safety and efficiency of navigation, and protection of the marine environment. Many maritime countries operate Ship Reporting Systems, they are useful in the event of a search and rescue (SAR) incident. Certain administrations are making wider use of automated means, such as Automatic Identification System (AIS) and long-range identification and tracking of ships (LRIT) schemes, both of which are now compulsory fitted systems on vessels bound by the 1974 SOLAS Convention.

船舶报告系统（SRS）有助于海上人命安全、航行安全和效率以及海洋环境保护。许多海运大国都有船舶报告系统，它们在发生搜救(SAR)事件时非常有用。某些主管机关正在更广泛地使用自动化手段，如船舶自动识别系统（AIS）和船舶远程识别与跟踪（LRIT）系统，这两种系统现在都是受 1974 年《国际海上人命安全公约》要求的船舶必须安装的系统。

The SRS may be voluntary or obligatory. The voluntary reporting systems are based on mutual solidarity, and they are usually set up in the areas where unfavorable weather conditions prevail. The obligatory reporting systems rest on the stipulations of the 1974 SOLAS Convention. In keeping with these provisions, the only authorized organization for issuing instructions, defining conditions and rules with a view to founding and regulating the SRS is the IMO. In compliance with the 1974 SOLAS Convention, the obligatory SRS may refer to all or some individual types of ships, excepting military and subsidiary merchant shipping, or some other non-commercial types of ships in charge of the government. Ships Masters are obligated to send in the following reports about the movement of the ship:

· Sailing Plan;

- Position Report;

- Deviation Report; and

- Final Report.

SRS 可以是自愿性的,也可以是强制性的。自愿报告制度以互助为基础,通常在天气条件恶劣的地区建立。强制性报告系统以 1974 年《国际海上人命安全公约》的规定为基础。根据这些规定,IMO 是唯一被授权发布指令、确定条件和规则以建立和管理 SRS 的组织。根据 1974 年《国际海上人命安全公约》的规定,强制性船舶报告系统可适用于所有或个别类型的船舶,但不包括军舰和附属商船,也不包括由政府管理的其他非商业类型的船舶。船长有义务提交以下船舶航行报告:

- 航行计划;

- 船位报告;

- 偏航报告;以及

- 最终报告。

There exists an obligation to report in cases of real or possible sea contamination (pollution) through the use of reports on:

- Dangerous Goods Report;

- Harmful Substances Report; and

- Marine Pollutants Report.

在实际发生或可能发生的海洋污染时,有义务通过以下报告进行报告:

- 危险货物报告;

- 有害物质报告;以及

- 海洋污染物报告。

Individual systems vary in that some countries make reporting mandatory only for vessels of their own flag. The purpose of such schemes is to provide an information data bank about shipping present in a particular area for use during SAR incidents. Vessels would normally report their position to shore authorities through coast radio stations. The most well-known of these systems is the Automated Mutual-assistance Vessel Rescue (AMVER) service, operated by the US Coast Guard (USCG).

各系统的情况各不相同,有些国家只强制要求悬挂本国国旗的船舶提交报告。此类计划的目的是提供一个有关特定区域航行的信息数据库,供发生搜救事件时使用。船舶通常会通过海岸电台向海岸当局报告其位置。这些系统中最著名的是由美国海岸警卫队(USCG)运营的船舶自动互救系统(AMVER)业务。

6.2　Automated Mutual-assistance Vessel Rescue System（AM-VER）船舶自动互救系统（AMVER）

6.2.1　The AMVER Organization Introduction AMVER 组织简介

The AMVER service is operated by the USCG and is available to any merchant vessel of greater than 1000 gross tonnage on a voyage greater than 24 h. However, it is also open to cruise ships, research vessels and fish factory ships, etc. Ships registered with AMVER can send messages via many overseas coast stations, as well as to USCG radio stations. These messages can be transmitted using RT or telex for onward transmission to USCG New York, where the data is stored on computer. All AMVER messages should be addressed as follows：

AMVER 业务由 USCG 负责运营,适用于超过 1000 总吨、航行时间超过 24 h 的任何商船。不过,它也向邮轮、科学研究船和渔船等开放。在 AMVER 注册的船舶可以通过许多海外海岸电台以及 USCG 无线电台发送电文。这些电文可以通过无线电话或电传发送到 USCG 纽约分部,将数据存储在计算机中。所有 AMVER 电文的地址如下。

AMVER, followed by the name of the participating radio station.

For example：

AMVER NEW YORK RADIO

AMVER messages may also be forwarded over the INMARSAT system using special code "43".

AMVER,后跟参与电台的名称。

例如：

纽约 AMVER 海岸电台

AMVER 电文也可使用特殊代码"43"通过 INMARSAT 系统转发。

However, the use of E-mail via the Internet is now the preferred method for sending AMVER reports using the following address：amvermsg@ amver.com.

不过,通过互联网发送电子邮件是目前发送 AMVER 报告的首选方法,地址如下：amvermsg@ amver.com。

If a marine incident occurs, the computer will produce a picture of vessels in the area（a surface picture, or SURPIC）that may be in a position to render assistance.

如果发生海上事故,计算机将生成该区域内可能有能力提供援助的船舶的图像（水面图像,或水面图像监视系统）。

Merchant vessels of all nations making offshore voyages are encouraged to send movement reports and periodic position reports to the US Coast Guard Operation System Center in Martinsburg,

West Virginia through selected radio stations or the INMARSAT. Information from these reports is entered into a computer, which generates and maintains dead reckoning positions for vessels while they are within the plotting area. Characteristics of vessels, which are valuable for determining SAR capability, are also entered into the computer from available sources of information. Appropriate information concerning the predicted location and SAR characteristics of each vessel known to be within the area of interest, is made available upon request to recognized SAR agencies of any nation, or person in distress, for use during an emergency. Predicted locations are only disclosed for reasons connected with maritime safety.

鼓励进行近海航行的各国商船通过选定的无线电台或 INMARSAT 向位于西弗吉尼亚州马丁斯堡的美国海岸警卫队业务系统中心发送移动报告和定期船位报告。这些报告中的信息被输入计算机,当船舶在标绘区域内时,计算机会生成并保持船舶的推算位置。此外,系统还通过现有的信息来源将那些确定对搜救有价值的船舶的特征输入计算机。如果任何国家的公认搜救机构或遇险人员提出要求,可向其提供有关预测位置的适当信息,以及已知在相关区域内的每艘船舶的搜救特征,供其在紧急情况下使用。只有出于与海上安全有关的原因,才会披露预测位置。

In case of emergencies, all distress messages must be sent to the nearest RCC, NOT the AMVER Center.

在紧急情况下,所有遇险求救信息必须发送到最近的 RCC,而不是 AMVER 中心。

6.2.2 Requirement for Messages 对电文的要求

There are four types of report used in AMVER system, they are Sailing Plan (SP), Position Report (PR), Arrival Report (FR) and Deviation Report (DR). If required, the Sailing Plan and Departure Report can be combined into a single report.

AMVER 系统使用四种类型的报告,即航行计划 (SP)、船位报告 (PR)、抵港报告 (FR) 和偏航报告 (DR)。如有需要,航行计划和离港报告可合并为一份报告。

Sailing Plan 航行计划

·   Report identifier：AMVER/SP//

·   Required information：Lines A,B,E,F,G,I,L,Z

·   Optional information：Lines M, V, X, Y (Not optional for US vessels)

·   Sailing Plans may be sent within a few hours prior to or after departure

·   报告标识符:AMVER/SP//

·   所需信息:A、B、E、F、G、I、L、Z 行

·   可选信息:M、V、X、Y 行(对于美国船舶不是可选信息)

·   航行计划可在出发前或出发后数小时内发送

Position Report 船位报告

- Report identifier：AMVER/PR//

- Required information：Lines A,B,C,E,F,Z

- Optional information：Lines 1（Strongly recommended）M，X，Y（Not optional for US vessels）

- 报告标识符:AMVER/PR//

- 所需信息:A、B、C、E、F、Z 行

- 可选信息:第 1 行(强烈建议) M、X、Y 行(美国船舶非可选信息)

Position Report should be sent within 24 hours of departure and subsequently at intervals not exceeding 48 h until arrival.

应在出发后 24 小时内发送位置报告,随后每隔不超过 48 h 发送一次,直至抵达。

Arrival Report 抵港报告

- Report identifier:AMVER/FR//

- Required information：Lines A,K,Z

- Optional information:Line X,Y（Not optional for US vessels）

- 报告标识符:AMVER/FR//

- 所需信息:A、K、Z 行

- 可选信息:X、Y 行(美国船舶非可选信息)

Arrival Report should be sent immediately prior to or upon arrival at the port of destination.

抵港报告应在抵达目的港之前或之后立即发送。

Deviation Report 偏航报告

- Report identifier：AMVER/DR//

- Required information:Lines A, B, C, E, F, Z. Lines changed if destination or route changes.

- Optional information：One or more of the following lines（Strongly recommended）L, M, X, Y（Not optional for US vessels）

- 报告标识符:AMVER/DR//

- 必要信息:A、B、C、E、F、Z 行。如果目的地或路线发生变化,请换行。

- 可选信息: 以下一行或多行(强烈建议) L、M、X、Y 行(美国船舶非可选信息)

Used to report changes to the Sailing Plan.

用于报告航行计划的变更。

Form of Messages 电文的形式

The first line of each report is the report text identifier. Each line of report text starts with a line identifier. The line identifier and the data items on a line are separated from each other by a single slash"/", lines are terminated by a double slash "//".

每份报告的第一行是报告文本标识符。每行报告文本都以行标识符开头。行标识符和一行中的数据项之间用单斜线"/"分隔,行以双斜线"//"结束。

Key to line identifiers:

A/　Vessel's name/international radio call sign//

B/　Date and time (GMT)//

C/　Latitude/Longitude//

E/　Current course// (3-digit group)

F/　Estimated average speed// (3-digit group in knots and tenths of knots without decimal point)

G/　Port of departure/Latitude/Longitude//

I/　Port of destination/Latitude/Longitude/Estimated time of arrival//

K/　Port name/Latitude/Longitude/Time of arrival//

L/　Rout information. . . //

M/　Current coast radio station or satellite number/next station, if any//

V/　On board medical resources//(one or more of the following MD for physician/PA for physician's assistant/NURSE//or NONE//)

X/　Up to 65 characters of amplifying comments//

Y/　For forwarding of messages to JASREP and MAREP request//

Z/　(End of Report)—For computer processing of messages//

关键行标识符:

A/　船名/国际无线电呼号//

B/　日期和时间(格林尼治标准时间)//

C/　纬度/经度//

E/　当前航向// (3 位数字组)

F/　估计平均速度//(三位数字组,单位为节和 0.1 节,不含小数点)

G/　出发港/纬度/经度//

I/　目的港/纬度/经度/预计抵达时间//

K/　港口名称/纬度/经度/抵达时间//

L/　航线信息 ……//

M/　当前海岸电台或卫星编号/下一个电台（如果有）//

V/　船上医疗资源//（以下一个或多个 MD 代表医生/PA 代表医生助理/护士//或无//）

X/　最多 65 个字符的补充内容//

Y/　用于将电文转发给 JASREP 和 MAREP 请求//

Z/　（报告结束）——用于计算机处理电文//

Transmissions of Messages 发送电文

All AMVER messages should be addressed to the participating AMVER radio station to which the message is sent. AMVER (name of station), e. g., AMVER VALENTIA.

所有 AMVER 电文都应发送给参与的 AMVER 无线电台。AMVER（电台名称），例如：AMVER VALENTIA。

AMVER messages should be sent during regular watchkeeping periods. They are considered to comply with the US regulations regarding notification of the Coast Guard Captain 24 h before arrival at a port.

AMVER 电文应在正常值班期间发送。这些电文被视为符合美国关于在抵达港口前 24 h 通知海岸警卫队队长的规定。

Detailed instructions in English and a number of other languages, are contained in AMVER User's Manual which may be obtained free of charge by request to AMVER Maritime Relations Office.

AMVER 用户手册载有英文和其他一些语言的详细说明，可向 AMVER 海事关系办公室免费索取。

6.3　Japanese Ship Reporting System（JASREP）日本船舶报告系统（JASREP）

6.3.1　Introduction 简介

The Japanese Ship Reporting System (JASREP) has been established to assist in the coordination of SAR operations in the sea area bounded by the mainland of Asia, the parallel of latitude 17° N, and the meridian of longitude 165° E. Vessels send regular reports, through Japan Coast Guard stations at which a computer keeps a continuous record of the predicted position of each vessel. Should an expected report not be received, SAR action may be initiated.

日本船舶报告系统（JASREP）的建立是为了协助协调以亚洲大陆、北纬 17 度平行线和东经 165 度经线为界的海域的搜救行动。船舶通过日本海上保安厅站定期发送报告，该站的计算机持续记录每艘船舶的预测位置。如果没有收到预期报告,则可能启动搜救行动。

The JASREP System provides up-to-date information on the movements of vessels in order, in the event of a distress incident:

- To reduce the interval between the loss of contact with a vessel and the initiation of search and rescue operations in cases where no distress signal has been received;

- To permit rapid determination may be called upon to provide of vessels with assistance;

- To permit delineation of a search area of limited size in case the position of a vessel in distress is unknown or uncertain: and

- To facilitate the provision of urgent medical assistance or advice to vessels not carrying a doctor.

一旦发生遇险事件,JASREP 系统可提供有关船舶动态的最新信息:

- 在没有收到求救信号的情况下,缩短与船舶失去联系到启动搜救行动的间隔时间;

- 以便迅速确定可能需要提供援助的船舶;

- 在遇险船舶位置不明或不确定的情况下,划定一定范围的搜索区;以及

- 为没有携带医生的船舶提供紧急医疗援助或建议。

6.3.2　Types of Reports and Timing 报告类型和时间安排

There are four types of JASREP Reports: Sailing Plan, Position Report, Deviation Report and Final Report.

JASREP 报告有四种类型:航行计划、船位报告、偏航报告和最终报告。

Sailing Plan 航行计划

Sailing Plan is the basic information to estimate ship's position, and it should be sent at the time when a ship participates in this system. Reports should therefore be made when the ship departs from a port within the service area or when the ship enters the area.

航行计划是估算船位的基本信息,应在船舶加入该系统时发送。因此,应在船舶离开服务区内的港口或进入服务区时进行报告。

The essential lines listed are A, B, G, I, L, M, X, V and Y.

列出的基本项目有 A、B、G、I、L、M、X、V 和 Y。

When Sailing Plan is sent after departure from a port or after entering the service area, such reporting should be made as soon as practicable. When Sailing Plan is to be sent before departure from a port, such a report may be sent in a written document.

如果航行计划在离港后或进入服务区后发送,则应在可行的情况下尽快报告。如果航行计划在离港前发送,则可以书面形式发送。

Position Report 船位报告

Position Report is the information to verify if ship's position input according to the Sailing Plan is correct. The 1st report should therefore be sent at an optional time within 24 h of departure from a port or entering the service area, and then the reports should be sent subsequently no less frequently than every 24 h until Final Report.

船位报告是用来核实根据航行计划输入的船位是否正确的信息。因此,第一份报告应在离开港口或进入服务区后的 24 h 内发送,随后至少每 24 h 发送一次,直至最终报告。

The report comprises lines A, B, C, E, F, M, X and Y.

报告由 A、B、C、E、F、M、X 和 Y 行组成。

In case where delayed reporting is anticipated due to change of radio operator's duty hours or else, reports should be sent earlier than the scheduled time of reporting as far as practicable. Reports should be sent more frequently than the above schedule, when the ship is in heavy weather or under other adverse conditions. In the JASREP service area, no coordination with weather reporting service is made.

如果由于无线电报务员的值班时间改变或其他原因预计会延迟报告,则应尽可能在预定报告时间之前发送报告。当船舶处于恶劣天气或其他不利条件下时,发送报告的频率应高于上述时间安排。在 JASREP 服务区,其不与气象报告服务协调播发。

Deviation Report 偏航报告

Deviation Report is the information to be used for necessary correction of pre-reported Sailing Plan when a ship deviates from the intended course due to change in Sailing Plan. Reports should be sent whenever the ship's position deviates 25 n mile or more from the original track, or the port of destination is changed, or other changes occur with resultant change in Sailing Plan.

偏航报告是当船舶因航行计划改变而偏离预定航线时,用于对预先报告的航行计划进行必要修正的信息。每当船位偏离原航道 25 n mile 或以上,或目的港改变,或发生其他变化而导致航行计划改变时,均应发送报告。

Final Report 最终报告

Final Report is the information to terminate participation in the system. Accordingly, reports should be sent prior to or on arrival at port, or when a ship departed from the service area of the system.

最终报告是终止参与该系统的信息。因此,报告应在船舶到港前、到港时或离开系统服务区时发送。

When Final Report is intended to be sent after departing from the service area, such a report should be sent as soon as practicable.

如果打算在离开服务区后发送最终报告,则应在可行的情况下尽快发送。

If report is sent after arrival at port, such a report may be sent in a written document.

如果报告是在抵达港口后发送的,则可以书面形式发送。

6.3.3　**Reporting Instructions 报告说明**

As far as practicable, report should be sent by shortwave radiotelegraphy to the shortwave coastal radio station designated by Japan Coast Guard in Reporting will be charged free. Table 6.1, 6.2 and 6.3 show the useful information of JASREP.

在可行的情况下,应通过短波无线电报向日本海上保安厅指定的海岸短波电台发送报告, 报告将免费。表 6.1、6.2 和 6.3 列出了 JASREP 的有用信息。

JASREP reports may be sent by other means of communications such as telex addressed to Japan Coast Guard, submission of documents or reporting by telegram or telephone to 11th Regional Coast Guard Headquarters, a coast guard office or station, or district communications center.

JASREP 报告可通过其他通信方式发送,如发给日本海上保安厅的电传、提交文件或通过电报或电话向第 11 区海上保安总部、海上保安厅办事处或站或地区通信中心报告。

HF Radiocommunications 高频无线电通信

Table 6.1　HF Radio Telegram（NBDP）

表 6.1　高频无线电传（NBDP）

Identification signals 识别信号	Receiving frequency(kHz) 接收频率(kHz)	Transiting frequency (kHz) 发射频率(kHz)
2400/004310001	F1B 4179 8379.5 12487.5 16688.5	F1B 4216.5 8419.5 12590 16812

Table 6.2　NBDP or HF Radiotelephone After DSC Calling

表 6.2　拨打 DSC 后的 NBDP 或高频无线电话

Identification signals 识别信号	Mode 模式	Receiving frequency(kHz) 接收频率(kHz)	Transiting frequency (kHz) 发射频率(kHz)
004310001	F1B （DSC）	4208 8415 12577.5 16805	4219.5 8436.512657 16903
TOKYO COAST GUARD RADIO 东京海岸警卫队电台	F1B（NBDP）	4179 8379.5 12487.5 16688.5	4216.5 8419.5 12590 16812
	J3E	4354 8707 8710 12326 12332 16513 16519	4354 8707 8710 13173 13179 17395 17401

Table 6.3   MF and VHF Coastal Radio Stations
表 6.3   中频和甚高频海岸电台

Identification signals 识别信号	Receiving frequency （kHz） 接收频率(kHz)	Transmitting frequency （kHz） 发射频率(kHz)
HOKKAIDO COAST GUARD RADIO 004310101 JNL 北海道海岸警卫队无线电台 004310101 JNL SHIOGAMA COAST GUARD RADIO 004310201 JNN 盐釜海岸警卫队电台 004310201 JNN YOKOHAMA COAST GUARD RADIO 004310301 JGC 横滨海岸警卫队电台 004310301 JGC NAGOYA COAST GUARD RADIO 004310401 JNT 名古屋海岸警卫队电台 004310401 JNT KOBE COSAT GUARD RADIO 004310501 JGD 神户海岸警卫队无线电台 004310501 JGD HIROSHIMA COAST GURARD RADIO 004310601 JNE 广岛海岸古拉电台 004310601 JNE MOJI COAST GUARD RADIO 004310701 JNR 莫吉海岸警卫队电台 004310701 JNR MAIZURU COAST GUARD RADIO 004310801 JNC 舞鹤海岸警卫队电台 004310801 JNC NIIGATA COAST GUARD RADIO 004310901 JNV 新潟海岸警卫队电台 004310901 JNV KAGOSHIMA COAST GUARD RADIO 004311001 JNJ 鹿儿岛海岸警卫队电台 004311001 JNJ OKINAWA COAST GUARD RADIO 004311101 JNB 冲绳海岸警卫队无线电台 004311101 JNB	F3E： 156.6 MHz 156.8 MHz F1B： 2189.5（DSC）	F3B： 156.6 MHz F1B： 2177（DSC） J3E： 2150 2394.5

Operation Center of Japan Coast Guard：Telex No. 722225193 JMSAHQ J.

日本海上保安厅行动中心:电传号 722225193 JMSAHQ J.

Form of Messages 电文的形式

The first line of a message is always JASREP/message type（SP, PR, DR or FR）// and, in subsequent lines, strokes（/）are used to separate sub-items, with two strokes to mark the end of the line.

电文的第一行总是 JASREP/电文类型(SP、PR、DR 或 FR)//,在随后的行中,斜线(/)用来分隔子项目,两个斜线用来标记行尾。

The following lines are essential in messages of one or more types.

以下各行在一种或多种类型的电文中是必不可少的。

A/   Vessel's name/call sign//

B/   Date and time of departure or report//

C/   Latitude/longitude//

E/   Present course, in degrees//

F/   Estimated average speed//

G/   Port of departure/latitude/longitude//

I/   Port of destination/latitude/longitude/ETA//

K/   Port of arrival/time of arrival//

L/   Navigation method: rhumb line (RL) or great circle (GC)/average speed/latitude/longitude//ETA/name of place, if appropriate// (any number of "L" lines may be included, so as to define the route)

M/   CRS being worked/next CRS//

V/   Medical personnel on board: doctor (MD), paramedic (PA), NURSE or NON-E//

X/   Up to 65 characters of amplifying comments

Y/   AMVER// (to be included in every message, if it is desired to participate in AMVER as well as JASREP)

A/   船名/呼号//

B/   出发或报告的日期和时间//

C/   纬度/经度//

E/   现在的航向,以度为单位//

F/   估计平均速度//

G/   出发港/纬度/经度//

I/   目的港/纬度/经度/ETA //

K/   抵达港口/抵达时间//

L/   航法:直线(RL)或大圆(GC)/平均速度/纬度/经度//ETA/地名(如适用)//(可包含任意数量的"L"行,以确定航线)

M/   当前海岸无线电台/下一个海岸无线电台 //

V/   机上医务人员:医生(MD)、辅助医务人员(PA)、护士或无//

X/   最多65个字符的扩展内容

Y/   AMVER//(如果希望参加 AMVER 和 JASREP,则应包括在每份电文中)

6.4 Australian Ship Reporting System（AUSREP）澳大利亚船舶报告系统（AUSREP）

6.4.1 Introduction 简介

The Australian Ship Reporting System（AUSREP）has been established in accordance with the 1974 SOLAS Convention, which requires signatories to the convention to provide marine search and rescue（SAR）for prescribed areas, and also recommends the establishment of a Ship Reporting System. Australia, as a signatory to the 1974 SOLAS Convention, has accepted SAR responsibility for the area.

澳大利亚船舶报告系统（AUSREP）是根据 1974 年《国际海上人命安全公约》建立的,该公约要求公约签署国为规定区域提供海上搜救（SAR）服务,并建议建立船舶报告系统。澳大利亚作为 1974 年《国际海上人命安全公约》的签约国,已承担对规定区域的搜救责任。

AUSREP is a Ship Reporting System designed to contribute to safety of life at sea and is operated by the Australian Maritime Safety Authority（AMSA）through the Australian Rescue Coordination Center（RCC Australia）in Canberra.

AUSREP 是一个船舶报告系统,旨在促进海上人命安全,由澳大利亚海事安全局（AMSA）通过位于堪培拉的澳大利亚搜救协调中心（RCC）运营。

Participation in AUSREP is mandatory for certain ships but other commercial ships visiting Australia or transiting Australian waters are encouraged to participate voluntarily. It is a "positive" system, that is, if a Position Report or Final Report is not received, the RCC Australian will initiate checks to establish the safety of the vessel. These checks are aimed solely at establishing whether a vessel is safe, and include broadcasts to shipping and communications with owners, agents or charters. If these checks are unsuccessful, then air search action will be initiated. As a "positive" system, it is important that Masters comply with the defined procedures as closely as circumstances permit.

某些船舶必须参加 AUSREP,但鼓励其他驶往澳大利亚或在澳大利亚水域航行的商船自愿参加。这是一个"积极"的系统,即如果没有收到船位报告或最终报告,澳大利亚 RCC 将启动检查以确定船舶的安全。这些检查的唯一目的是确定船舶是否安全,包括向航运界广播以及与船东、代理或租船人联系。如果这些检查不成功,就会启动空中搜索行动。AUSREP 作为一个"积极"的系统,船长必须在情况允许的情况下严格遵守其规定的程序。

The AUSREP's objectives are:

a. To limit the time between the loss of a vessel and the initiation of search and rescue action, in cases where no distress signal is sent out;

b. To limit the search area for a rescue action;

c. To provide up-to-date information on shipping resources available in the area, in the event of a search and rescue incident.

AUSREP 的目的是：

a.在未发出求救信号的情况下,减少船舶失联与启动搜救行动之间的时间;

b.限制救援行动的搜索范围;

c.在发生搜救事件时,提供该地区现有船舶数据的最新信息。

The Commonwealth of Australia Navigation Act 1912 makes participation in AUSREP compulsory for the following ships.

a. All Australian-registered ships engaged in interstate of overseas trade and commerce, while in the AUSREP area.

b. Ships not registered in Australia, but engaged in the coasting trade between Australia and an external territory, or between external territories, while in the AUSREP area.

c. Ships not registered in Australia but demised under charter parties to charter whose, residences or principal places of business are in Australia, while in the AUSREP area.

d. Foreign ships, other than the above-mentioned ships, from their arrival at their first Australian port until their departure from their final Australian port. However, they are encouraged to participate from their entry into and final departure from the AUSREP area.

e. Australian fishing vessels which are GMDSS compatible, fitted with 1974 SOLAS Convention compliant AIS and proceeding on overseas voyages, while in the AUSREP area, but not including those ships operating from Queensland ports, which may call at ports in Papua New Guinea as an incidental part of their fishing operations.

澳大利亚联邦 1912 年《航海法》规定,下列船舶必须加入 AUSREP:

a.所有在澳大利亚注册、在 AUSREP 区域内从事洲际或海外贸易和商业活动的船舶。

b.未在澳大利亚注册,但从事澳大利亚与外部领土之间或外部领土与外部领土之间沿海贸易的并在 AUSREP 区域内的船舶。

c.未在澳大利亚注册,但根据租船合同租给住所或主要营业地在澳大利亚的租船人的船舶,且船舶在 AUSREP 区域内。

d.除上述船舶外,其他外国船舶从抵达第一个澳大利亚港口到离开最后一个澳大利亚港口。然而,鼓励这些船舶从进入 AUSREP 区域到最后离开该区域期间参与该系统。

e.与 GMDSS 兼容、配备符合 1974 年《国际海上人命安全公约》的 AIS 并在 AUSREP 区域进行海外航行的澳大利亚渔船,但不包括在昆士兰港口作业的船舶,这些船舶可能在其捕鱼作业中附带停靠巴布亚新几内亚的港口。

6.4.2　Types of AUSREP Reports AUSREP 报告的类型

Main Report Types 主要报告类型

a. Sailing Plan；

b. Position Report（these will be obtained automatically from the ship's AIS transmitter）；

c. Deviation Report，where applicable；

d. Final Report.

a. 航行计划；

b. 船位报告（这些报告将从船舶的 AIS 发射机自动获取）；

c. 偏航报告（如适用）；

d. 最终报告。

Special Reports Types 特别报告类型

a. Dangerous Goods Report；

b. Harmful Substances Report；

c. Marine Pollutants Report.

a. 危险货物报告；

b. 有害物质报告；

c. 海洋污染物报告。

Table 6.4 shows the IMO message format for AUSREP reports.

表 6.4 显示了 AUSREP 报告的 IMO 电文格式。

Table 6.4　IMO Message Format for AUSREP Reports

表 6.4　AUSREP 报告的 IMO 电文格式

A	(1) Ship's name；(2) call sign；and (3) IMO number (1) 船名；(2) 呼号；以及(3)IMO 编号
B	Date/Time of event（UTC） 事件发生日期/时间（UTC）
C	Position（latitude and longitude in degrees and minutes）or when within a 2 n mile radius of a REEFREP reporting point，the name of that reporting point 位置（以度和分表示的经度和纬度），或者在大堡礁船位报告系统（REEFREP）报告点半径 2 n mile 范围内的报告点的名称
D	（Not to be used in AUSREP messages） （不可用于 AUSREP 电文）

Continued　续表

E	Course 航向
F	Speed（ship's anticipated average speed until next report in knots & tenths of knots） 航速（到下次报告前的预计平均航速,以节和十分之一节为单位）
G	Name of last non-Australian port of call 最后停靠的非澳大利亚港口名称
H	Date/Time（UTC）and point of joining the AUSREP system. The point of joining must be either the Australian port the ship is departing from, or if joining from overseas, the latitude/longitude of crossing the AUSREP boundary 日期/时间（UTC）和加入 AUSREP 系统的地点。加入点必须是船舶出发的澳大利亚港口,如果从海外加入,则必须是穿越 AUSREP 边界的经度/纬度
I	Next non-Australian port of destination and estimated time of arrival at that port 下一个非澳大利亚目的港以及预计抵达该港口的时间
J	Coastal pilotage details:（1）Yes/No;（2）last name of pilot; and（3）license number of pilots 沿海引航详情:(1) 是/否;(2)引航员姓氏;以及(3)引航员执照号码
K	Date/Time（UTC）and point of exit from the AUSREP system（point of exit is either the latitude/longitude of crossing the AUSREP boundary or the Australian port to which the ship is bound） 日期/时间（UTC）和离开 AUSREP 系统的时间点(离开时间点为穿越 AUSREP 边界的经度/纬度,或船舶前往的澳大利亚港口)
L	Route information 航线信息
M	Radiocommunication arrangements. State in full: names of stations/frequencies guarded including MMSI and INMARSAT numbers（B, C, F77, etc.） 无线电通信安排详细说明:所保护的台站/频率名称,包括 MMSI 和 INMARSAT 编号（B、C、F77等）
N	Use word "POLL" if the ship is to be polled by INMARSAT-C. If not, enter nominated Date/Time of next report（UTC）and reason why ship cannot be polled 如果该船应由 INMARSAT-C 轮询,请使用 "POLL"（轮询）字样。如果不是,请输入下次报告的指定日期/时间（UTC）以及无法对船舶进行轮询的原因
O	Draught（fore and aft in meters and tenths of meters） 吃水（前后,以米和十分之一米为单位）
P *	Cargo information may be passed by non-voice means if required.（1）Normal name of the cargo; and（2）indicate Yes or No if cargo is classified as hazardous 如有需要,可通过非语音方式发送货物信息。(1)货物的正常名称;以及 (2)如果货物被归类为危险品,请注明是或否
Q *	Defects or other limitations such as damage, failure or breakdown affecting the safety of the ship, including any AIS malfunction 影响船舶安全的缺陷或其他限制,如损坏、失灵或故障,包括任何 AIS 故障

Continued　续表

R	Brief details of type of pollution lost overboard（oil，chemicals，etc.）and also report if any pollution sighted 简要说明落海污染物的类型(油类、化学品等)，并报告是否发现任何污染
S	Weather conditions in area 该地区的天气状况
T	Ship's agents 船舶代理
U	（1）Ship type；（2）ship length（meters）；and（3）gross tonnage (1)船舶类型;(2)船舶长度(米);以及(3)总吨位
V	Medical personnel carried 船上医务人员
W	Number of persons on board 船上人数
X	Remarks 备注

6.4.2.1　Sailing Plan（SP）航行计划（SP）

The Sailing Plan（SP）contains information necessary for Australia RCC to initiate a vessel plot and gives an outline of the intended passage. You may send your AUSREP SP up to 24 h prior to joining the system；but：

a.At ports within the REEFREP area the SP must be sent prior to departure；and at other Australian ports the SP may be sent up to 2 h after departure；

b.When joining AUSREP at the ocean boundary the SP may be sent 24 h prior to entering the area or up to 2 h after crossing the boundary.

航行计划（SP）包含澳大利亚 RCC 启动船舶航行计划所需的信息，并概述预定航程。您可以在加入系统前 24 h 内发送您的 AUSREP SP;但是：

a.在 REEFREP 区域内的港口，必须在启航前发送 SP;在澳大利亚其他港口，可在启航后 2 h 内发送 SP;

b.在海洋边界加入 AUSREP 时，可在进入该区域前 24 h 或穿越边界后 2 h 内发送 SP。

If the ship does not sail or cross the boundary more than 2 h after the time specified in the Sailing Plan，the Sailing Plan is deemed to be cancelled and another sent within 2 h of the format fields for your AUSREP SP.

如果船舶在航行计划规定的时间超过 2 h 后仍未启航或越过边界,则视为取消航行计划,并在 AUSREP SP 格式字段的 2 h 内发送另一份航行计划。

Mandatory fields:A, F, H, K, L, M, U, V.

必填字段:A、F、H、K、L、M、U、V。

Additional fields:G, I, N, Q, R, X (include if appropriate).

附加字段:G、I、N、Q、R、X(请酌情填写)。

Where polling is selected as the method of position reporting, Masters should include the word "POLL" in section N.

如果选择询呼作为船位报告的方法,"船长"应在 N 部分注明"POLL"(轮询)一词。

6.4.2.2　Position Report (PR) 船位报告 (PR)

Position Reports will be obtained using fitted automatic identification system (AIS) transmissions in accordance with 1974 SOLAS Convention Ⅴ, Regulation 19.2.4. Masters are required to ensure an operational AIS transmitter.

根据 1974 年《国际海上人命安全公约》第五章第 19.2.4 条的规定,将通过安装的自动识别系统(AIS)传输获取位置报告。船长必须确保 AIS 发射机正常工作。

If a ship's AIS is not operational, then the deficiency must be reported. A vessel with a faulty AIS will NOT be provided with a SAR watch. A Position Report transmitted by AIS should include the following information about the ship.

如果船舶的 AIS 无法运行,则必须报告该缺陷。如果船舶的 AIS 出现故障,则不会为其提供搜救守班。由 AIS 发送的位置报告应包括以下有关船舶的信息。

a.Static information:

- Identity, including IMO number, call sign & name;

- Length and beam;

- Type of ship.

a.静态信息:

- 身份信息,包括 IMO 编号、呼号和船名;

- 长度和宽度;

- 船舶类型。

b.Dynamic information:

- Ship's position;

- Time in UTC;

- Course over ground；

- Speed over ground；

- Navigational status（e.g. NUC, at anchor, etc. —manual input）.

b.动态信息：

- 船位；

- UTC 时间；

- 对地航向；

- 对地航速；

- 航行状态(如失控、抛锚等—手动输入)。

c.Voyage related：

- Ship's draught；

- Destination and ETA.

c.与航行有关：

- 船舶吃水；

- 目的地和预计到达时间。

6.4.2.3 Deviation Report（DR） 偏航报告（DR）

You must send a DR when you realize that your ship is more than 2 h steaming from the position that would be predicted from the ship's voyage plan. A DR can also be sent when any other voyage details are altered.

当您发现您的船舶与航行计划所预测的位置相差 2 h 以上时,您必须发送偏航报告。当任何其他航行细节发生变化时,也可发送偏航报告。

Mandatory fields：A, B, C, N, X.

必填字段:A、B、C、N、X。

Additional fields：E, F, I, K, L, M should be included where appropriate. The reason for deviation should be included in Field X.

附加字段:应酌情包括 E、F、I、K、L、M 字段。偏航的原因应包括在字段 X 中。

6.4.2.4 Final Report（FR） 最终报告(FR)

The Final Report（FR）is used by Australia RCC to remove a ship from the plot.

最终报告（FR）被澳大利亚 RCC 用于删除船舶。

a.For ships enroute overseas and departing the AUSREP area send your AUSREP FR at the AUSREP boundary.

b.For ships ending a voyage at an Australian port within the REEFREP area，at the last refits reporting point；

c.For ships ending a voyage at any other Australian port，when within 2 h steaming of the port or pilot station.

a.对于驶往海外并离开 AUSREP 区域的船舶，请在 AUSREP 边界发送 AUSREP FR。

b.对于在 REEFREP 区域内的澳大利亚港口结束航程的船舶，在最后一个报告点。

c.在澳大利亚任何其他港口结束航程的船舶，在距离港口或引航站 2 h 航程内。

For ships ending a voyage at any other Australian ports send your AUSREP FR when your ship is within two hours steaming of the port or pilot station.

对于在澳大利亚其他港口结束航行的船舶，当您的船舶距离港口或引航站不到 2 h 航程时，请发送 AUSREP FR。

Mandatory fields：A，K.

必填字段：A、K。

Masters must ensure that an FR is always sent to Australia RCC to prevent unnecessary SAR action and a waste of valuable resources.

船长必须确保始终向澳大利亚 RCC 发送最终报告，以防止不必要的搜救行动和资源的浪费。

6.4.3　Overdue AUSREP Reports AUSREP 逾期未上报处置

As AUSREP is a positive reporting system，if a PR（where polling not being used）or FR is not received by Australia RCC within 2 h of the expected time，action is taken to ascertain the ship's whereabouts and confirm the safety of its crew. Masters should note that in some parts of the AUSREP area the ability to conduct an air search may be restricted by aircraft range limitations.

由于 AUSREP 是一个积极的报告系统，如果澳大利亚 RCC 在预计时间的 2 h 内没有收到 PR(在不使用轮询的情况下)或 FR，则会采取行动以确定船舶的行踪并确认船员的安全。船长应注意，在 AUSREP 区域的某些地方，进行空中搜索的能力可能会受到飞机航程的限制。

The action taken by Australia RCC if your report is not received as expected will depend on prevailing circumstances，but will generally include：

a.Internal checks to establish if your report has been received by Australia RCC.

b.For INMARSAT equipped ships，attempts to contact the ship directly.

c.Electronic communications，including E-mail，INMARSAT and LRIT polling attempt to

contact ship directly by calling on HF DSC to ship's MMSI.

d.An all station broadcast indicating concern for the safety of the ship due to non-receipt of the PR or FR.

e.Extensive communication checks with overseas Coast Radio Stations, owners, agents and other ships are carried.

f.Out to trace the last sighting or contact with the ship.

g.At twenty-one hours overdue an Urgency Signal PAN PAN will be broadcast.

如果报告没有如期收到,澳大利亚 RCC 将根据当时的情况采取相应措施,但一般包括:

a.进行内部检查,以确定澳大利亚 RCC 是否已收到报告。

b.对于配备 INMARSAT 的船舶,可尝试直接与船舶联系。

c.电子通信,包括电子邮件、INMARSAT 和 LRIT 轮询尝试通过高频 DSC 呼叫船舶的 MMSI 直接与船舶联系。

d.向所有船广播,表示因未收到 PR 或 FR 而对船舶安全的关注。

e.与海外海岸电台、船东、代理和其他船舶进行广泛的通信检查。

f.追踪最后一次看到或接触这艘船的时间。

g.逾期 21 h 后,将播发紧急信号 PAN PAN。

By the time the report is twenty-four hours overdue, positive SAR action will have been started to locate the ship. This action may include the launching of search aircraft.

在报告逾期 24 h 后,将开始采取积极的搜救行动以确定船舶的位置。这一行动可能包括出动搜索飞机。

6.4.4　Method to Provide Reports 提供报告的方法

Masters should note that recent changes have been implemented to AUSREP including the use of shipboard AIS equipment to provide Position Reports:

a.The preferred mode of communications for all reports (Sailing Plans, Position Reports, Deviation Reports and Final Reports) is INMARSAT-C. A Master must make their ship available to be polled by AMSA using INMARSAT-C to obtain position reports. When INMARSAT-C polling cannot be used or when Australia RCC directs a Master, the Master must report positions using INMARSAT-C or HF DSC.

b.When reporting via INMARSAT-C, terminals should be logged into LES 212 for Pacific Ocean Region and LES 312 for Indian Ocean Region using Special Access Code (SAC) 1243.

c.Note: If AUSREP reports are sent through other LES using (SAC) 1243, there is no guarantee that the message will be received by AMSA.

d.If required to report manually, Masters are requested to send a Position Report each day at a convenient time nominated by the ship between 2200 UTC and 0800 UTC. The maximum time between any two reports is not to exceed 24 h.

e.Position reports obtained via the ship's AIS must be transmitted in accordance with 1974 SOLAS Convention, Chapter 5, Regulation 19.2.4.

船长应注意,最近对 AUSREP 进行了修改,包括使用船载 AIS 设备提供船位报告:

a.所有报告(航行计划、船位报告、偏航报告和最终报告)的首选通信方式是 INMARSAT-C。船长必须允许 AMSA 使用 INMARSAT-C 对其船舶进行轮询,以获取位置报告。当 INMARSAT-C 轮询无法使用或澳大利亚 RCC 指示船长时,船长必须使用 INMARSAT-C 或高频 DSC 报告位置。

b.通过 INMARSAT-C 进行报告时,终端应使用特别接入码(SAC)1243 登录太平洋区域的 LES 212 和印度洋区域的 LES 312。

c.注:如果通过其他 LES 使用(SAC)1243 发送 AUSREP 报告,则不能保证 AMSA 收到电文。

d.如果需要人工报告,请船长每天在 2200 UTC 至 0800 UTC,船舶指定的方便时间发送位置报告。任何两次报告之间的间隔时间最长不得超过 24 h。

e.通过 AIS 获得的位置报告必须按照 1974 年《国际海上人命安全公约》第 5 章第 19.2.4 条的规定发送。

Operating Authority 运营机构

The Australian Maritime Safety Authority through the Maritime Rescue Coordination Center.

澳大利亚海事安全局下设海上搜救协调中心。

Address:MRCC AUSTRALIA

地址:MRCC 澳大利亚

Telephone：Canberra (06)279 5916

电话:堪培拉 (06)279 5916

Telex:62349 (computer connected)—Answerback MRCCAUS AA

电传:62349(电脑连接)——应答码 MRCCAUS AA

Facsimile：Canberra (06)257 2036

传真:堪培拉 (06)257 2036

6.5 West European Tanker Reporting System（WETREP）西欧油船报告系统（WETREP）

The West European Tanker Reporting System（WETREP）is established in the Western Euro-

pean Particularly Sensitive Sea Area.

在西欧特别敏感海域建立了西欧油船报告系统(WETREP)。

6.5.1 Categories of Ships Required to Participate in the System 参加该系统船舶类别

Ships required to participate in the mandatory WETREP are shown as follow.

Every kind of oil tanker of more than 600 tonnes deadweight, carrying a cargo of:

- heavy crude oil, meaning crude oils with a density at 15 ℃ of higher than 900 kg/m^3;

- heavy fuel oils, meaning fuel oils with a density at 15 ℃ of higher than 900 kg/m^3, or a kinematic viscosity at 50 ℃ of higher than 180 mm^2/s;

- bitumen and tar.

需要参加强制 WETREP 的船舶如下。

载重量超过 600 吨的各种油船,载运的货物包括:

- 重原油,指 15 ℃ 时密度大于 900 kg/m^{3}的原油;

- 重燃油,指 15 ℃ 时密度大于 900 kg/m^{3}或 50 ℃ 时运动黏度大于 180 mm^2/s 的燃油;

- 沥青和焦油。

Ships on voyage to and from the Western European Reporting Area shall send reports:

- on entry into the Reporting Area; or

- immediately on departing from a port, terminal or anchorage within the Reporting Area; or

- when they deviate from routing to their original declared destination port/terminal/anchorage or position "for orders" given at time of entry into the Reporting Area; or

- when deviation from planned route is necessary due to weather or equipment malfunction or a change in the navigational status; and

- when finally exiting from the Reporting Area.

进出西欧油船报告区的船舶应提交报告:

- 进入报告区时;或

- 立即离开报告区内的港口、码头或锚地;或

- 在进入报告区时"奉命"偏离原申报的目的港/终点站/停泊地或位置的航线;或

- 因天气、设备故障或航行状态改变而必须偏离计划航线时;以及

- 最后离开报告区时。

Ships need not report if, while on normal passage routing during transit of the Reporting Area, the boundary of the Reporting Area is crossed on other occasions apart from the initial entry and final exit.

如果船舶在报告区过境期间的正常航行路线上,除最初进入和最后离开外,在其他场合跨越了报告区的边界,则无须报告。

The area covered by the WETREP is defined within the coordinates shown in Table 6.5 and 6.6.

WETREP 所覆盖的区域如表 6.5 和 6.6 所示。

Table 6.5　Geographical Coverage of the System
表 6.5　系统的地理覆盖范围

Number 数量	Latitude 纬度	Longitude 经度
1 (UK) (英国)	58°30′N	UK coast
2 (UK) (英国)	58°30′N	000°W
3 (UK) (英国)	62°N	000°W
4 (UK) (英国)	62°N	003°W
5 (UK+ Irl) (英国+爱尔兰)	56°30′N	012°W
6 (Irl) (爱尔兰)	54°40′40″.91N	015°W
7 (Irl) (爱尔兰)	50°56′45″.36N	015°W
8 (Irl+UK+F) (爱尔兰+英国+法国)	48°27′N	006°25′W
9 (F) (法国)	48°27′N	008°W
10 (F+S) (法国+西班牙)	44°52′N	003°10′W
11 (S) (西班牙)	44°52′N	010°W
12 (S) (西班牙)	44°14′N	011°34′W
13 (S) (西班牙)	42°55′N	012°18′W

Continued 续表

Number 数量	Latitude 纬度	Longitude 经度
14（S+P） （西班牙+葡萄牙）	41°50′N	011°34′W
15（P） （葡萄牙）	37°N	009°49′W
16（P） （葡萄牙）	36°20′N	009°00′W
17（P） （葡萄牙）	36°20′N	007°47′W
18（P） （葡萄牙）	Guadiana River mouth 瓜迪亚纳河口 37°10′N	007°25′W
19（B） （比利时）	51°22′25″N	003°21′52″.5E （border between B and NL）
20（UK） （英国）	52°12′N	UK east coast 英国东海岸
21（Irl） （爱尔兰）	52°10′.3″N	006°21′.8″W
22（UK） （英国）	52°01′.52″N	005°04′.18″W
23（UK） （英国）	54°51′.43″N	005°08′.47″W
24（UK） （英国）	54°40′.39″N	005°34′.34″W

Table 6.6　Position Coordinates of WETREP

表 6.6　WETREP 的位置坐标

MRCC	Tel. 电话	Fax 传真	Telex 电报	VHF/MF 甚高频/中频	INM-C/E-mail 电子邮件
Oostende 奥斯滕德 002059981	+3259701000 +3259701100	+3259703605	82125	9, 16, 67, 70 2182	
Gris-Nez 格利内角 002275100	+33321872187	+33321877855	130680	16, 70	422799256
Corsen 科森 002275300	+33298893131	+33298896575	940086	16, 70	

Continued　续表

MRCC	Tel. 电话	Fax 传真	Telex 电报	VHF/MF 甚高频/中频	INM-C/E-mail 电子邮件
Dublin 都柏林	+35316620922	+3531662079			mrccdublin@ irishcoastguard.ie
Lisbon 里斯本	+351214401950	+351214401954	60747 P		mrcclisboa@ netc.pt
Madrid 马德里	+34917559133	+34915261440	+5241210 +5241224		cncs@ sasemar.es
Finisterre 菲尼斯特雷	+34981767500	+34981767740	+5282268 +5286207	16 ,11 2182	
Bilbao 毕尔巴鄂	+34944839286	+34944839161		16, 10	bilbao@ sasemar.es
Falmouth 法尔茅斯	+(0)1326317575	+(0)1326318342	+5142981		falmouthcoastguard@ mcga.gov.uk

6.5.2　Types of Reports 报告类型

The reports shall be drawn up in accordance with Table 6.7. The designators A，B，C，E，F，G，I，P，T，W and X are mandatory for a Sailing Plan, A，B，C，E and F for a Final Report, A，B，C，E，F, and I for a Deviation Report. The designator Q shall also be included at any time where defects including breakdown，damage，deficiencies，circumstances affecting normal navigation should occur within the reporting area.

报告应按表 6.7 编制。A、B、C、E、F、G、I、P、T、W 和 X 是航行计划的必填项，A、B、C、E 和 F 是最终报告的必填项，A、B、C、E、F 和 I 是偏航报告的必填项。在报告区域内出现故障、损坏、缺陷、影响正常航行的情况等缺陷时，也应加上代号 Q。

Table 6.7　Designator of WETREP

表 6.7　WETREP 代号

Designator 代号	Function 功能	Text 文本
	Type of report： Sailing Plan Final Report Deviation Report 报告类型： 航行计划 最终报告 偏航报告	One of the following 2-letter identifiers： "SP"（Sailing Plan） "FR"（Final Report—on final leaving the Reporting Area） containing only A，B，C，E & F "DR"（Deviation Report）containing only A,B,C,E,F, and I 以下 2 个字母标识符之一： "SP"（航行计划） "FR"（最终报告——最终离开报告区时） 仅包含 A、B、C、E 和 F "DR"（偏航报告）仅包含 A、B、C、E、F 和 I

Continued　续表

Designator 代号	Function 功能	Text 文本
A	Ship 船舶	Name and call sign (ship's name, call sign, IMO identification number and MMSI Number) (e.g.: NONESUCH/KTOI) 名称和呼号(船名、呼号、IMO 识别号和 MMSI 号码)(例如:NONESUCH/KTOI)
B	Date Time Group corresponding to the position under designator C given in UTC 与代号 C 下的位置相对应的日期时间组,以 UTC 表示	A 6-digit group followed by a Z. The first 2 digits giving date of month, the next 2 digits giving hours and the last 2 digits minutes. The Z indicates that the time is given in UTC (e.g.: 081340Z) 一个 6 位数组后跟 Z。前两位数表示月份日期,后两位数表示小时,最后两位数表示分钟。Z 表示时间,以 UTC 表示(例如:081340Z)
C	Position by latitude and longitude 经纬度位置	A 4-digit group giving latitude in degrees and minutes suffixed with N, and a 5-digit group giving longitude in degrees and minutes suffixed with W(e.g.: 5512N 03420W) 一个 4 位数组,以度和分表示纬度,后缀为 N;一个 5 位数组,以度和分表示经度,后缀为 W(例如:5512N 03420W)
E	Course 航向	True course. A 3-digit group (e.g.: 083) 真航向。一个三位数组(如:083)
F	Speed 速度	Speed in knots. A 2-digit group (e.g.: 14) 速度(节)。2 位数组(例如:14)
G	Name of last port of call 最后停靠港名称	The name of the last port of call (e.g.: New York) 最后停靠港口的名称(如:纽约)
I	Destination and ETA (UTC) 目的地和预计到达时间 (UTC)	The name of the destination followed by expected time of arrival, expressed as under designator B(e.g.: Milford Haven 181400Z) 目的地名称和预计到达时间,以代号 B 表示(例如:Milford Haven 181400Z)
P	Cargo 货物	Oil cargo type(s), quantity, grade(s) and density of heavy crude oil, heavy fuel oil and bitumen and tar. If those tankers carry other hazardous cargo simultaneously: the type, quantity and IMO class of that cargo, as appropriate 重质原油、重燃油、沥青和焦油的油品类型、数量、等级和密度。如果这些油船同时运载其他危险货物:货物的类型、数量和 IMO 等级(视情况而定)
Q	Defect, damage, deficiency, limitations 缺陷、损坏、不足、限制	Brief details of defects including breakdown, damage, deficiencies or other circumstances affecting normal navigation 故障的简介,包括故障、损坏、缺陷或影响正常航行的情况

Designator 代号	Function 功能	Text 文本
T	Address for the communications of cargo information 货物信息地址	Name, telephone number and either: facsimile, E-mail address or URL 姓名、电话号码和传真、电子邮件地址或 URL
W	Total number of persons on board 船上总人数	State the number 说明数量
X	Various information 各种信息	Various information applicable for those tankers: characteristics and estimated quantity of bunker fuel, for tankers carrying more than 5000 tonnes of bunker fuel; navigational status (for example, under way with engines, at anchor, not under command, restricted in ability to manoeuvre, constrained by draught, moored, aground, etc.): 适用于这些油船的各种信息: 船用燃料的特性和估计数量,运载燃料超过 5000 吨的油船; 航行状态(例如在航、锚泊、失控、操纵能力受限、限制水域航行、系泊、搁浅等)

6.5.2.1　Sailing Plan (SP) 航行计划 (SP)

Sailing Plan is sent as a first report when:

a.On entering the Reporting Area as defined.

b.Immediately on departing from a port located within the Reporting Area.

当出现以下情况时,航行计划将作为第一份报告发送:

a.进入规定的报告区域。

b.从位于报告区内的港口启航时立即离开。

Example:

例如:

Name of station to which the report is being sent 接收报告的电台名称

WETREP-SP

A. NONESUCH/KTOI

B. 161520Z

C. 4105N1115W

E. 026

F. 15

G. RAS TANNURAH

I. ROTTERDAM 230230Z

P. 56000 TONNES HEAVY FUEL OILS

T. J. Smith, 004722315610, Facsimile 004722315611

W. 23

X. NONE, NONE

6.5.2.2　Final Report 最终报告

a.On leaving the Reporting Area.

b.On arrival in a port situated within the Reporting Area.

a.离开报告区时。

b.抵达位于报告区内的港口。

Example：

例如：

Name of station to which the report is being sent 发送报告的电台名称

WETREP-FR

A. NONESUCH/KTOI

B. 201520Z

C. 5145N0238E

E. 044

F. 16

6.5.2.3　Deviation Report 偏航报告

a. When they deviate from routing to their original declared destination/port/terminal/anchorage or position "for orders" given at time of entry into the Reporting Area.

b.When deviation from planned route is necessary due to weather or equipment malfunction or a change in navigational status.

a.在进入报告区时"奉命"偏离原申报目的地/港口/终点站/锚地或位置的航线。

b.因天气、设备故障或导航状态改变而必须偏离计划航线时。

Example：

例如：

Name of station to which the report is being sent 发送报告的电台名称

WETREP-FR

A. NONESUCH/KTOI

B. 201520Z

C. 4957N0207W

E. 073

F. 14

I. ROTTERDAM 270230Z

X. NONE, SATISFACTORY

6.5.3   Measures to Be Taken If a Ship Fails to Comply with the Requirements 船舶不符合要求时应采取的措施

The objectives of the system are to initiate SAR and measures to prevent pollution as fast and effective as possible if an emergency is reported or a report from a ship fails to appear, and it is impossible to establish communications with the ship. All means will be used to obtain the full participation of ships required to submit reports. If reports are not submitted and the offending ship can be positively identified, then information will be passed on to the relevant Flag State Authorities for investigation and possible prosecution in accordance with national legislation. The WETREP is for the exchange of information only and does not provide any additional authority for mandating changes in the vessel's operations. This reporting system will be implemented consistent with UNCLOS, SOLAS and other relevant international instruments so that the reporting system will not provide the basis to impinge on a transiting vessel's passage through the Reporting Area.

该系统的目标是在接到紧急情况报告或船舶未提交报告,且无法与船舶建立联系的情况下,尽可能快速有效地启动搜救和防止污染的措施。系统将采取一切手段,让需要提交报告的船舶充分参与。如果未提交报告,且能确定违规船舶,则会将信息传递给相关船旗国当局,以便根据国家立法进行调查和可能的起诉。WETREP 仅用于信息交流,并不提供任何强制改变船舶操作的额外权力。该报告系统的实施将符合《联合国海洋法公约》《国际海上人命安全公约》和其他相关国际文书的规定,因此该报告系统不会成为影响过境船舶通过报告区的依据。

6.6   Chinese Ship Reporting System（CHISREP）中国船舶报告系统（CHISREP）

Chinese Ship Reporting System（CHISREP）undertakes to ensure the safety of life at sea and navigation to improve the efficiency of search and rescue operations and provide information service for the prevention and control of marine pollution from ships.

中国船舶报告系统(CHISREP)致力于保障海上人命和航行安全,提高搜救效率,为防治船

舶污染海洋提供信息服务。

The area of coverage for CHISREP are: thence 9 N northward, 130 E westward, excluding other country's terrestrial seas and inland water areas. It combines ship management with its sailing safety, makes share of resources. With command of information about sailing ships, it is much easier to do searching at sea, to salvage ships in danger, to avoid ocean pollution, to supply safe insurance for ship sailing, and improve searching efficiency. CHISREP's completion changes the history when there's no integral dynamic information about sailing ship in China's coastal area, signs a new age of China's safe management at sea.

CHISREP 的覆盖区域为:北纬 9°以北,东经 130°以西,不包括其他国家的陆地海域和内陆水域。它将船舶管理与其航行安全相结合,实现了资源共享。掌握了航行船舶的信息,海上搜寻、救助遇险船舶、避免海洋污染、为船舶航行提供安全保障、提高搜寻效率等都变得更加容易。CHISREP 的建成,改变了中国沿海没有完整的船舶动态信息的历史,标志着中国海上安全管理进入了一个新时代。

The following ships which navigate more than 6 hours within CHISREP areas are mandatory to participate the system:

· All 300 GT or more, China-registered ships engaged in international routes.

· 1600 GT or more, China-registered ships engaged in domestic coastal routes.

· 300 GT or more but under 1600 GT, China-registered ships engaged in domestic coastal routes was mandatory to participate in the system since January 1st, 2005.

在 CHISREP 区域内航行超过 6 小时的下列船舶必须参加该系统:

· 所有 300 总吨或以上中国籍且从事国际航线的船舶。

· 1600 总吨或以上中国籍从事国内沿海航线的船舶。

· 自 2005 年 1 月 1 日起,从事国内沿海航线的 300 总吨以上、1600 总吨以下中国籍船舶必须参加。

The main purpose of CHISREP are as follows:

· Even in the absence of the distress signal, the time from the notification for the loss of a ship to the initiation of Search and Rescue action is to be reduced.

· Quick assistance by ships proceeding in the vicinity can be expected and confirmed.

· When the position of a person or a ship in distress is unknown or uncertain, a certain area for Search and Rescue operations can be delimited.

· Emergency medical assistance or advice can be obtained.

CHISREP 的主要目的如下:

· 即使在没有遇险信号的情况下,也要缩短从发出船舶失联通知到启动搜救行动的时间。

- 可以预期并确认附近船舶会迅速提供援助。

- 当遇险人员或船舶的位置不明或不确定时,可以划定一定的搜救区域。

- 可获得紧急医疗援助或建议。

CHISREP contains several kinds of reports, there are four general reports and three special reports:

CHISREP 包含多种报告,其中有四种一般报告和三种特别报告:

General reports:

SP:sailing Plan Report;

PR:ship's Position Report;

DR:Deviation Report;

FR:Final Report.

一般报告:

SP:航行计划报告;

PR:船位报告;

DR:偏航报告;

FR:最终报告。

Special reports:

DG:Dangerous Goods Report;

HS:Harmful Substances Report;

MP:Marine Pollutants Report.

特别报告:

DG:危险货物报告;

HS:有害物质报告;

MP:海洋污染物报告。

It can receive and examine data, E-mail and fax automatically, point out incompetent report and track all kinds of ship on electronic chart, give an alarm and demo assistant rescue function, calculate ship's position and dynamically replay.

它可以自动接收和检查数据、电子邮件和传真,在电子海图上指出不合格报告并跟踪各种船舶,发出警告并演示辅助救援功能,计算船位并动态回放。

Ships should give report when they enter or leave China's water area. If there is an incident, the system can make a rescue plan quickly to assist RCC effectively. The system can offer ship's

static information and supply emergency medical aid and consultation. It's proved to be very safe, reliable and advanced after undergoing a simulated operation with this system.

　　船舶进出中国水域时应及时报告。如果发生事故,该系统可迅速制订救援计划,有效协助搜救协调中心。该系统可提供船舶静态信息,并提供紧急医疗救助和咨询。该系统经过模拟运行,被证明是非常安全、可靠和先进的。

习题

Modernization of GMDSS

GMDSS 的现代化

Chapter 7

7.1 General Introduction 概述

Technological progress in electronics, radiocommunications and information technology results in the constant emergence of new proposals for modifications to the equipment and systems used on sea-going vessels. The principles and scope of equipment for these vessels, related to ensuring their safety, are strictly regulated by the International Maritime Organization (IMO), with merit-related support by its committees and sub-committees.

电子技术、无线电通信和信息技术的技术进步促使新的修改远洋船舶设备和系统的建议不断出现。国际海事组织(IMO)严格规定了与确保船舶安全有关的这些船舶设备的原则和范围,并由其委员会和分委员会提供相关支持。

In 2006, several countries submitted a proposal to the IMO Maritime Safety Committee (IMO-MSC) for preparing a broad strategy for the inclusion of new technologies in a comprehensive manner, to ensure their compatibility with existing navigation and communication technologies and services.

2006 年,一些国家向 IMO 海事安全委员会(IMO-MSC)提交了一份提案,建议制定一项全面的战略,全面纳入新技术,确保其与现有的导航和通信技术及服务相兼容。

In 2008 at the 85th session of the IMO Maritime Safety Committee (MSC 85), the "E-navigation Strategy" was adopted. As a consequence of this decision, another project was adopted: "Preparation of the E-navigation Strategy Implementation Plan", and added to the agenda of the IMO sub-committee on Navigation, Communications, Search and Rescue (NCSR), as well as the sub-committee on Standards of Training and Watchkeeping (STW), with completion scheduled for 2012.

2008 年,IMO 海事安全委员会第 85 届会议(MSC 85)通过了"电子航海战略"。作为该决定的结果,另一个项目得到通过:"编制电子航海战略实施计划",并列入了 IMO 航行、通信和搜救(NCSR)分委员会以及培训和值班标准(STW)分委员会的议程,于 2012 年完成。

The integration of communications and navigation equipment that is being considered as part of the E-navigation project is seen as being desirable but with numerous hurdles to overcome. The E-navigation concept itself is still somewhat nebulous and its development direction is still unclear; in recent years the emphasis has been more on emissions reduction than safety related issues.

作为电子航海项目的一部分,通信和导航设备的整合被认为是可取的,但需要克服许多障碍。电子航海概念本身仍有些模糊,其发展方向也仍不明确;近年来,其重点更多的是减排,而不是与安全相关的问题。

A draft Modernization Plan of the GMDSS was completed at NCSR 4 in March 2017 and submitted to the MSC for approval. The aim is to eventually adopt a revised and updated SOLAS Chapter Ⅳ, enabling the use of modern communication systems in GMDSS, while removing the requirement to carry obsolete systems, at the same time maintaining the requirements for ships to carry specified terrestrial and satellite radiocommunications equipment for sending and receiving distress alerts and Maritime Safety Information, as well as for other communications.

GMDSS 现代化计划草案已于 2017 年 3 月在 NCSR 第 4 次会议上完成,并提交 MSC 批准。其目的是最终通过经修订和更新的《国际海上人命安全公约》第四章,使现代通信系统能够在 GMDSS 中使用,取消携带老旧系统的要求,同时保留船舶携带特定地面和卫星无线电通信设备的要求,用于发送和接收遇险报警和海上安全信息以及其他通信。

7.2 Technical and Equipment Improvements in Terrestrial Communications 地面通信技术和设备改进

7.2.1 VHF Data Exchange System (VDES) 甚高频数据交换系统(VDES)

The VHF Data Exchange System (VDES) was developed by International Association of Marine Aids to Navigation and Lighthouse Authorities (IALA) to address emerging indications of overload of the Automatic Identification System (AIS) VHF Data Link (VDL) and simultaneously enabling a wider seamless data exchange for the maritime community. The initial concept of VDES includes the function of the AIS, Applications Specific Messages (ASM), VDE terrestrial component and VDE satellite component. The VDES is one of the potential elements of E-navigation. VDES is capable of exchanging ASM, facilitating numerous applications for safety and security of navigation, protection of marine environment, efficiency of shipping and others. VDES will prospectively have a significant beneficial impact on the maritime information services including Aids to Navigation (AtN) and Vessel Traffic Service (VTS) in the future.

甚高频数据交换系统(VDES)是由国际航标协会(IALA)开发的,旨在解决新出现的自动识别系统(AIS)甚高频数据链路(VDL)超负荷问题,同时为海事界提供更广泛的无缝数据交换。VDES 的初步概念包括 AIS、特定应用信息（ASM）、VDE 地面部分和 VDE 卫星部分的功能。VDES 是电子航海的潜在要素之一。VDES 能够交换 ASM，为航行安全和安保、海洋环境保护、航运效率等方面的众多应用提供便利。未来，VDES 将对包括导航辅助系统（AtN）和船舶交通服务（VTS）在内的海事信息服务产生重大的有益影响。

The VDES concept includes a satellite component. This system component might be suitable to be used for the transmission of MSI information in remote areas. Figure 7.1 shows the basic concept of VDES.

VDES 的概念包括一个卫星组件。该系统组件可能适用于在偏远地区传输 MSI 信息。图 7.1 为 VDES 系统概念图。

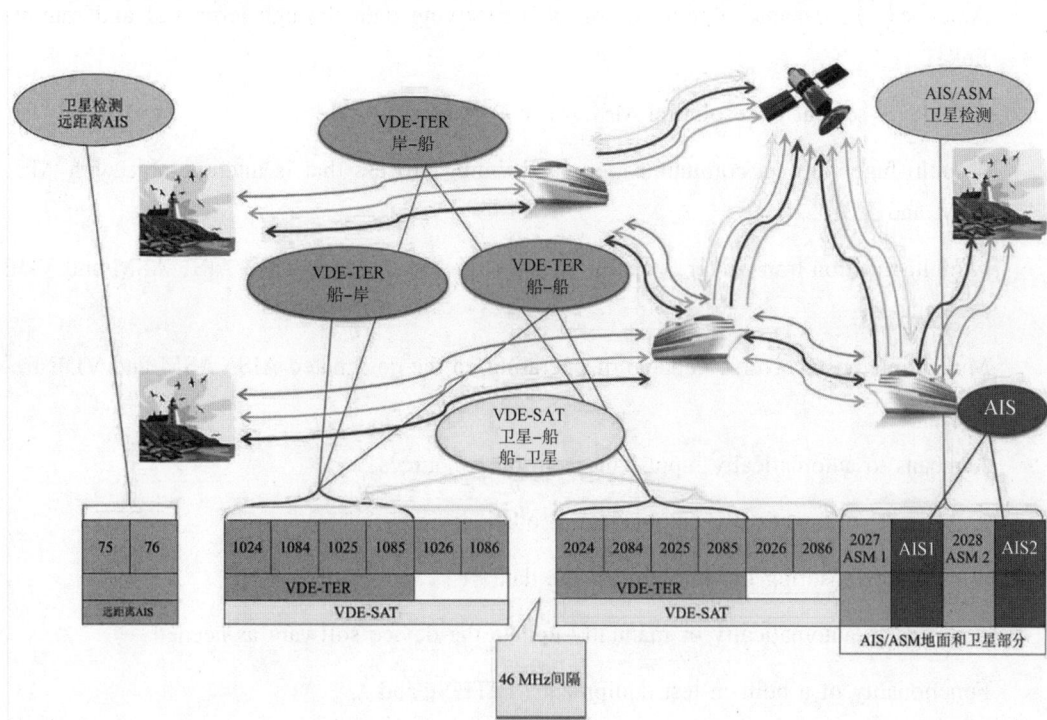

Figure 7.1　The Conceptual Diagram of the VDES System
图 7.1　VDES 系统概念图

The VDES should improve the safety of life at sea, the safety and efficiency of navigation, and the protection of marine environment and enhance maritime safety and security. These goals will be achieved through efficient and effective use of maritime radiocommunications, incorporating the following functional requirements:

a.As a means of AIS.

b.As a means of radiocommunications equipment through exchange of digital data between ship to ship, ship to shore including satellite, via AIS, ASM and VDE.

c.As a means of applications external to the VDES equipment itself. These applications use AIS, ASM or VDE separately or combined.

VDES 可改进海上人命安全、航行安全和运营效率,保护海洋环境,加强海上安全和安保。这些目标通过高效和有效地利用海上无线电通信来实现,并包含以下功能要求:

a.作为 AIS 的一种手段。

b.作为无线电通信设备的一种手段,通过 AIS、ASM 和 VDE 在船与船、船与岸(包括卫星)之间交换数字数据。

c.作为 VDES 设备本身外部应用的一种手段。这些应用单独或合并使用 AIS、ASM 或 VDE。

The VDES includes:

· Antenna(s), capable of transmitting and receiving data through terrestrial and satellite link;

· An AIS as set out in resolution MSC.74(69) Annex 3;

· A multi-function data communications and timing process that is interoperable with AIS, ASM and VDE;

· A multi-function transmitter, capable of operating on the designated AIS, ASM and VDE frequencies;

· Multi-function receivers, capable of operating on the designated AIS, ASM and VDE frequencies;

· A means to automatically input data from other sources;

· A means to automatically output data to other devices;

· A means of ensuring the integrity of the data;

· A means to automatically or manually update the device software as needed;

· Functionality of a built-in test equipment (BITE); and

· GNSS receiver to support AIS and to possibly serve as a secondary source of Positioning Navigation and Timing (PNT).

VDES 包括:

· 能够通过地面和卫星链路收发数据的天线;

· MSC.74(69) 号决议附件 3 规定的 AIS;

· 与 AIS、ASM 和 VDE 可互操作的多功能数据通信和定时程序;

· 多功能发射机,能够在指定的 AIS、ASM 和 VDE 频率上运行;

· 多功能接收机,能够在指定的 AIS、ASM 和 VDE 频率上运行;

· 自动输入其他来源数据的装置;

· 自动向其他设备输出数据的装置;

- 确保数据完整性的装置；

- 根据需要自动或手动更新设备软件的方法；

- 内置测试设备（BITE）的功能；以及

- GNSS 接收机，用于支持 AIS，并可作为定位导航和定时(PNT)的辅助来源。

The following aspects may be of help when deciding on implementation of VDES as a transport for maritime services. VDES shore station operations should consider：

- AIS system load；

- Services to be provided；

- Existing equipment（for existing sites）；

- Antenna requirements，including interaction with other services/systems；

- Power requirements；

- Installation costs（which may include mobile station，tower access）；

- Operational costs；and

- Coordination with other administrations may be required.

在决定将 VDES 作为传输工具时以下方面可能会对海事业务有所帮助。VDES 岸基站运行应考虑以下方面：

- AIS 系统负载；

- 要提供的服务；

- 现有设备(针对现有站点)；

- 天线要求，包括与其他服务/系统的交互；

- 电力要求；

- 安装成本(可能包括移动电站、塔台接入)；

- 运营成本；以及

- 可能需要与其他管理部门协调。

Provision of VDES shore infrastructure may be managed through：

- A regular scheduled lifecycle process for existing AIS shore stations；

- Through an upgrade of existing AIS shore stations；or

- Through the implementation of VDES at a new location where there is no existing AIS shore station.

VDES 岸上基础设施的提供可通过以下方式管理：

- 现有 AIS 岸基站到计划使用周期后处理;

- 升级现有的 AIS 岸基站;或

- 在没有现有 AIS 岸基站的新地点实施 VDES。

The services offered by a VDES system will allow for priority with essential services/safety related services having the highest priority and non-essential/commercial service having the lowest priority.

VDES 系统提供的服务有优先级之分,基本服务/安全相关服务的优先级最高,非基本服务/商业服务的优先级最低。

The transfer of data using VDES should consider that the available VDES data transfer capacity is shared by all users within the coverage range of a VDES base station.

使用 VDES 传输数据时,应考虑到 VDES 数据传输能力由 VDES 基站覆盖范围内的所有用户共享。

Other means could be considered but take into account specific characteristics of these communication systems:

- Near real time short messages;

- No streaming or large files;

- Doesn't need shore infrastructure;

- No need for subscription at provider.

还可以考虑其他方式,但要考虑到这些通信系统的具体特点:

- 接近实时的短信息;

- 无流媒体或大文件;

- 不需要岸上基础设施;

- 无须在提供商处订购。

7.2.2 Navigational Data（NAVDAT）航行数字（NAVDAT）

Navigational Data（NAVDAT）MF is the radio system, for use in the maritime mobile service, operating in the 500 kHz band for digital broadcasting of maritime safety and security related information from shore-to-ship.

航行数字(NAVDAT)MF 是一种用于海上移动业务的无线电系统,在 500 kHz 频段内运行,用于岸对船的海上安全和安保相关信息的数字广播。

The NAVDAT system uses a time-slot allocation similar to the NAVTEX system which could be coordinated by IMO in the same manner. That system can also work on Single Frequency Network（SFN）. In this case transmitters are frequency synchronized and the transmit data must be the same for all transmitter.

NAVDAT 系统使用的时隙分配,类似于 NAVTEX 系统,可由 IMO 以同样的方式进行协调。该系统也可在单频网(SFN)上运行。在这种情况下,发射机频率同步,所有发射机的发射数据必须相同。

The NAVDAT 500 (495-505) kHz digital system offers a broadcast transmission of any kind of message from shore-to-ships with possibility of encryption. The frequency band 495-505 kHz is used for the international NAVDAT system as described in the most recent version of Recommendation ITU-R M.2010. NAVDAT transmitting stations are limited to coast stations (WRC-19). Any broadcasting message should be provided by a secure and controlled source.

NAVDAT 500(495~505) kHz 数字系统可由岸对船广播发射任何类型的电文,并可进行加密。根据最新版本的 ITU-R M.2010 建议,495~505 kHz 频段用于国际 NAVDAT 系统。NAVDAT 发射台仅限于海岸电台(WRC-19)。任何广播电文均应由安全可控的来源提供。

Message types broadcast can include, but are not limited to, the following:

· Safety of navigation;

· Security;

· Piracy;

· Search and rescue;

· Meteorological messages;

· Piloting or harbour messages;

· Vessel traffic system files transfer.

广播的电文类型可包括但不限于以下内容:

· 航行安全;

· 安全;

· 海盗;

· 搜救;

· 气象电文;

· 引航或港口电文;

· 船舶交通系统文件传输。

These messages are broadcasted for the attention of all ships, a group of ships or in a specific navigation area. These messages can be addressed to one ship, using the maritime mobile service identity (MMSI) as well.

这些电文是为了引起所有船舶、一组船舶或特定航行区域的注意而广播的。这些电文也可

使用海事移动服务识别码（MMSI）发送给一艘船。

The NAVDAT system is organized upon five vectors performing the following functions：

a. System of information and management（SIM）：

· Collects and controls all kinds of information；

· Creates message files to be transmitted；

· Creates transmitting programme according to message files priority and need of repetition.

b. Shore network：

· Assures the transportation of the message files from sources to the transmitters.

c. Shore transmitter：

· Receives the message files from SIM；

· Translates message files to Orthogonal Frequency Division Multiplexing（OFDM）signal；

· Transmits RF signal to the antenna for broadcast to ships.

d. Transmission channel：

· Transports the 500 kHz RF signal.

e. Ship receiver：

· Demodulates the RF OFDM signal；

· Reconstructs the message files；

· Sorts and makes the message files available for the dedicated equipment according to the message files applications.

NAVDAT 系统由五个部分组成,具有以下功能：

a. 信息和管理系统(SIM)：

· 收集和控制各种信息；

· 创建要传送的电文文件；

· 根据信息文件的优先级和重复需要创建传送程序。

b. 岸上网络：

· 确保将电文文件从信息源传送到发射机。

c. 岸上发射机：

· 接收 SIM 发送的电文文件；

· 将电文文件转换为正交频分复用(OFDM)信号；

· 向天线发射射频信号,以便向船舶广播。

d.传送频道：

· 传输 500 kHz 射频信号。

e.船舶接收机：

· 解调射频 OFDM 信号；

· 重建电文文件；

· 根据电文文件应用程序，为专用设备整理和提供电文文件。

Figure 7.2 shows the diagram of the NAVDAT broadcast chain.

图 7.2 是 NAVDAT 广播链示意图。

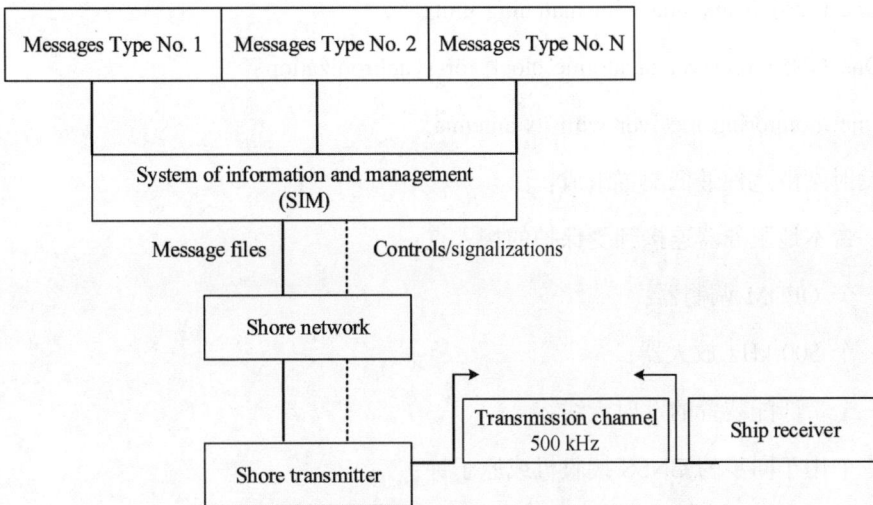

Figure 7.2　The Diagram of the NAVDAT Broadcast Chain
图 7.2　NAVDAT 广播链示意图

The SIM term includes：

· All the sources that deliver message files（e.g. meteorological office, safety and security organizations, etc.）；

· The file multiplexer which is an application running on a server；

· The file multiplexer manager；

· The shore transmitter manager.

SIM 术语包括：

· 所有传送电文文件的来源(如气象局、安全和保安组织等)；

· 文件多路复用器是运行在服务器上的一个应用程序；

· 文件多路复用器管理器；

· 岸上发射机管理器。

All the sources are connected to the file multiplexer through a network. The shore network can use a broadband link, a low data rate link or a local file sharing.

所有信号源都通过网络连接到文件多路复用器。岸上网络可以使用宽带链路、低数据速率链路或本地文件共享。

A coastal transmitting station consists of this minimum configuration：

· One local server connected to a protected access；

· One OFDM modulator；

· One 500 kHz amplifier；

· One transmit antenna with matching unit；

· One GNSS receiver or atomic clock for synchronization；

· One monitoring receiver with its antenna.

沿岸发射站由这种最低配置组成：

· 一台本地服务器连接到受保护的接入点；

· 一个 OFDM 调制器；

· 一个 500 kHz 放大器；

· 一个带匹配装置的发射天线；

· 一个用于同步的 GNSS 接收机或原子钟；

· 一个带天线的监测接收机。

A typical NAVDAT 500 kHz digital receiver is composed of several basic blocks：

· Reception antenna and GNSS antenna；

· RF front end；

· Demodulator；

· File demultiplexer；

· Controller；

· Power supply.

典型的 NAVDAT 500 kHz 数字接收机由几个基本模块组成：

· 接收天线和 GNSS 天线；

· 射频前端；

· 解调器；

· 文件解复用器；

- 控制器；

- 电源。

The system uses Orthogonal Frequency Division Multiplexing（OFDM）which is a modulation technology for digital transmissions. In the 10 kHz channel bandwidth with 500 kHz propagation, the raw data rate available for the data stream（DS）is typically around 25 kbit/s with 16-QAM signal.

该系统采用正交频分复用技术(OFDM)，这是一种数字传输调制技术。在传播频率为 500 kHz 的 10 kHz 信道带宽中，数据流(DS)的原始数据速率通常约为 25 kbit/s，信号为 16-QAM。

With respect to the GMDSS Modernization Plan：

- SOLAS Chapter Ⅳ should be revised to allow ships to use NAVDAT service in addition to or in place of NAVTEX in places where NAVDAT is available.

- When the NAVDAT concept is sufficiently developed, IMO and ITU should develop the necessary technical recommendations and performance standards for international NAVDAT service. This work should be closely followed by the development of IMO, IHO, ITU, WMO and IEC standards as appropriate, for shipborne NAVDAT and/or combined NAVTEX/NAVDAT equipment.

- The need for a NAVDAT coordination scheme needs to be considered taking account that it should retain the existing NAVTEX service areas, but other aspects may not be compatible with the existing NAVTEX coordination scheme（allocation of transmission times, duration etc.）

关于 GMDSS 现代化计划：

- 应修订《国际海上人命安全公约》第四章，允许船舶在有 NAVDAT 的地方使用 NAV-DAT 服务，以补充或取代 NAVTEX。

- 当 NAVDAT 概念得到充分发展时，国际海事组织和国际电联应为国际 NAVDAT 服务制定必要的技术建议和性能标准。在开展这项工作的同时，应酌情制定国际海事组织、国际水道测量组织、国际电联、世界气象组织和国际电工委员会关于船载 NAVDAT 和/或 NAVTEX/NAVDAT 组合设备的标准。

- 需要考虑建立 NAVDAT 协调机制的必要性，该机制应保留现有的 NAVTEX 业务区，但其他方面可能与现有的 NAVTEX 协调机制不兼容（传输时间的分配、持续时间等）。

7.2.3　Search and Rescue Technologies 搜救技术

When considering amendments to the SOLAS Convention, a decision needs to be made as to whether all lifeboats, and whether some or all inflatable liferafts should be equipped with installed search and rescue locating devices：AIS-SART or 9 GHz radar SART, and how that requirement should be introduced, taking into account the regulatory scheme of survey and certification and the

environmental conditions inside of the survival craft.

在考虑《国际海上人命安全公约》修正案时,需要决定是否所有救生艇、部分或所有气胀救生筏都应安装搜救定位装置:AIS-SART 或 9 GHz radar SART,以及如何引入这一要求,同时考虑到检验和认证的监管计划以及救生艇内部的环境条件。

Appropriate revisions need to be made to SOLAS Chapter Ⅳ and the Record of Equipment List in the certificates. Consideration on the development of a circular or other instrument to advise Member Governments to encourage shipowners of certain categories of ships to carry VHF direction finders to detect 121.5 MHz signals and VHF marine band transmissions (for instance offshore industry vessels) is needed. Consideration should be given to the possible SAR benefits of the inclusion of text messaging, digital data, and chat messaging capabilities. The possibility to allow for the addition of an AIS technology locating device to the EPIRB should also be considered.

需要对《国际海上人命安全公约》第四章和证书中的设备记录清单进行适当修订。需要考虑制定一份通告或其他文书,建议成员国政府鼓励某些类别船舶的船东携带 VHF 测向仪,以探测 121.5 MHz 信号和 VHF 海洋波段传输(例如近海工程船舶)。应考虑增加文本信息、数字数据和聊天信息功能可能给搜救带来的好处。还应考虑在 EPIRB 上增加 AIS 技术定位装置的可能性。

MSC/Circ.1039 on Guidelines for shore-based maintenance of satellite EPIRBs needs to be revised to delete references to L-Band EPIRBs. MSC/Circ.1039 and MSC/Circ.1040/Rev.1 on Guidelines on Annual Testing of 406 MHz Satellite EPIRBs need to be revised, as appropriate, to include AIS locators, and reviewed for other needed changes in respect of Second-Generation Beacons.

需要修订关于卫星 EPIRB 岸基维护准则的 MSC/Circ.1039,删除提及 L 波段 EPIRB 的内容。MSC/Circ.1039 和 MSC/Circ.1040/Rev.1 关于 406 MHz 卫星 EPIRB 的年度测试准则需要酌情修订,以包括 AIS 定位器,并审查有关第二代信标的其他必要改动。

7.2.4 HF Communications 高频通信

The list of HF stations in the GMDSS Master Plan needs to be updated, including information on coast stations capable of receiving and responding to test messages. The technical basis and the governance for determining the minimum number of HF GMDSS coast stations and their geographical distribution should be reviewed and, if necessary, consequential changes should be included in Resolution A.801(19) on Provision of radio services for the GMDSS. Consideration on the future role for HF data exchange under ITU-R Recommendation 1798-1 on Characteristics of HF radio equipment for the exchange of digital data and electronic mail in the maritime mobile service is needed.

GMDSS 总体规划中的 HF 电台列表需要更新,包括能够接收和响应测试消息的海岸电台信息。应审查确定高频 GMDSS 海岸电台最低数量及其地理分布的技术基础和管理,如有必要,应在为 GMDSS 提供无线电服务的 A.801(19)号决议中做出相应修改。需要根据国际电信联盟关于在海上移动业务中交换数字数据和电子邮件的高频无线电设备的特点的第 1798-1 号

建议,考虑高频数据交换的未来作用。

Technological improvements can make HF easier to use. Consider revising Resolutions A.806 (19) on Performance Standards for Shipborne MF/HF Radio Installations Capable of Voice Communication, Narrow Band Direct Printing and Digital Selective Calling and MSC.68(68) on Adoption of amendments to performance standards for shipborne radiocommunication equipment, Annexe 3, to include a requirement for frequency scanning and/or Automatic Link Establishment (ALE). MSC.1/Circ.1460 on Guidance on the validity of radiocommunications equipment installed and used on ships should be revised to delete the references to HF radiocommunication equipment capable of operating NBDP. Alternatively, it may be revoked since it relates to the 2012 revisions to the Radio Regulations.

技术改进可使高频更易于使用。考虑修订 A.806(19)号决议"可进行语音通信、窄带直接印字和数字选择性呼叫的船载中频/高频无线电装置性能标准" 和 MSC.68(68)号决议"通过船载无线电通信设备性能标准修正案"附件 3,纳入频率扫描和/或自动链路建立(ALE)的要求。应修订关于船舶上安装和使用的无线电通信设备有效性指南的 MSC.1/Circ.1460,删除有关能够操作 NBDP 的高频无线电通信设备的内容。或者可以废除该指南,因为它涉及 2012 年对《无线电规则》的修订。

Automatic Link Establishment (ALE) was developed to automatically select a frequency that will support automatic linking between stations in a network or point-to-point communications without operator assistance. This new technology has given HF radio a renewed sense of being. ALE offers a new approach in adaptive automated control via the HF medium. Once, skilled radio operators knowledgeable in HF propagation were the only answer to mastering long-haul HF communication. With ALE, significant training and cost is no longer required. ALE takes the guesswork out of the frequency selection process. Under microprocessor control, ALE modes include automatic signaling, selective calling, and automatic handshaking. Other automatic functions related to ALE are channel scanning and selection, link quality analysis, polling, sounding, and message store-and-forward capabilities.

自动链路建立(ALE)的开发是为了自动选择一个频率,以支持网络中电台之间的自动链路或点对点通信,而无须操作员的协助。这项新技术赋予了高频无线电新的作用。ALE 提供了一种通过高频媒介进行自适应自动控制的新方法。以往精通高频传播知识的熟练的无线电操作员是掌握远程高频通信的唯一方法。有了 ALE,就不再需要大量的培训和费用。ALE 使频率选择过程不再需要多次尝试。在微处理器的控制下,ALE 模式包括自动信令、选择性呼叫和自动连接。与 ALE 有关的其他自动功能包括信道扫描和选择、链路质量分析、轮询、发声和电文存储转发功能。

An adaptive system automates this process, dispenses with the need for a skilled operator and improves the quality of service and the efficiency of the link.

自适应系统可使这一过程自动化,无须熟练的操作员,并提高服务质量和链路效率。

ALE may be used:

a.For point-to-point links.

b.For a network, with selective calling procedure, carried out by the control station, which may be:

· General (all stations);

· Group (several stations);

· Individual (a single station with which a point-to-point link is established).

ALE 可以用来进行:

a.点对点链接。

b.在网络中,控制台可以执行选择性呼叫程序:

· 一般(所有台);

· 组(一组台);

· 单台(与之建立点对点链接的单个台)。

All the user has to do is to operate the peripheral equipment corresponding to the type of service indicated in the call sequence (telephone, teleprinter, picture transmission equipment, data terminal), there being no need whatever for him to intervene in connection with the establishment, control and interruption of the radio connections.

用户只需根据呼叫序列中显示的业务类型(电话、电传打印机、图像传输设备、数据终端)操作相应的外围设备即可,无须对无线电连接的建立、控制和中断过程进行任何干预。

Basically, an adaptive system has a triple function:

· automatic selection of the frequency to be used;

· automatic operation as regards calling, establishing the communication (with possible switch-over to the peripheral equipment needed for the type of service to be provided), and disconnecting;

· adaptivity during the communications so as to optimize at all times the quality of service according to the ionospheric conditions and spectrum congestion.

基本上,自适应系统具有三重功能:

· 自动选择使用的频率;

· 自动操作,包括呼叫、建立通信(可能切换到所提供服务类型所需的外围设备)和断开连接;

· 通信过程中的自适应能力,以便随时根据电离层条件和频谱拥塞情况优化服务质量。

7.3　Technical and Equipment Improvements in Satellite Communications 卫星通信技术和设备改进

IMO is modernizing the GMDSS and expanding the worldwide radio navigation system. In January 2020, IMO's Sub-Committee on Navigation, Communications and Search and Rescue (NCSR) endorsed upgrade work, approved rule amendments and recognized new satellite constellations for emergency communications and ship positioning.

IMO 正在对 GMDSS 进行现代化改造,并扩大全球无线电航行系统。2020 年 1 月,IMO NCSR 分委员会批准了升级工作,批准了规则修正案,并承认了用于紧急通信和船舶定位的新卫星星座。

As part of this modernization process, Iridium Communications received formal verification of its rival GMDSS service, which uses the Next constellation of Low Earth orbit (LEO) satellites. IMO currently recognizes the US-funded Global Positioning System (GPS), Russia's GLONASS, China's BeiDou satellites and European Union-developed Galileo satellites as providers of this information.

作为现代化进程的一部分,铱星通信公司通过了 GMDSS 业务的正式验证,该服务使用 Next 低轨道(LEO)卫星群。IMO 目前认可美国资助的全球定位系统(GPS)、俄罗斯的全球导航系统(GLONASS)、中国的北斗卫星和欧盟开发的伽利略(Galileo)卫星作为该信息的提供者。

7.3.1　INMARSAT-Fleet Broadband（FBB）国际海事卫星组织–船队宽带（FBB）

Fleet Broadband provides cost-effective voice and data through a compact antenna, delivered globally via the I-4 satellite and ground network, which maintains over 99.9% network availability. It can provide unlimited back-up to high-speed Fleet Xpress service, ensuring global seamless mobility connection. It boosts morale onboard by enabling crew to stay in touch with family and friends, use social media, and watch news and entertainment.

船队宽带通过一个小巧的天线提供具有成本效益的语音和数据,通过 I-4 卫星和地面网络向全球提供服务,网络可用率超过 99.9%。它可以为高速 Fleet Xpress 服务提供近乎无限容量,确保全球无缝移动连接。它可以让船员与家人和朋友保持联系、使用社交媒体、观看新闻和娱乐节目,从而改善船上人员的精神状态。

Crucially, Fleet Broadband delivers safety services to non-SOLAS vessels so that in an emergency vessel can immediately get through to a Maritime Rescue and Coordination Center (MRCC) by pressing the distress button or simply dialling 505.

最重要的是,船队宽带可为非 SOLAS 船舶提供安全服务,因此在紧急情况下,船舶只需按下求救按钮或拨打 505,就能立即与海上救援和协调中心(MRCC)取得联系。

There are three types of Fleet Broadband terminals supported by INMARSAT, see Table 7.1.

INMARSAT 支持三种类型的船队宽带终端,见表 7.1。

Table 7.1　Fleet Broadband Terminals
表 7.1　船队宽带终端

Data 数据	FB150	FB250	FB500
Standard IP 标准 IP	Up to 150 kbit/s	Up to 284 kbit/s	Up to 432 kbit/s
Streaming IP 流媒体 IP	—	8, 16, 32, 64, 128 kbit/s	8, 16, 32, 64, 128, 256 kbit/s
ISDN 综合业务数据网	—	—	64 kbit/s
Voice 声音	4 kbit/s AMBE+2	4 kbit/s AMBE+2 and 3.1 kHz audio	
Fax 传真	—	Group 3 fax via 3.1 kHz audio, access to E-fax applications 通过 3.1 kHz 音频发送第 3 组传真,访问电子传真应用程序	
SMS 短信	Standard 3G (up to 160 characters)		
Antenna 天线			
Diameter 直径	27.5 cm	32 cm	60 cm
Height 高度	22.1 cm	28 cm	63 cm
Weight 重量	2.5 kg	3.9 kg	16 kg

Fleet Broadband supports an extensive range of commercially available, off-the-shelf software, as well as specialized user applications. It is ideal for:

· E-mail and webmail;

· Real-time electronic chart and weather updates;

· Remote company intranet and internet access;

· Secure communications;

· Large file transfer;

· Crew communications;

· Vessel/engine telemetry;

- SMS and instant messaging;

- Videoconferencing;

- Store and forward video.

船队宽带支持广泛的现成的商用软件以及专门的用户应用程序。它适用于：

- 电子邮件和网络邮件；

- 实时电子海图和天气更新；

- 远程访问公司内部网和互联网；

- 安全通信；

- 大文件传输；

- 船员通信；

- 船舶/发动机遥测；

- 短信和即时消息；

- 视频会议；

- 存储和转发视频。

7.3.2   INMARSAT Global Express（GX） INMARSAT 全球高速网络（GX）

In May 2019, the INMARSAT Company has revealed the deployment of Global Xpress (GX) system. GX system already fitted in number of vessels and it covers the earth's surface except at the high latitude areas near the North Pole and the South Pole.

2019 年 5 月，INMARSAT 公司透露部署 Global Xpress 系统。GX 系统已安装在多艘船舶上，除北极和南极附近的高纬度地区外，该系统已覆盖地球表面。

INMARSAT GX terminals are available for many types of vessels and operating in the resilient Ka-band, GX also integrates seamlessly with L-band network to deliver connectivity.

INMARSAT GX 终端适用于多种类型的船舶，在弹性 Ka 波段运行，GX 还可与 L 波段网络无缝集成以提供连接。

GX terminal is specifically suitable for Mobile Earth Stations for any type of vessel navigating the world's ocean. The GX terminal delivers services that are provided by INMARSAT Company Ka-band high speed data communications using Internet Protocol techniques up to 50 Mbps data rate, voice communications and multimedia sessions over IP networks (need NSD).

GX 终端特别适用于在全球海洋中航行的任何类型船舶的移动地球站。GX 终端通过 IP 网络（需要 NSD）提供 INMARSAT 公司使用互联网协议技术的 Ka 波段高达 50 Mbps 的高速数据通信、语音通信和多媒体会话服务。

INMARSAT GX system coverage map displays the area of four satellite regions, namely：

- · I5-F1 Europe, the Middle East, Africa and Asia；

- · I5-F2 The Americas and the Atlantic Ocean Region；

- · I5-F3 The Pacific Ocean Region；

- · I5-F4 Asia.

INMARSAT GX 系统覆盖图显示了四个卫星区域的面积,即

- · I5-F1 欧洲、中东、非洲和亚洲；

- · I5-F2 美洲和大西洋地区；

- · I5-F3 太平洋地区；

- · I5-F4 亚洲。

GX6A launched in 2021 and is INMARSAT's largest and most advanced satellite ever built. Delivering twice the capacity of the entire existing GX fleet, it features 20 Ka-spot beams that can be directed to meet customer demand second-by-second, and will power greater capacity, coverage and speeds for customers into the 2040s and beyond. GX6A came into service in 2023 over the Indian Ocean. Currently served by a fleet of six satellites, we have an additional six satellites scheduled to launch or come into service by 2025.

INMARSAT GX 卫星群的第六代第一颗卫星于 2021 年发射,是 INMARSAT 有史以来最大、最先进的卫星。GX6A 提供的容量是现有整个 GX 卫星群的两倍,具有 20 个 Ka 点波束,可按秒定向以满足客户需求,并将为客户提供更大的容量、覆盖范围和速度至 21 世纪 40 年代及以后。GX6A 于 2023 年在印度洋上空投入使用。目前,GX 网络由六颗卫星组成,另有六颗卫星计划于 2025 年之前发射或投入使用。

GX7, 8 & 9, scheduled to launch by 2025, will employ dynamic beam forming to simultaneously create thousands of independent beams of different sizes, bandwidth and power that can be reconfigured and repositioned across the globe in real time.

GX7、8 和 9 号卫星计划于 2025 年发射,将采用动态波束成形技术,同时形成数千个不同大小、带宽和功率的独立波束,可在全球范围内实时重新配置和重新定位。

Two HEO (Highly Elliptical Orbit) payloads, GX10A & 10B will become the world's first mobile broadband payloads dedicated to the Arctic region, through a partnership with Space Norway and its subsidiary Space Norway HEOSAT. The satellite carrying payloads is currently scheduled to launch in 2024. Figure 7.3 shows the satellite constellation map of GX.

通过与挪威航天局及其子公司挪威航天局 HEOSAT 合作,两个 HEO(高椭圆轨道)有效载荷 GX10A 和 10B 将成为世界上第一个专门用于北极地区的移动宽带有效载荷。携带有效载荷的卫星目前计划于 2024 年发射。图 7.3 展示了目前 GX 全球卫星星座图。

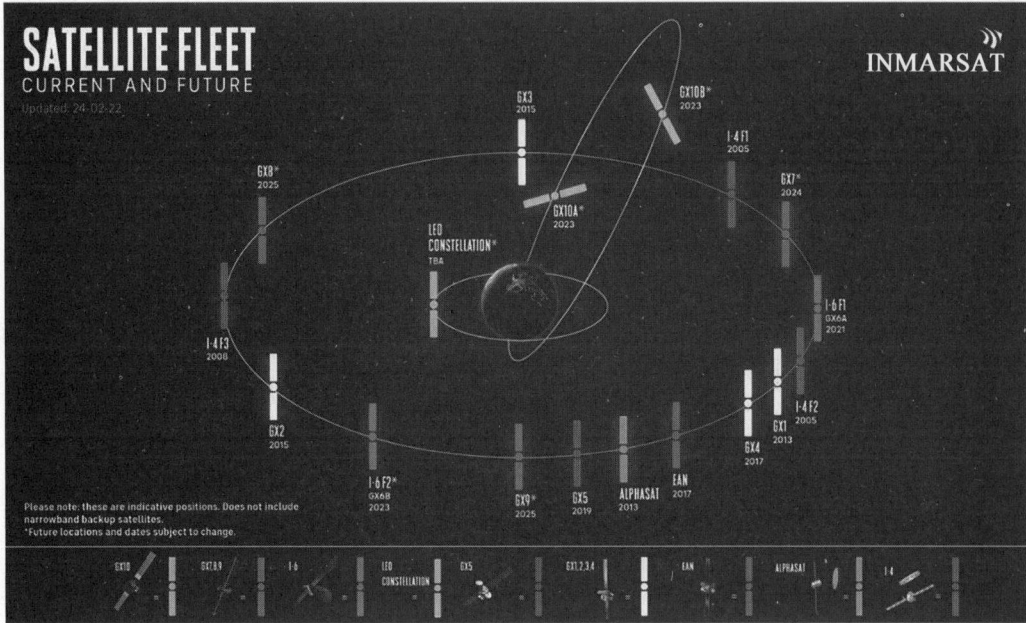

Figure 7.3　The Satellite Constellation Map of GX

图 7.3　GX 全球卫星星座图

7.3.2.1　INMARSAT Global Xpress Service Network INMARSAT 全球高速服务网络

The GX service network was developed by INMARSAT Company based on the GX satellite regions(see Figure 7.4). The INMARSAT Global Xpress network consists of Network Operation Center (NOC) and Satellite Access Stations (SAS), Network Operation Center (NOC) is located at the INMARSAT headquarters in London, UK., and coordinates communication lines of the network. The NOC maintains contact via dedicated satellite and terrestrial links with the NCSs and SASs in all ocean regions covered by INMARSAT GX map. The NOC performs the following:

· Coordinates with the Satellite Control Center (SCC) for operation of satellites.

· Coordinates with NCS and SAS for system operation.

· Collect of any status data in operation.

· Coordinates with any test of satellite's performance verification.

GX 服务网络由 INMARSAT 公司根据 GX 卫星区域开发而成(见图 7.4)。INMARSAT Global Xpress 网络由网络运行中心 (NOC) 和卫星接入站 (SAS) 组成,网络运行中心 (NOC) 位于英国伦敦的 INMARSAT 总部,负责协调网络的通信线路。NOC 通过专用卫星和地面链路与 INMARSAT GX 地图覆盖的所有海区的 NCS 和 SAS 保持联系。NOC 执行以下任务:

· 与卫星控制中心(SCC)协调卫星运行。

· 与 NCS 和 SAS 协调系统运行。

· 收集运行中的任何状态数据。

- 与任何卫星性能验证测试进行协调。

Operational Backup Center（OBC）—back up data of NOC.

运行备份中心（OBC）——备份 NOC 的数据。

Satellite Access Station（SAS）—located in Fucino（Italy）, Burum（Holland）and Hawaii（America）which are the gateway systems operating inter-working with public network, such as telephone and internet services.

卫星接入站(SAS)——位于意大利 Fucino、荷兰 Burum 和美国夏威夷,是与电话和互联网服务等公共网络互联互通的网关系统。

Points of Presence（POP）is the gateway to public communication lines.

接入点（POP）是公共通信线路的网关。

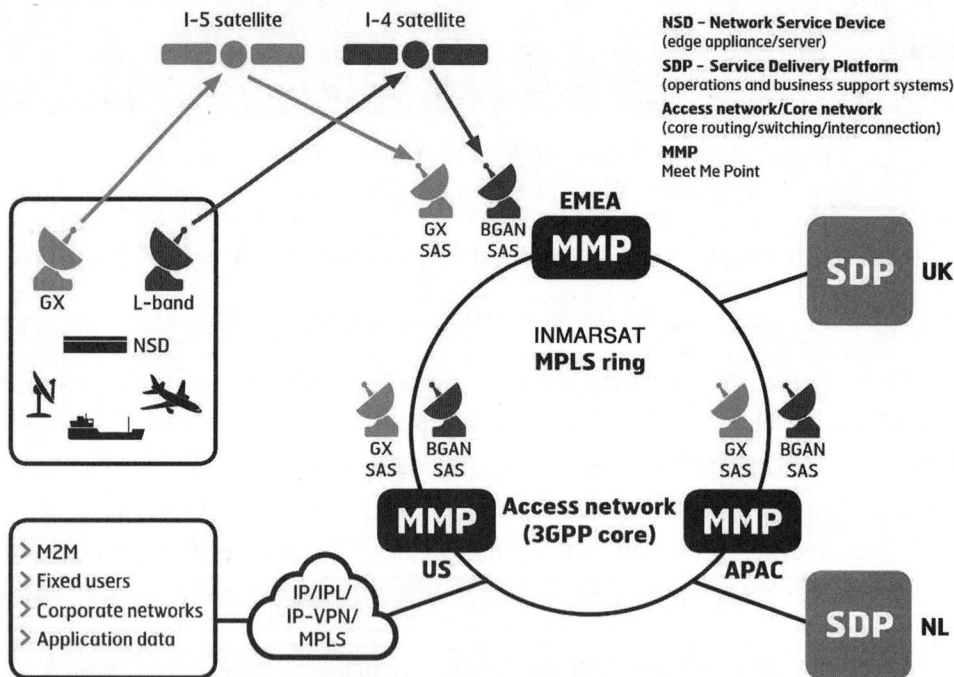

Figure 7.4　Global Xpress Service Network Architecture
图 7.4　全球高速服务网络架构

7.3.3　Iridium Maritime Satellite Service 铱星海事卫星服务

Iridium Company is one of the major competitors of INMARSAT. In the early days the Iridium Company was specializing with satellite phones and today it is a leading company for satellite communications. In March 2019, the Iridium have unveiled the Lars Thrane（LT）3100S Terminal designed to operate on Iridium network for GMDSS vessel carriage requirements. The Low Earth Orbit Iridium network with interconnected satellites allow the system to offer multiple services throughout all the world's waterways in a single, compact terminal. In other words, the system is all-in-one that meet 1974 SOLAS Convention vessel carriage requirements, whilst also serving as primary or companion communications system.

铱星公司是 INMARSAT 的主要竞争对手之一。铱星公司早期专门从事卫星电话业务,如今已成为卫星通信领域的领先企业。2019 年 3 月,铱星公司发布了 Lars Thrane(LT)3100S 终端,该终端设计用于在铱星网络上运行,以满足 GMDSS 船舶运输要求。低轨道铱星网络与相互连接的卫星相结合,使该系统能够在一个紧凑的终端中为全球所有航道提供多种服务。换句话说,该系统是满足 1974 年《国际海上人命安全公约》船舶运输要求的一体化系统,同时也可作为主用或配套通信系统。

Iridium GMDSS terminal is unlike the competitive INMARSAT-C, its terminal is small and solid. It offers GMDSS services, along with voice communications through satellite, texting, and data services with a built in GNSS/GPS receiver. The multi-service terminal also supports the integration of Ship Security Alert System (SSAS), Anti-Piracy communications and Long Range Identification and Tracking (LRIT). Iridium Company is the one and only satellite communication company that delivers services in all sea areas (including A4 Sea Area). The system also offers the navigational and meteorological warnings from the terminals, Marine Safety Information broadcasts. This will help mariners to avoid danger zones. If they cannot, then the terminal's distress alert and distress voice features will be able to help.

铱星 GMDSS 终端与具有竞争力的 INMARSAT-C 不同,它的终端小巧而坚固。它提供 GMDSS 服务,以及卫星语音通信、短信和数据服务,并内置 GNSS/GPS 接收机。该多服务终端还支持整合船舶安全警告(SSAS)、反海盗通信以及远程识别和跟踪(LRIT)。铱星公司是唯一一家在所有海域(包括 A4 海区)提供服务的卫星通信公司。该系统还提供来自终端的导航和气象警告、海洋安全信息广播。这将帮助航海者避开危险区域。如果无法避开,终端的遇险报警和遇险语音功能也能提供帮助。

In April 2019, Iridium Company and the International Mobile Satellite Organization (IMSO) announced the signing of a Public Services Agreement (PSA) which detailed the conditions for IMSO to act as regulator and maintain oversight of Iridium's GMDSS services. This was a main step in the process towards IMSO hand out Iridium a letter of compliance, testifying that the company is prepared to begin providing its GMDSS services.

2019 年 4 月,铱星公司与国际移动卫星组织(IMSO)宣布签署公共服务协议(PSA),详细规定了 IMSO 作为监管机构并对铱星公司的 GMDSS 服务进行监督的条件。这是 IMSO 向铱星公司颁发合规函的主要一步,证明该公司已准备好开始提供 GMDSS 服务。

Iridium Company has began to provide services for GMDSS from 2020.

目前,铱星公司已经于 2020 年起为 GMDSS 提供服务。

Iridium Company operates the Iridium satellite constellation, a system of 141 active satellites used for worldwide voice and data communications from handheld satellite phones and other transceiver systems. The Iridium network is unique in such a way that it covers the whole earth, including the poles and all ocean regions, with 95 satellites in Low Earth Orbit (LEO) launched so far (see Figure 7.5). The Iridium LEO satellite orbits are at height of 780 km above the earth surface,

at an inclination of 86.4 degrees to the equatorial plane. Iridium satellites are often visible in the night sky as satellite flares, usually they can be observed as short-lived bright flashes of light.

铱星公司运营着由 141 颗现役卫星组成的铱星星座系统,用于通过手持卫星电话和其他收发系统进行全球语音和数据通信。铱星网络的独特之处在于它覆盖了整个地球,包括两极和所有海洋区域,迄今已发射了 95 颗低轨道卫星(见图 7.5)。铱星低轨道卫星的轨道距离地球表面 780 km,与赤道面的倾角为 86.4 度。铱星卫星在夜空中经常以卫星耀斑的形式出现,通常可以观察到短暂的强光闪烁。

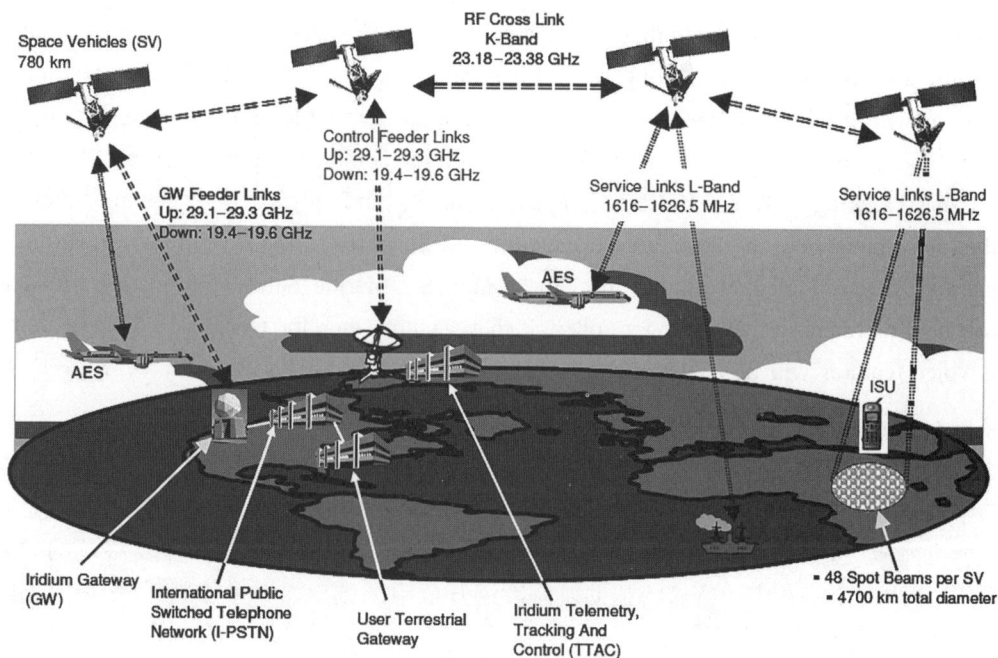

Figure 7.5   Iridium-NEXT-Spacecraft & Satellites
图 7.5   Iridium-NEXT-航天器和卫星

Iridium Company accomplishes numerous operation centers, including Tempe, Arizona and Leesburg, Virginia, United States. The US Department of Defence, through its own dedicated gateway, depends on Iridium for global communication capabilities.

铱星公司拥有众多运营中心,包括美国亚利桑那州坦佩和弗吉尼亚州利斯堡。美国国防部通过自己的专用网关,依靠铱星公司提供全球通信能力。

Iridium Service Network 铱星服务网络

The Iridium network uses radio frequency assignments that have been coordinated and notified according to the requirements of the International Telecommunication Union (ITU) Radio Regulations (RR). The service links between the mobile terminal and the satellites use assignments in the frequency band of 1616.0–1626.5 MHz (which is L-Band). The Iridium service links are unique in that uplink and downlink use the same frequencies and are in the same range (allocation). The uplink being primary and the downlink secondary. This arrangement was made at the 1992 World Radio Administrative Conference (WARC92). The system also harnesses inter-satellite communication links to inter-connect the in-orbit satellites in the band of 23.15–23.55 GHz（which is K-band）. The system operates through feeder links in the L-band of 19.4–19.6 GHz（space to earth）and 29.1–29.3 GHz（earth to space）（Ka-band）for connecting to the public switched through the gateway.

铱星网络使用的无线电频率分配是根据国际电信联盟(ITU)《无线电规则》(RR)的要求进行协调和通知的。移动终端与卫星之间的服务链路使用 1616.0～1626.5 MHz 频段(即 L 波段)。铱星服务链路的独特之处在于上行链路和下行链路使用相同的频率,并且在相同的范围内(分配)。上行链路为主,下行链路为辅。这一安排是在 1992 年世界无线电管理大会(WARC92)上做出的。该系统还利用卫星间通信链路将 23.15～23.55 GHz 波段(即 K 频段)的在轨卫星相互连接起来。该系统通过 L 波段 19.4～19.6 GHz(空间到地面)和 29.1～29.3 GHz(地面到空间)(Ka 波段)的馈电链路运行,通过网关与公共交换机连接。

7.3.4　Satellite AIS 卫星自动识别系统

Satellite AIS was created as a low-cost solution for VTS, providing the individual position of each vessel registered in the network, the activities it performs and the type of cargo carried. Monitoring maritime traffic from shore stations is limited by the range of VHF radios, which is about 40 n mile. A growing interest in extending the area monitored led to the deployment of several satellite constellations for this purpose.

卫星 AIS 是 VTS 的一种低成本解决方案,可提供在网络中注册的每艘船舶的具体位置、所从事的活动和运载的货物类型。岸基站对海上交通的监控受限于甚高频无线电的覆盖范围,约为 40 n mile。人们对扩大监测范围的兴趣日益浓厚,为此部署了多个卫星星座。

Small LEO satellites are often used in these constellations since a satellite takes approximately 90 min to circle the earth and therefore it is a simple solution. Since it takes sixteen days to pass through the same point again, a constellation of several satellites is required.

这些星座通常使用小型低轨道卫星,因为一颗卫星环绕地球一周大约需要 90 min,因此这是一个简单的解决方案。由于再次经过同一点需要 16 天,因此需要多个卫星。

The footprint of an LEO satellite is about 6000 km in diameter and, since SOTDMA cells have a radius of approximately 40 n mile, several hundred SOTDMA cells that are not synchronised with each other are included within the FoV of each satellite. Besides, the standard defines that the method of access to the medium for AIS-S is RATDMA, which comprises the main problem of Satellite AIS reception.

低轨道卫星的覆盖范围直径约为 6000 km,由于 SOTDMA 小区的半径约为 40 n mile,因此每颗卫星的 FoV 范围内包括几百个彼此不同步的 SOTDMA 小区。此外,该标准规定,AIS-S 的介质访问方法是 RATDMA,这也是卫星 AIS 接收的主要问题。

The task of these satellites is to receive messages with the identifier "27" of the AIS standard, in some cases to decode them and, finally, download them to the earth station so that they are delivered to the final client. As already specified above, the ITU defines in two channels within the

maritime VHF band reserved exclusively for the operation of AIS: AIS 1 (161.975 MHz) and AIS 2 (162.025 MHz). The AIS-S service has two independent AIS 1 and AIS 2 channels for proper operation Channels 75 (156.775 MHz) and 76 (156.825 MHz).

这些卫星的任务是接收带有 AIS 标准标识符"27"的电文,在某些情况下对其进行解码,最后将其下载到地球站,以便将其发送给最终用户。如上所述,ITU 在 VHF 海上波段中规定了两个专门用于 AIS 操作的频道:AIS 1(161.975 MHz)和 AIS 2(162.025 MHz)。AIS-S 服务有两个独立的 AIS 1 和 AIS 2 频道,分别用于 75 频道(156.775 MHz)和 76 频道(156.825 MHz)的正常运行。

Appendixes

附　录

Appendix 1　IMO Guidelines for the Avoidance of False Distress Alerts

1.1　Administrations Should

a.Inform shipowners and seafarers about the implications of the rising number of false distress alerts;

b.Take steps to enable ships properly to register all GMDSS equipment, and ensure that this registration data is readily available to RCCs;

c.Consider establishing and using national enforcement measures to prosecute those who:

(1)Inadvertently transmit a false distress alert without proper cancellation, or who fail to respond to a distress alert due to misuse or negligence;

(2)Repeatedly transmit false distress alerts; and

(3)Deliberately transmit false distress alerts;

d.Use the International Telecommunication Union violation reporting process for false distress alerts, or for failure to respond to a distress alert relayed from shore-to-ship;

e. Ensure that all relevant ship personnel know how GMDSS equipment operates, the importance of avoiding false distress alerts, the steps to be taken to prevent the transmission of such false distress alerts, and the procedures to be followed when a false distress alert has been transmitted;

f.Inform type-approval authorities of false distress alert problems, in order to draw their atten-

tion to the testing and alerting functions of radio equipment during the type approval process;

g. Urge companies installing radio equipment to ensure that relevant ship personnel are made familiar with the operation of the installed equipment;

h. Investigate the cause when a specific model of GMDSS equipment repeatedly transmits unwanted distress alerts, and inform the appropriate organizations accordingly;

i. Ensure that surveyors and inspectors are informed about GMDSS equipment, and particularly about how to operate and test it without transmitting a false distress alert; and

j. Require that GMDSS radio operators be appropriately certificated.

1.2 Manufacturers, Suppliers and Installers Should

a. Design equipment for distress alerting so that:

(1) It will not be possible to transmit a distress alert unintentionally;

(2) The panel for emergency operation is separated from the one for normal operation and is partially fitted with a cover, and the switches on the panel are clearly classified by colouring; and

(3) There are standardized arrangements of operation panels and operational procedures;

b. Design test features so that the testing of GMDSS equipment will not result in transmission of false distress alerts;

c. Ensure that any distress alert activation is indicated visually or acoustically; or both, and shows that the equipment is transmitting a distress alert until manually deactivated;

d. Ensure that the satellite EPIRB position onboard, installations (including the release and activation mechanisms) and handling procedures preclude unwanted activation (designing the EPIRB so that when it is out of its bracket it must also be immersed in water to activate automatically, and so that, when operated manually, a two-step activation action is required);

e. Provide clear and precise operational instructions that are easy to understand (maintenance and operational instructions should be separated, and should be written both in English and in any other language deemed necessary);

f. Ensure that when any GMDSS equipment has been installed, the necessary instructions are given to ship personnel, drawing specific attention to operational procedures (a record should be kept that such instructions have been given); and

g. Ensure that supply and installation personnel understand how the GMDSS works, and the consequences of transmitting a false distress alert.

1.3 Trainers and Educators Should

a. Ensure that maritime education centers are informed about false distress alert problems and their implications for SAR, the GMDSS, etc., and procedures to be followed if a false distress alert is transmitted, and include them in their teaching programmes;

b. Obtain and use actual case histories as examples;

c. Emphasize the need to avoid false distress alerts; and

d. Ensure that no inadvertent transmission of a false distress alert occurs when training on GMDSS equipment.

1.4 Companies, Masters and Seafarers Should, as Appropriate

a. Ensure that all GMDSS certificated personnel responsible for sending a distress alert have been instructed about, and are competent to operate, the particular radio equipment on the ship;

b. Ensure that the person or persons responsible for communications during distress incidents give the necessary instructions and information to all crew members on how to use GMDSS equipment to send a distress alert;

c. Ensure that as part of each "abandon ship" drill, instruction is given on how emergency equipment should be used to provide GMDSS functions;

d. Ensure that GMDSS equipment testing is only undertaken under the supervision of the person responsible for communications during distress incidents;

e. Ensure that GMDSS equipment testing or drills are never allowed to cause false distress alerts;

f. Ensure that encoded identities of satellite EPIRBs, which are used by SAR personnel responding to emergencies, are properly registered in a database accessible 24 h a day or automatically provided to SAR authorities (Masters should confirm that their EPIRBs have been registered with such a database, to help SAR services identify the ship in the event of distress and rapidly obtain other information which will enable them to respond appropriately);

g. Ensure that EPIRB, INMARSAT and DSC registration data is immediately updated if there is any change in information relating to the ship such as owner, name or flag, and that the necessary action is taken to reprogramme the ship's new data in the GMDSS equipment concerned;

h. Ensure that, for new ships, positions for installing EPIRBs are considered at the earliest stage of ship design and construction;

i. Ensure that satellite EPIRBs are carefully installed in accordance with manufacturers, instructions and using qualified personnel (sometimes satellite EPIRBs are damaged or broken due to improper handling or installation. They must be installed in a location that will enable them to float free and automatically activate if the ship sinks. Care must be taken to ensure that they are not tampered with or accidentally activated. If the coding has to be changed or the batteries serviced, manufacturers, requirements must be strictly followed. There have been cases where EPIRB lanyards were attached to the ship so that the EPIRB could not float free; lanyards are only to be used by survivors for securing the EPIRB to a survival craft or person in water);

j. Ensure that EPIRBs are not activated if assistance is already immediately available (EPIRBs are intended to call for assistance if the ship is unable to obtain help by other means, and to provide position information and homing signals for SAR units);

k. Ensure that, if a distress alert has been accidentally transmitted, the ship makes every reasonable attempt to communicate with the RCC by any means to cancel the false distress alert using the procedures given in the appendix;

l. Ensure that, if possible, after emergency use, the EPIRB is retrieved and deactivated; and

m. Ensure that when an EPIRB is damaged and needs to be disposed of if a ship is sold for scrap, or if for any other reason a satellite EPIRB will no longer be used, the satellite EPIRB is made inoperable, either by removing its battery and, if possible, returning it to the manufacturer, or by demolishing it.

Note: If the EPIRB is returned to the manufacturer, it should be wrapped in tin foil to prevent transmission of signals during shipment.

1.5   Instructions for Mariners and Others on How to Cancel a False Distress Alert

1.5.1   DSC

1.5.1.1   VHF

a. Switch off transmitter immediately;

b. Switch equipment on and set to Channel 16; and

c. Make broadcast to "all stations" giving the ship's name, call sign and DSC number, and cancel the false distress alert.

Example

All Stations, All Stations, All Stations,

THIS IS NAME, CALL SIGN,

DSC NUMBER, POSITION.

Cancel my distress alert of

DATE, TIME UTC,

Master NAME, CALL SIGN,

DSC NUMBER, DATE, TIME UTC.

1.5.1.2   MF

a. Switch off equipment immediately;

b. Switch equipment on and tune for radiotelephony transmission on 2182 kHz; and

c. Make broadcast to "all stations" giving the ship's name, call sign and DSC number, and cancel the false distress alert.

Example

All Stations, All Stations, All Stations,

THIS IS NAME, CALL SIGN,

DSC NUMBER, POSITION.

Cancel my distress alert of

DATE, TIME UTC,

Master NAME, CALL SIGN,

DSC NUMBER, DATE, TIME UTC.

1.5.1.3 HF

As for MF, but the alert must be cancelled on all the frequency bands on which it was transmitted. Hence, in stage 1.5.1.2 (b) the transmitter should be tuned consecutively to the radiotelephony distress frequencies in the 4, 6, 8, 12 and 16 MHz bands, as necessary.

1.5.1.4 INMARSAT-C

Notify the appropriate RCC to cancel the alert by sending a distress priority message via the same CES through which the false distress alert was sent.

Example of message

NAME, CALL SIGN, IDENTITY NUMBER,

POSITION,

Cancel my INMARSAT-C distress

alert of DATE, TIME UTC,

Master.

1.5.1.5 EPIRBs

If for any reason an EPIRB is activated accidentally, the ship should contact the nearest coast station or an appropriate Coast Earth Station or RCC and cancel the distress alert.

1.5.1.6 General

Notwithstanding the above, ships may use any means available to them to inform the appropriate authorities that a false distress alert has been transmitted and should be cancelled.

No action will normally be taken against any ship or mariner for reporting and cancelling a false distress alert. However, in view of the serious consequences of false alerts, and the strict ban on their transmission, Governments may prosecute in cases of repeated violations.

Appendix 2   Standard Marine Communication Phrases

In the interests of accuracy, brevity and clarity it is sound practice for operators to use the Standard Marine Communication Phrases (SMCPs) when possible. A selection of the standard vocabulary and phrases is contained in the following paragraphs.

2.1 Message Markers

If necessary, messages passed by radiotelephony may be preceded by the following message markers.

"Question" indicates the following message is of interrogative character.

"Answer" indicates that the following message is the reply to a previous question.

"Request" indicates that the content of the following message is asking for action with respect

to the ship.

"Information" indicates that the following message is restricted to observed facts.

"Intention" indicates that the following message informs others about immediate navigational actions intended to be taken.

"Warning" indicates that the following message informs other traffic participants about dangers.

"Advice" indicates that the following message implies the intention of the sender to influence the recipient(s) by a recommendation.

"Instruction" indicates that the following message implies the intention of the sender to influence the recipient(s) by a regulation.

2.2 Responses

Where the answer to a question is in the affirmative, say: "Yes" followed by the appropriate phrase in full.

Where the answer to a question is in the negative, say: "No" followed by the appropriate phrase in full.

Where the information is not immediately available, but soon will be, say: "Stand by".

Where the information cannot be obtained, say: "No information".

Where a message is not properly heard, say: "Say again".

Where a message is not understood, say: "Message not understood".

2.3 Miscellaneous Phrases

What is your name (and call sign)?

How do you read me? I read you bad/1 poor/2 fair/3 good/4 excellent/5.

Stand by on Channel…

Change to Channel…

I cannot read you (Pass your message through./Advise try channel.)

I cannot understand you. Please use the Standard Marine Communications Phrases/International Code of Signals.

I am passing a message for vessel…

2.4 Correction

If a mistake is made in a message, say: "mistake" followed by the word: "correction", plus the correct message.

2.5 Repetition

If any parts of the message are considered sufficiently important to need particular emphasis, use the word "repeat", e.g. "Do not overtake, do not overtake".

2.6 Position

When latitude and longitude are used, these should be expressed in degrees and minutes (and decimals of a minute, if necessary), north or south of the Equator and east or west of Greenwich (zero degrees longitude).

When the position is related to a mark, the mark shall be a well-defined charted object. The bearing shall be in the 360-degree notation from true north and shall be that of the position from the mark.

2.7 Courses

Courses should always be expressed in the 360-degree notation from true north (unless otherwise stated). Whether this is to, or from, a mark can be stated.

2.8 Bearings

The bearing of the mark or vessel concerned is the bearing in the 360-degree notation from true north (unless otherwise stated), except in the case of relative bearings.

Bearings may be either from the mark or from the vessel.

2.9 Distances

Distances should be expressed in nautical miles or cables (tenths of a nautical mile). The unit should always be stated.

2.10 Speed

Speed should be expressed in kn (without further notation meaning speed through the water). "Ground speed" meaning speed over the ground.

2.11 Numbers

Numbers should be transmitted by speaking each digit separately, e.g. "one five zero" for 150.

2.12 Geographical Names

Place names used should be those on the chart or Sailing Directions in use. Should these not be understood, latitude and longitude should be used.

2.13 Time

Time should be expressed in the 24-h notation indicating whether UTC, zone-time or local shore time is being used.

Appendix 3 Allocation of Maritime Identification Digit (MID) Series 110

In Numerical Order by MID

MID	Country/State
201	Albania (Republic of)
202	Andorra (Principality of)
203	Austria
204	Portugal—Azores
205	Belgium
206	Belarus (Republic of)
207	Bulgaria (Republic of)
208	Vatican City State
209	Cyprus (Republic of)
210	Cyprus (Republic of)
211	Germany (Federal Republic of)
212	Cyprus (Republic of)
213	Georgia
214	Moldova (Republic of)
215	Malta
216	Armenia (Republic of)
218	Germany (Federal Republic of)
219	Denmark
220	Denmark
224	Spain

Continued

MID	Country/State
225	Spain
226	France
227	France
228	France
229	Malta
230	Finland
231	Denmark—Faroe Islands
232	United Kingdom of Great Britain and Northern Ireland
233	United Kingdom of Great Britain and Northern Ireland
234	United Kingdom of Great Britain and Northern Ireland
235	United Kingdom of Great Britain and Northern Ireland
236	United Kingdom of Great Britain and Northern Ireland—Gibraltar
237	Greece
238	Croatia (Republic of)
239	Greece
240	Greece
241	Greece
242	Morocco (Kingdom of)
243	Hungary
244	Netherlands (Kingdom of the)
245	Netherlands (Kingdom of the)
246	Netherlands (Kingdom of the)
247	Italy
248	Malta
249	Malta
250	Ireland
251	Iceland
252	Liechtenstein (Principality of)
253	Luxembourg
254	Monaco (Principality of)
255	Portugal—Madeira
256	Malta

Continued

MID	Country/State
257	Norway
258	Norway
259	Norway
261	Poland（Republic of）
262	Montenegro
263	Portugal
264	Romania
265	Sweden
266	Sweden
267	Slovak Republic
268	San Marino（Republic of）
269	Switzerland（Confederation of）
270	Czech Republic
271	Turkey
272	Ukraine
273	Russian Federation
274	North Macedonia（Republic of）
275	Latvia（Republic of）
276	Estonia（Republic of）
277	Lithuania（Republic of）
278	Slovenia（Republic of）
279	Serbia（Republic of）
301	United Kingdom of Great Britain and Northern Ireland—Anguilla
303	United States of America—Alaska（State of）
304	Antigua and Barbuda
305	Antigua and Barbuda
306	Netherlands（Kingdom of the）—Bonaire, Sint Eustatius and Saba
306	Netherlands（Kingdom of the）—Curaçao
306	Netherlands（Kingdom of the）—Sint Maarten（Dutch part）
307	Netherlands（Kingdom of the）—Aruba
308	Bahamas（Commonwealth of the）
309	Bahamas（Commonwealth of the）

Continued

MID	Country/State
310	United Kingdom of Great Britain and Northern Ireland—Bermuda
311	Bahamas（Commonwealth of the）
312	Belize
314	Barbados
316	Canada
319	United Kingdom of Great Britain and Northern Ireland—Cayman Islands
321	Costa Rica
323	Cuba
325	Dominica（Commonwealth of）
327	Dominican Republic
329	France—Guadeloupe（French Department of）
330	Grenada
331	Denmark—Greenland
332	Guatemala（Republic of）
334	Honduras（Republic of）
336	Haiti（Republic of）
338	United States of America
339	Jamaica
341	Saint Kitts and Nevis（Federation of）
343	Saint Lucia
345	Mexico
347	France—Martinique（French Department of）
348	United Kingdom of Great Britain and Northern Ireland—Montserrat
350	Nicaragua
351	Panama（Republic of）
352	Panama（Republic of）
353	Panama（Republic of）
354	Panama（Republic of）
355	Panama（Republic of）
356	Panama（Republic of）
357	Panama（Republic of）
358	United States of America—Puerto Rico

Continued

MID	Country/State
359	El Salvador (Republic of)
361	France—Saint Pierre and Miquelon (Territorial Collectivity of)
362	Trinidad and Tobago
364	United Kingdom of Great Britain and Northern Ireland—Turks and Caicos Islands
366	United States of America
367	United States of America
368	United States of America
369	United States of America
370	Panama (Republic of)
371	Panama (Republic of)
372	Panama (Republic of)
373	Panama (Republic of)
374	Panama (Republic of)
375	Saint Vincent and the Grenadines
376	Saint Vincent and the Grenadines
377	Saint Vincent and the Grenadines
378	United Kingdom of Great Britain and Northern Ireland—British Virgin Islands
379	United States of America—United States Virgin Islands
401	Afghanistan
403	Saudi Arabia (Kingdom of)
405	Bangladesh (People's Republic of)
408	Bahrain (Kingdom of)
410	Bhutan (Kingdom of)
412	China (People's Republic of)
413	China (People's Republic of)
414	China (People's Republic of)
416	China (People's Republic of)—Taiwan (Province of China)
417	Sri Lanka (Democratic Socialist Republic of)
419	India (Republic of)
422	Iran (Islamic Republic of)
423	Azerbaijan (Republic of)
425	Iraq (Republic of)

Continued

MID	Country/State
428	Israel（State of）
431	Japan
432	Japan
434	Turkmenistan
436	Kazakhstan（Republic of）
437	Uzbekistan（Republic of）
438	Jordan（Hashemite Kingdom of）
440	Korea（Republic of）
441	Korea（Republic of）
443	State of Palestine（In accordance with Resolution 99 Rev. Dubai, 2018）
445	Democratic People's Republic of Korea
447	Kuwait（State of）
450	Lebanon
451	Kyrgyz Republic
453	China（People's Republic of）—Macao（Special Administrative Region of China）
455	Maldives（Republic of）
457	Mongolia
459	Nepal（Federal Democratic Republic of）
461	Oman（Sultanate of）
463	Pakistan（Islamic Republic of）
466	Qatar（State of）
468	Syrian Arab Republic
470	United Arab Emirates
471	United Arab Emirates
472	Tajikistan（Republic of）
473	Yemen（Republic of）
475	Yemen（Republic of）
477	China（People's Republic of）—Hong Kong（Special Administrative Region of China）
478	Bosnia and Herzegovina
501	France—Adelie Land
503	Australia
506	Myanmar（Union of）

Continued

MID	Country/State
508	Brunei Darussalam
510	Micronesia (Federated States of)
511	Palau (Republic of)
512	New Zealand
514	Cambodia (Kingdom of)
515	Cambodia (Kingdom of)
516	Australia—Christmas Island (Indian Ocean)
518	New Zealand—Cook Islands
520	Fiji (Republic of)
523	Australia—Cocos (Keeling) Islands
525	Indonesia (Republic of)
529	Kiribati (Republic of)
531	Lao People's Democratic Republic
533	Malaysia
536	United States of America—Northern Mariana Islands (Commonwealth of the)
538	Marshall Islands (Republic of the)
540	France—New Caledonia
542	New Zealand—Niue
544	Nauru (Republic of)
546	France—French Polynesia
548	Philippines (Republic of the)
550	Timor—Leste (Democratic Republic of)
553	Papua New Guinea
555	United Kingdom of Great Britain and Northern Ireland—Pitcairn Island
557	Solomon Islands
559	United States of America—American Samoa
561	Samoa (Independent State of)
563	Singapore (Republic of)
564	Singapore (Republic of)
565	Singapore (Republic of)
566	Singapore (Republic of)
567	Thailand

Continued

MID	Country/State
570	Tonga (Kingdom of)
572	Tuvalu
574	Viet Nam (Socialist Republic of)
576	Vanuatu (Republic of)
577	Vanuatu (Republic of)
578	France—Wallis and Futuna Islands
601	South Africa (Republic of)
603	Angola (Republic of)
605	Algeria (People's Democratic Republic of)
607	France—Saint Paul and Amsterdam Islands
608	United Kingdom of Great Britain and Northern Ireland—Ascension Island
609	Burundi (Republic of)
610	Benin (Republic of)
611	Botswana (Republic of)
612	Central African Republic
613	Cameroon (Republic of)
615	Congo (Republic of the)
616	Comoros (Union of the)
617	Cabo Verde (Republic of)
618	France—Crozet Archipelago
619	Côte d'Ivoire (Republic of)
620	Comoros (Union of the)
621	Djibouti (Republic of)
622	Egypt (Arab Republic of)
624	Ethiopia (Federal Democratic Republic of)
625	Eritrea
626	Gabonese Republic
627	Ghana
629	Gambia (Republic of)
630	Guinea—Bissau (Republic of)
631	Equatorial Guinea (Republic of)
632	Guinea (Republic of)

Continued

MID	Country/State
633	Burkina Faso
634	Kenya (Republic of)
635	France—Kerguelen Islands
636	Liberia (Republic of)
637	Liberia (Republic of)
638	South Sudan (Republic of)
642	Libya (State of)
644	Lesotho (Kingdom of)
645	Mauritius (Republic of)
647	Madagascar (Republic of)
649	Mali (Republic of)
650	Mozambique (Republic of)
654	Mauritania (Islamic Republic of)
655	Malawi
656	Niger (Republic of)
657	Nigeria (Federal Republic of)
659	Namibia (Republic of)
660	France—Reunion (French Department of)
661	Rwanda (Republic of)
662	Sudan (Republic of the)
663	Senegal (Republic of)
664	Seychelles (Republic of)
665	United Kingdom of Great Britain and Northern Ireland—Saint Helena
666	Somalia (Federal Republic of)
667	Sierra Leone
668	Sao Tome and Principe (Democratic Republic of)
669	Eswatini (Kingdom of)
670	Chad (Republic of)
671	Togolese Republic
672	Tunisia
674	Tanzania (United Republic of)
675	Uganda (Republic of)

Continued

MID	Country/State
676	Democratic Republic of the Congo
677	Tanzania (United Republic of)
678	Zambia (Republic of)
679	Zimbabwe (Republic of)
701	Argentine Republic
710	Brazil (Federative Republic of)
720	Bolivia (Plurinational State of)
725	Chile
730	Colombia (Republic of)
735	Ecuador
740	United Kingdom of Great Britain and Northern Ireland—Falkland Islands (Malvinas)
745	France—Guiana (French Department of)
750	Guyana
755	Paraguay (Republic of)
760	Peru
765	Suriname (Republic of)
770	Uruguay (Eastern Republic of)
775	Venezuela (Bolivarian Republic of)

Appendix 4　Table of Transmitting Frequencies in the VHE Maritime Mobile Band 118

Channel Designator	Transmitting Frequencies（MHz）		Inter-ship	Port Operations and Ship Movement		Public Correspondence
	From Ship Stations	From Coast Stations		Single Frequency	Two Frequencies	
60	156.025	160.625		Y	Y	Y
01	156.050	160.650		Y	Y	Y
61	156.075	160.675		Y	Y	Y
02	156.100	160.700		Y-	Y	Y
62	156.125	160.725		Y	Y	Y
03	156.150	160.750		Y	Y	Y
63	156.175	160.775		Y	Y	Y
04	156.200	160.800		Y	Y	Y
64	156.225	160.825		Y	Y	Y
05	156.250	160.850		Y	Y	Y
65	156.275	160.875		Y	Y	Y
06	156.300		Y			
2006	160.900	160.900				
66	156.325	160.925		Y	Y	Y
07	156.350	160.950		Y	Y	Y
67	156.375	156.375	Y	Y		
08	156.400		Y			
68	156.425	156.425		Y		

Continued

| Channel Designator | Transmitting Frequencies (MHz) | | Inter-ship | Port Operations and Ship Movement | | Public Correspondence |
	From Ship Stations	From Coast Stations		Single Frequency	Two Frequencies	
09	156.450	156.450	Y	Y		
69	156.475	156.475	Y	Y		
10	156.500	156.500	Y	Y		
70	156.525	156.525	Digital Selective Calling for Distress, Safety and Calling			
11	156.550	156.550		Y		
71	156.575	156.575		Y		
12	156.600	156.600		Y		
72	156.625		Y			
13	156.650	156.650	Y	Y		
73	156.675	156.675	Y	Y		
14	156.700	156.700		Y		
74	156.725	156.725		Y		
15	156.750	156.750	Y	Y		
75	156.775	156.775		Y		
16	156.800	156.800	Distress, Safety and Calling			
76	156.825	156.825		Y		
17	156.850	156.850	Y	Y		
77	156.875		Y			
18	156.900	161.500		Y	Y	Y
78	156.925	161.525		Y	Y	Y
1078	156.925	156.925		Y		
2078		161.525		Y		
19	156.950	161.550		Y	Y	Y
1019	156.950	156.950		Y		
2019		161.550		Y		
79	156.975	161.575		Y	Y	Y
1079	156.975	156.975		Y		
2079		161.575		Y		
20	157.000	161.600		Y	Y	Y
1020	157.000	157.000		Y		

Continued

Channel Designator	Transmitting Frequencies（MHz）		Inter-ship	Port Operations and Ship Movement		Public Correspondence
	From Ship Stations	From Coast Stations		Single Frequency	Two Frequencies	
2020		161.600		Y		
80	157.025	161.625		Y	Y	Y
21	157.050	161.650		Y	Y	Y
81	157.075	161.675		Y	Y	Y
22	157.100	161.700		Y	Y	Y
82	157.125	161.725		Y	Y	Y
23	157.150	161.750		Y	Y	Y
83	157.175	161.775		Y	Y	Y
24	157.200	161.800		Y	Y	Y
1024	157.200	157.200	Y（digital）	Y（digital）		
2024	161.800	161.800	Y（digital）	Y（digital）		
84	157.225	161.825		Y	Y	Y
1084	157.225	157.225	Y（digital）	Y（digital）		
2084	161.825	161.825	Y（digital）	Y（digital）		
25	157.250	161.850		Y	Y	Y
1025	157.250	157.250	Y（digital）	Y（digital）		
2025	161.850	161.850	Y（digital）	Y（digital）		
85	157.275	161.875		Y	Y	Y
1085	157.275	157.275	Y（digital）	Y（digital）		
2085	161.875	161.875	Y（digital）	Y（digital）		
26	157.300	161.900		Y	Y	Y
1026	157.300					
2026		161.900				
86	157.325	161.925		Y	Y	Y

Continued

| Channel Designator | Transmitting Frequencies (MHz) | | Inter-ship | Port Operations and Ship Movement | | Public Correspo-ndence |
	From Ship Stations	From Coast Stations		Single Frequency	Two Frequencies	
1086	157.325					
2086		161.925				
1027	157.350	157.350		Y		
ASM 1	161.950	161.950				
87	157.375	157.375		Y		
1028	157.400	157.400		Y		
ASM 2	162.000	162.000				
88	157.425	157.425		Y		
AIS 1	161.975	161.975				
AIS 2	162.025	162.025				

Specific Notes

a. The frequencies 156.300 MHz (Channel 06), 156.525 MHz (Channel 70), 156.800 MHz (Channel 16), 161.975 MHz (AIS 1) and 162.025 MHz (AIS 2) may also be used by aircraft stations for the purpose of search and rescue operations and other safety-related communication.

b. The frequencies 156.525 MHz (Channel 70), 161.975 MHz (AIS 1) and 162.025 MHz (AIS 2) may also be used by autonomous maritime radio devices Group A that enhance the safety of navigation, using DSC and/or AIS technology. Such use should be in accordance with the most recent version of Recommendation ITU-R M.2135. (WRC-19).

c.These channels may be operated as single frequency channels, subject to coordination with affected administrations.

The following conditions apply for single frequency usage:

- The lower frequency portion of these channels may be operated as single frequency channels by ship and coast stations.
- Transmission using the upper frequency portion of these channels is limited to coast stations.
- If permitted by administrations and specified by national regulations, the upper frequency portion of these channels may be used by ship stations for transmission. All precautions should be taken to avoid harmful interference to Channels AIS 1, AIS 2, ASM 1 and ASM 2. (WRC-19)

d.Transmission on these channels is limited to coast stations. If permitted by administrations and specified by national regulations, these channels may be used by ship stations for transmission. All precautions should be taken to avoid harmful interference to Channels AIS 1, AIS 2, ASM 1 and ASM 2. (WRC-19)

e. In the maritime mobile service, the frequency 160.9 MHz (Channel 2006) is designated for autonomous maritime radio devices Group B that do not enhance the safety of navigation, using AIS technology, in accordance with the most recent version of Recommendation ITU-R M.2135. Auton-

omous maritime radio devices Group B are limited to a transmitter e.i.r.p. of 100 mW and an antenna height not exceeding 1 m above the surface of the sea.

In the maritime mobile service, this frequency may also be used for experimental use for future applications or systems (e.g. new AIS applications, man overboard systems, etc.). If authorized by administrations for experimental use, the operation shall not cause harmful interference to, or claim protection from, stations operating in the fixed and mobile services, including the use of autonomous maritime radio devices Group B. (WRC-19)

f. The frequency bands 157. 1875 – 157. 3375 MHz and 161. 7875 – 161. 9375 MHz (corresponding to Channels: 24; 84; 25; 85; 26; 86; 1024; 1084; 1025; 1085; 1026; 1086; 2024; 2084; 2025; 2085; 2026 and 2086) are identified for the utilization of the VHF Data Exchange System (VDES). The VDES terrestrial and satellite components are described in the most recent version of Recommendation ITU-R M.2092. These channels shall not be used for feeder links.

g.The channels may be merged using multiple 25 kHz contiguous channels to form channel bandwidths of 50, 100 or 150 kHz. The channel usage is shown below:

- The Channels 1024; 1084; 1025 and 1085 are identified for ship-to-shore, shore-to-ship and ship-to-ship communications, but ship-to-satellite and satellite-to-ship communications may be possible without imposing constraints on ship-to-shore, shore-to-ship and ship-to-ship communications.
- The Channels 2024; 2084; 2025 and 2085 are identified for shore-to-ship and ship-to-ship communications, but ship-to-satellite and satellite-to-ship communications may be possible without imposing constraints on shore-to-ship and ship-to-ship communications.
- The Channels 1026; 1086; 2026 and 2086 are identified for ship-to-satellite and satellite-to-ship.
- Communications are not used by the terrestrial component of VDES.
- The Channels 24, 84, 25 and 85 are identified for ship-to-shore and shore-to-ship communications.

The earth-to-space component of the VDES shall not cause harmful interference to, nor claim protection from, nor restrict future development of, terrestrial systems operating in the same frequency bands.

Until 1 January 2030, the Channels 24, 84, 25, 85, 26 and 86 may also be used for analogue modulation described in the most recent version of Recommendation ITU-R M.1084 by an administration that wishes to do so, subject to not causing harmful interference to, or claiming protection from other stations in the maritime mobile service using digitally modulated emissions and subject to coordination with affected administrations. (WRC-19)

h.In Regions 1 and 3:

The frequency bands 157.0125–157.1125 MHz and 161.6125–161.7125 MHz (corresponding to Channels: 80, 21, 81 and 22) are identified for utilization of the digital systems described in the most recent version of Recommendation ITU-R M.1842 using multiple 25 kHz contiguous channels.

The frequency bands 157.1375–157.1875 MHz and 161.7375–161.7875 MHz (corresponding to Channels: 23 and 83) are identified for utilization of the digital systems described in the most recent version of Recommendation ITU-R M.1842 using two 25 kHz contiguous Channels. The frequencies 157.125 MHz and 161.725 MHz (corresponding to Channel: 82) are identified for the utilization of the digital systems described in the most recent version of Recommendation ITU-R M.1842.

The frequency bands 157.0125–157.1875 MHz and 161.6125–161.7875 MHz (corresponding to Channels: 80, 21, 81, 22, 82, 23 and 83) can also be used for analogue modulation described in the most recent version of Recommendation ITU-R M.1084 by an administration that wishes to do so, subject to not claiming protection from other stations in the maritime mobile service using digitally modulated emissions and subject to coordination with affected administrations. (WRC-19)

i. In Angola, Botswana, Eswatini, Lesotho, Madagascar, Malawi, Mauritius, Mozambique, Namibia, Democratic Republic of the Congo, Seychelles, South Africa, Tanzania, Zambia and Zimbabwe, the frequency bands 157.1125–157.3375 MHz and 161.7125–161.9375 MHz (corresponding to Channels: 82, 23, 83, 24, 84, 25, 85, 26 and 86) are designated for digitally modulated emissions.

In China, the frequency bands 157.1375–157.3375 MHz and 161.7375–161.9375 MHz (corresponding to Channels: 23, 83, 24, 84, 25, 85, 26 and 86) are designated for digitally modulated emissions. (WRC-19)

j. These channels may be operated as single or duplex frequency channels, subject to coordination with affected administrations. (WRC-12)

k. Channels ASM 1 and ASM 2 are used for application specific messages (ASM) as described in the most recent version of Recommendation ITU-R M.2092. (WRC-19)

l. Channels 1027, 1028, 87 and 88 are used as single-frequency analogue channels for port operation and ship movement. (WRC-19)

Appendix 5   INMARSAT-C Non-delivery Notification (NDN) Failure Codes

ABS   Absent subscriber. The mobile terminal is not logged in to the ocean region.
ACB   Access barred.
ADR   Addressee refuses to accept message.
ANU   Deleted. The message has not been delivered within an hour and is therefore deleted.
ATD   Attempting to deliver the message.
BK   Message aborted. Is used when a fax or PSTN-connection is cleared abnormally.
BUS   Busy.
CCD   Call cut or disconnected.
CI   Conversation impossible.
CIE   The LESO ran out of processing/communications capacity to process the message.
CNS   Call not started.

DTE	Data terminal equipment. Used when an X.25 subscriber has cleared the connection during the call attempt.
ERR	Error.
FAU	Faulty.
FMT	Format error.
FSA	Fast select acceptance not subscribed.
IAB	Invalid answerback from destination.
IAM	Was unable to process the address information in the following message.
IDS	Invalid data from ship.
IDT	Input data time-out.
IFR	Invalid facility request.
IMS	Message size is invalid; 7932 characters maximum.
IND	Incompatible destination.
INH	Was unable to establish the type of message from the following header.
INV	Invalid.
ISR	Invalid ship request.
LDE	Maximum acceptable message length or duration has been exceeded.
LEF	Local equipment failure.
LPE	Local procedure error.
MBB	Message broken by higher priority.
MCC	Message channel congestion.
MCF	Message channel failure.
MKO	Message killed by operator.
MSO	Machine switched off.
NA	Correspondence with this subscriber is not permitted.
NAL	No address line is present.
NC	No circuits.
NCH	Subscriber's number has changed.
NDA	No delivery was attempted.
NFA	No final answerback.
NIA	No initial answerback.
NOB	Not obtainable.
NOC	No connection.
NP	No party. The called party is not, or is no longer, a subscriber.
NTC	Network congestion.
OAB	Operator aborted.
OCC	Subscriber is occupied.
OOO	Out of order.
PAD	Packet assembler/disassembler.
PRC	Premature clearing.

PRF	Protocol failure.
RCA	Reverse charging acceptance not subscribed.
REF	There was a failure in the remote equipment.
RLE	Resource limit exceeded.
RPE	Remote procedure error.
RPO	RPOA out of order.
SCC	Call completed successfully.
SHE	MES hardware error.
SNF	The satellite network has failed.
SPE	MES protocol error.
SUC	Test results are being delivered.
TBY	Trunks busy.
TGR	TDM group reset.
TIM	Time-out.
TMD	Too many destinations.
UNK	Unknown. Is used when no other failure codes are suitable.
WFA	Wrong final answerback.
WIA	Wrong initial answerback.

Appendix 6　Terms and Definitions

AA (**Accounting Authority**): The organization named on a commissioning application form to administer the billing and settlement of the communication charges incurred by an MES.

AAIC (**Accounting Authority Identification Code**): A unique code assigned by the ITU to identify an accounting authority.

AMVER (**Automated Mutual-assistance Vessel Rescue System**): A vessel position-reporting system operated by the United States Coast Guard for any merchant vessel of 1000 grt or more on a voyage lasting longer than 24 h, to and from anywhere on the world.

Analogue: Any signal which represents a changing value over time.

Answerback: An identifier given to an INMARSAT MES and used in message transmissions. The format must be four letters (A–Z; no numbers) finishing with an x.

AOR-E: Atlantic Ocean Region (East).

AOR-W: Atlantic Ocean Region (West).

Applicant: The person who completes and signs a maritime commissioning application form when applying to have an INMARSAT MES commissioned. The applicant must submit the form to the national routing organization for the country where the vessel is registered.

ARQ (**Automatic Request Repeat**): The error correction process used in store-and-forward

messaging by which a receiver checks for errors in received data packets and requests the sending end to re-transmit any packets which were received containing an error.

ASCII (American Standard Code for Information Interchange): A standard alphanumeric character set based on 7-bit codes.

AUSREP: A vessel position-reporting system similar to AMVER, but operated by the Australian Authorities.

BBER: Bulletin Board Error Rate.

Bit: The basic unit of digital communications; may be either 1 or 0.

Bit Error Rate (BER): Used as a measure of the quality of reception by the MES of the Bulletin Board of a TDM Channel.

Bps (bits per second): A unit of measurement for speed of data transfer or throughput.

Bulletin Board (in a TDM Channel): A data packet transmitted in each frame of a TDM Channel which contains information about the status of the INMARSAT-B/M, Mini-M and C network configurations and the current frame number, used by the MES as a timing reference.

Bulletin Board Service (BBS): A notice board on which information can be exchanged or posted for others to download.

Byte: One byte comprises eight bits and may represent either one alphanumeric character or numeric information.

CAG: Customer Activation Group.

Case-approval: The official approval given by INMARSAT to an MES model which is typically still undergoing development by a manufacturer so as to permit the model to access an INMARSAT communication system. See also type-approval.

CCITT (Consultative Committee on International Telecommunications and Telegraph): An advisory committee to the International Telecommunication Union (ITU). The CCITT publishes standards and recommendations to enable telecommunications systems and equipment world-wide to communicate with each other. Examples of CCITT standards are the X.25 and X.400 protocols used on PSDN land-lines.

Channel number: The number representing the frequency of an INMARSAT communication channel.

Character: One element of an alphanumeric character set. One character is equivalent to one byte or 8 bits.

Class 1 INMARSAT-C MES: A Class 1 MES is capable of ship-to-shore and shore-to-ship message transfer and distress alerting, but is not capable of receiving EGC messages.

Class 2 INMARSAT-C MES: A Class 2 MES is capable of two modes of operation (selected by the operator):

- As Class 1, and also capable of receiving EGC messages when not engaged in INMARSAT-C traffic.
- Ready for EGC message reception exclusively (and not available in that mode for INMARSAT-C message transfer).

Class 3 INMARSAT-C MES: A Class 3 MES has two independent receivers, one for receiving two-way INMARSAT-C messages, the other for receiving EGC messages.

Closed network: A private network, with access limited to registered users. The INMARSAT-C system allows two types of closed networks: data reporting networks, identified by a Data Reporting Network Identification (DNID) code, and EGC FleetNET networks, identified by an EGC Network Identification (ENID) code.

Commissioning: The process by which an MES is registered for use via the INMARSAT network.

Commanded: A method of transmission, meaning "compressed/expanded", which is used to improve signal-to-noise ratio. At the sending end, a "compressor" electronic circuit amplifies low-level signals and reduces high levels to a mean level according to an algorithm. At the receiving end, an "expander" circuit uses similar methods to return the signal levels to their original values before passing them on to other circuits.

COSPAS-SARSAT: A satellite-based distress beacon locating system.

CSS: Coordinator Surface Search.

Data report (programmed unreserved, P): A short collection of data (up to 32 bytes in three packets) which is transmitted by an MES at random times in unreserved time slots of a signaling channel after receipt of a polling command from an operational center.

Data report (reserved, R): A small amount of data (up to 32 bytes in three packets) which is transmitted by an MES in reserved times slots in a signaling channel, in response to an earlier polling command from an operational center.

Data report (unreserved, U): A small amount of data (up to 32 bytes in three packets) which is transmitted in unreserved time slots of a signaling channel by an MES to an operational center.

Data services: This is how a terminal may send and receive electronic messages such as e-mail.

DCE: Data circuit terminating equipment: A component part of an INMARSAT-C MES. An MES contains a DCE receiver and a DCE transmitter which are used for communication between the MES and an INMARSAT-C LES.

DECCA navigator: A position-fixing system, based on chains of shore-based radio transmissions.

DHSD: Duplex high-speed data (see HSD).

Differential GPS: A global positioning system used with INMARSAT terminals and based on GPS satellites, with accuracy enhanced by the use of transmission of differential corrections from suitably located shore-based radio beacons.

Digital signal: A signal which represents values in the form of binary numbers.

Distress alerting: A facility available on all maritime MESs, enabling the MES to send distress priority messages through the INMARSAT system to a Rescue Coordination Center (RCC). This is not available on the INMARSAT Mini-M network.

Distress priority message: This is a message prepared and sent with distress priority using the INMARSAT system to a Rescue Coordination Center (RCC).

DMG: Distress Message Generator.

DNIC: Data Network Identification Code.

DNID：Data Reporting Network Identification Code. See data report (unreserved), data report (reserved) and data report (pre-assigned).

Downloading：The process by which an INMARSAT-C MES receives information from a service provider. For data reporting purposes, an operational center downloads a DNID code and Member Number to the MES. In the EGC FleetNET service, an information provider downloads an EGC Network Identification (ENID) code to an MES.

DTE (**Data Terminal Equipment**)：A component part of an INMARSAT-C MES, used primarily for storage and interfacing external devices (such as a keyboard or monitor). For other IN-MARSAT systems, this can be a computer connected to the MES for use for data communications.

Duplex：The ability of a communications channel to transmit data simultaneously in both directions. Also known as Full Duplex.

EGC：The EGC (Enhanced Group Call) services provided in the INMARSAT-C system are EGC SafetyNET, EGC FleetNET and INMARSAT system messages.

EIRP：Effective Isotopically Radiated Power, a measure of transmitted power.

E-mail：Electronic mail, a global message-handling system whereby subscribers to commercial e-mail services can exchange electronic messages and data files between computers. E-mail services are provided by some service providers and private organizations. Access to e-mail services may be via PSTN, PSDN networks or the Internet.

ENID：EGC network identification (ENID) code.

EPIRB：Emergency Position Indicating Radio Beacon.

ESAS：Electronic Service Activation System.

Fax：Abbreviation for "facsimile", a device used to transmit a copy of an original document. The INMARSAT-A, B/M and Mini-M systems support two-way fax transmissions. The INMAR-SAT-C system is able to send only text messages (no graphics) to a fax terminal in the ship-to-shore direction. It is only possible to send text messages (no graphics) in the shore-to-ship direction by using a third-party fax bureau.

Fax bureau service：A service offered by some private organizations and service providers to send and receive fax messages.

FleetNET：A service provided by FleetNET information providers to distribute commercial information to MESs belonging to a FleetNET group, identified by a unique ENID code.

Footprint (of a satellite)：The area on the Earth's surface (sea or land) covered by the satellite and where an antenna can obtain line-of-sight communications. In the INMARSAT systems, this area is also known as the ocean region or coverage area.

Gateway：An interface between communications systems such as the INMARSAT-C system and the national and international telecommunications networks.

GLONASS：A global positioning system similar to GPS but using satellites of the Soviet Union.

GMDSS：The Global Maritime Distress and Safety System：the INMARSAT-A/B and C systems are the only INMARSAT networks included in the GMDSS by the IMO International Maritime Organization.

Gold Franc (**GF**)：A nominal currency used by LESs and accounting authorities to calculate communication charges incurred by an MES. A fixed rate of exchange exists between the GF and the nominal currency the SDR: 1 SDR = 3.061 GF.

GPS (**Global Positioning System**): System which provides the geographic location of a vessel. This service uses American military satellites which have been made available for civilian use.

Ground segment: The network of LESs which provide a link between the space segment and the terrestrial telecommunication networks.

HSD: High-speed data. This service allows for data to be transferred at data rates of up to 64 kbit/s

IA5: International Alphabet 5—a standard alpha-numeric character set, also known as ASCII, based on 7-bit codes. Supports both upper- and lower-case characters.

IHO: International Hydrographic Organization.

IMN (**INMARSAT Mobile Number**): The number assigned by the national routing organization to an INMARSAT MES as its identity number. An INMARSAT-A maritime MN has the format 1×××××××××; an INMARSAT-B maritime IMN has the format 3×××××××××; an INMARSAT-C maritime IMN has the format 4×××××××××; an INMARSAT-M maritime IMN has the format 6×××××××××; and an INMARSAT Mini-M maritime IMN has the format 76×××××××.

IMO: International Maritime Organization.

Information provider: An organization which provides MSI messages for broadcasting to MESs via the EGC SafetyNET service, which can be received by vessels fitted with an EGC receiver.

INMARSAT: The operator of global mobile satellite communications, part of the INMARSAT Ventures Ltd group of companies.

INMARSAT-A: The original INMARSAT system, which has been operating since 1982, based on analogue techniques and capable of global two-way telephony, facsimile, data and telex communications.

INMARSAT-B: An INMARSAT system based on digital technology, and capable of high-quality telephony, facsimile, data and telex services.

INMARSAT-C: A digital system based on a low-cost MES with low power consumption. This system provides global two-way store-and-forward messaging, distress alerting, EGC SafetyNET and FleetNET, data reporting and polling.

INMARSAT-E: A distress alerting system based on EPIRBs.

INMARSAT-M: Introduced in 1993, based on digital technology and capable of two-way voice telephony, distress alerting, fax and data services at lower data rates.

INMARSAT Mini-M: Introduced in 1995, based on digital technology and capable of two-way voice telephony, alerting, fax and data services. Operates only in the reduced coverage offered by the spot beams.

Inter-station Signaling Links (**ISLs**): These signaling channels are used between an NCS and the LESs in its ocean region to pass system information around the system.

Internet: An international network of computers linked to enable information to be exchanged.

IOR: Indian Ocean Region.

ISDN (**Integrated Service Digital Network**): A high capacity digital line which lets users send voice and data at 64 kb/s over one telephone line from a common network interface.

ISP (**INMARSAT Service Provider**): An entity which establishes a contract with one or

more of the SPs to bill, promote and retail the services of the contracted SPs to end users. It can be an alternative to an AA.

ITA2 (International Telegraph Alphabet 2): A standard alphanumeric character set, generally used for sending messages on the international telex networks. The character set is based on 5-bit codes, also known as telex format, or 5-bit packed.

ITU: The International Telecommunication Union, which publishes a list of approved accounting authorities. See also CCITT.

JASREP: A vessel position-reporting system similar to AMVER, but operated by the Japanese authorities.

Kbytes: 1024 bits or 128 characters.

LAN (Local Area Network): A network which allows computers and printers to communicate with each other, have access to and share expensive peripherals such as fax servers, modem servers and centralized databases.

Land Earth Station (LES): The name used in the INMARSAT network for a shore-based receiving and transmitting station which acts as an interface between MESs and the terrestrial communications networks. LESs are owned and operated by service providers.

LES TDM Channel: A TDM Channel used by an LES to transmit system information and data addressed to an MES.

Log in: The action performed on an INMARSAT-C MES to inform the NCS in an ocean region that the MES is available for communications.

Log out: The action performed on an INMARSAT-C MES to inform the NCS in an ocean region that the MES is not available for communication.

LORAN-C: A position-fixing system, based on chains of shore-based, low-frequency radio transmissions.

MEM: Macro-encoded message.

Member number: The number downloaded with a DNID to an MES, when the MES is registered to a data reporting network.

MES (Mobile Earth Station): The generic name used to describe an INMARSAT-approved terminal which is allowed to access the network, and applicable to both maritime and land mobile communications.

Message channel: A channel assigned by the NCS for an MES to send a message through an LES to its required destination.

METAREA: Meteorological area corresponding to the NAVAREAs defined by the IMO.

MMSI (Maritime Mobile Service Identity): A 9-digit format assigned by the maritime authority to identify a vessel. The first three digits are the code of the country where the vessel is registered as defined by the ITU.

Modem: Modulator/Demodulator, a device used to transmit digital data, by converting (modulating) a digital signal into an analogue form and re-converting (demodulating) the analogue signal into digital form at the receiving end.

MSI (Maritime Safety Information): Information supplied by shore-based information providers and forwarded to an INMARSAT-C LES for broadcasting over the INMARSAT-C system to

MESs fitted with an EGC receive capability.

Multi-channel MES: An MES which is capable of making more than one call at a time. Most MESs are only single channel.

NAVAREA: One of 16 areas of sea as defined by the IMO, into which the world's oceans are divided for the dissemination of navigational and meteorological warnings. See also METAREA.

NAVTEX: The low-frequency system developed by the IMO for the broadcast and automatic reception of coastal MSI by means of direct-printing telegraphy.

NCS: An INMARSAT Network Coordination Station; a specially equipped LES appointed as the NCS for each INMARSAT system and ocean region, which monitors and coordinates the operation of all of the MESs and SPs within that ocean region.

NCS (Common Signaling Channel): Also known as the NCS Common Channel. A TDM Channel used by the NCS to transmit system information and message announcements to MESs.

Network: A group of communication channels which enable the sharing of information and resources between several users.

NOC: Network Operation Center, located at INMARSAT's headquarters in London, which monitors and controls the operation of the INMARSAT network.

NUA: Network user address.

Ocean region: The coverage area of an INMARSAT satellite within which an MES may send and receive messages.

Omega: A position-fixing system based on chains of shore-based, very low frequency radio transmissions.

Omni-directional antenna: An antenna which is capable of line-of-sight communications with a satellite without requiring any pointing. Generally used on an INMARSAT-C MES.

Operational center: A shore-based center for controlling a data-reporting network. The operational center initially downloads a DNID code and member number to an MES which joins the group. The center subsequently sends polling commands to instruct selected MESs to return pre-assigned data reports or to perform a defined task such as SCADA. The center also receives unreserved data reports from MESs belonging to the closed network.

Operator-assisted services: Communications services provided by some service providers, for example forwarding a text message from an MES as a voice message to a shore-based telephone.

Option 1 stand-alone EGC receiver: A type of stand-alone EGC receiver which can receive only EGC messages and cannot engage in non-EGC message transfer.

Option 2 stand-alone EGC receiver: This type of stand-alone EGC receiver may be added to the antenna of an INMARSAT-A or B MES so that the vessel may meet its GMDSS requirements.

Packet: An "envelope" or block of data sent over a network; each packet contains addressing information as well as the data being sent.

Polling: The facility whereby an operational center sends an instruction (a polling command) to selected MESs to perform a defined task, such as returning a preassigned data report or performing a SCADA operation.

POR: Pacific Ocean Region.

Presentation code: A code included in a transmission (ship-to-shore or shore-to-ship), indi-

cating to the recipient the presentation or formatting of the data contained in the message.

Protocol: A defined set of communications standards which lay down the parameters to which all users must abide. Protocols in general use are X.25 and X.400.

PSA: Point of Service Activation.

PSDN: Packet Switched Data Network.

PSTN: Public Switched Telephone Network.

PVT: Performance Verification Test; used to test the performance of INMARSAT-C.

RCC: Rescue coordination center.

SafetyNET: This service is provided by SafetyNET information providers to distribute MSI to MESs fitted with an EGC receive capability.

SAR: Search and Rescue.

SART: Search and Rescue Radar Transponder.

SCADA: Supervisory Control and Data Acquisition.

SCC: Satellite Control Center.

SDR (**Special Drawing Right**): A nominal currency used by service providers and accounting authorities to calculate communication charges incurred by an MES. A fixed rate of exchange exists between the SDR and the nominal currency of the GF: 1 SDR = 3.061 GF.

Service provider (**SP**): A company or organization which operates an LES.

Signaling channel (**MES-LES**): A random access TDMA Channel, used by an MES to transmit signaling information and data to an LES.

Signaling channels (**MES-NCS**): A random access TDMA Channel, used by an MES to transmit signaling information and data to an NCS.

SIM (**Subscriber Identity Module**) **card**: Used with INMARSAT Mini-M, SIM cards are easily installed and removed, allowing one terminal to be used by multiple users without having complex billing arrangements.

Simplex: The ability of a communication channel to carry communication traffic in one direction only.

SOLAS: Safety of Life at Sea.

Space segment: Consists of the communications satellites operated by INMARSAT.

Special access code: A destination address code used in a ship-to-shore or shore-to-ship message to access a special service provided by a service provider. The 2-digit codes are examples of special access codes.

Spot beam: A concentrated area offering coverage within the global footprint for particular regions in the world.

Store-and-forward messaging: The protocol used by the INMARSAT-C system to transfer text or data messages in data packets to receiving equipment.

System message: A message originated by INMARSAT containing information relevant to the INMARSAT system, broadcast on the NCS Common Channel and received by all MESs.

TCP/IP (**Transmission Control Protocol/Internet Protocol**): The set of protocols used to communicate via the Internet and between multiple networks.

TDM (**Time Division Multiplex**): The process by which multiple signals can share the same

communication channel, each using a different time slot.

TDM channel: The INMARSAT system uses different TDM Channels, each transmitted on a unique frequency. The TDM Channels are used for system control and message transfer to MESs. See LES TDM Channel and NCS Common Channel.

TDMA (**Time Division Multiple Access**): The process by which MESs communicate with an LES or NCS.

TNID: Terrestrial Network Identity.

Terrestrial telecommunication networks: The national and international telephone, telex and data networks with which the service providers interface to route calls to and from MESs via the space segment.

Time slot: Basic unit into which one-time frame of a TDM Channel is divided.

Type-approval: The official approval given by INMARSAT to an MES model produced by an independent manufacturer when the MES meets the technical standards defined by INMARSAT. Only models which have been granted type-approval (or case-approval) are permitted to operate via the INMARSAT network.

Uncompounded: A method of transmission which does not use commanding techniques and is used for data and fax transmission on the INMARSAT-A network.

UTC (**Universal Coordinated Time**): A term which, for practical purposes, has the same meaning as Greenwich Mean Time (GMT).

Value-added service (**VAS**) **provider**: A private organization which provides services such as weather forecasting to vessels using INMARSAT and other networks.

Video conferencing: Video and audio communication between two or more people via a video coder (coder/decoder) at either end and linked by digital circuits.

WAN (**Wide Area Network**): A network which connects users over large distances, often crossing geographical boundaries.

WMO: World Meteorological Organization.

X.25: The communications protocol used on the national and international PSDN networks to exchange digital data between devices attached to the network.

X.400: A message-handling protocol used to exchange electronic mail (e-mail) messages around the world. Able to use the X.25 (PSDN) networks.

2-digit codes: Special examples of Special Access Codes.

5-bit packed (**also known as telex format or ITA**2): A format based on 5-bit codes used for sending alphanumeric characters to and from telex terminals.

7-bit ASCII: A format based on 7-bit codes used for sending the alphanumeric characters of the ASCII character set.

8-bit data: A format based on 8-bit codes used for encoding information such as text, national character sets and numerical information.

Appendix 7   List of RCCS Associated with INMARSAT Land Earth Stations

No.	LES	Country	Ocean Region(s)	MRCC	Address	Contact Details
6	Emeq Haela	Israel	AOR-E IOR	Haifa Coast Radio Station	Bezeq, NETS/Transmissions Northern Dev. Solel Bobe Building Huir 1, Haifa Israel	Tel. :+972 4 869 9016 Fax:+972 4 869 9017 E-mail: haifaradio@ bezeqint. net
7	Fucino	Italy	AOR-E IOR	(M) RCC Rome	Italian Coast Guard Viale dell'Arte, 16 Rome I-00144 Italy	Tel. :+39 6 592 3569/4145 Fax:+39 6 592 2737/590 84793 Telex:+43 611172, 61456 COGECAP I E-mail: cgcp3rep4@ infrastrutturetrasporti. it
8	Ex Goonhilly @ Burum	The Netherlands	AOR-E AOR-W IOR	(M) RCC Falmouth (SARNET*)	HMCG Pendennis Point, Castle Drive Falmouth, Cornwall TR11 4WZ United Kingdom	Tel. :+44 1326 317575 Fax:+44 1326 315610 E-mail: falmouthcoastguard@ mcga. gov. uk
9	Hai Phong	Vietnam	IOR POR	RCC Vietnam	5th Floor, Vinamarine Building No.8, Phan Hung Str. Mai Dich Ward Cau Giay District Hanoi, Vietnam	Tel. :+84 4 768 3050 Fax:+84 4 768 3048 E-mail: vnrcc@ fpt. vn
10	Kumsan	Republic of Korea	IOR POR	KOMCC(Korea Mission Control Center)	Korea Coast Guard, 3 - 8 Songdo-Dong, Yeonsu-Gu, Incheon 406 741 Republic of Korea	Tel. :+82 32 8352352 Fax:+82 32 8589595 Telex:+801 24920 ROKNP K E-mail: mrcckorea@ kcg. go. kr

Continued

No.	LES	Country	Ocean Region(s)	MRCC	Address	Contact Details
11	Lakhadaria	Algeria	AOR-E	RCC D'Alger	123 Rue Tripoli Hussein Dey BP-428 Alger, Algeria	Tel. :+213 21 853256 Fax:+213 21 853260 E-mail: mcc_alger@mdn. dz
12	Nakhodka	Russian Federation	POR	MRCC Vladivostok	State Maritime Rescue Co-ordination Centre Nizhne-Portovaya Str. 3 Vladivostok 690019 Russian Federation	Tel. :+7 4232 495522, 227782 Fax:+7 4232 495895 Telex:+64 213115 MRF RU E-mail: vldvmrcc@vld. pma. ru
13	Nudol	Russian Federation	AOR-E IOR	SMRCC Moskva	State Maritime Rescue Co-ordination Centre Bldg 1, 1Rozhdestvenka Str. Moscow 109012 Russian Federation	Tel. :+7 495 626 1052 Fax:+7 495 6926 7476 E-mail: od_smrcc@morflot. ru
14	Perth	Australia	IOR POR	RCC Australia	Australian Maritime Safety Authority, Level 3, 25 Constitution Ave GPO Box 2181 Canberra, ACT 2601 Australia	Tel. :+61 2 6230 6811 Fax:+61 2 6230 6868 E-mail: rccaus@amsa. gov. au

Continued

No.	LES	Country	Ocean Region(s)	MRCC	Address	Contact Details
15	Psary	Poland	AOR-E IOR	(M) RCC Gdynia	Polish Maritime Search and Rescue Service P. O. Box 186 10Hryniewickiego Str. 81-340 Gdynia Poland	Tel.:+48 58 6610196, +48 58 4985745 Fax:+48 58 6610197 Telex:+63 54262 RCC PL E-mail: rcc-polratok@ polratok. com. pl
16	Pune	India	IOR	(M) RCC Mumbai	Indian Coast Guard Region West Golfa Devi Temple Road Prabha Devi Post Mumbai 400025 India	Tel.:+91 22 2431 6558 Fax:+91 22 2431 6558 (same number) Telex:+81 1171381 BMCG IN E-mail: indsar@ vsnl. net
17	Santa Paula	United States	POR	USCG Alameda	Pac Area Command Central Building 51-2, Coast Guard Island Alameda CA 94501-5100 United States	Tel.:+1 510 4373700 Fax:+1 510 437 3017 Telex:+230 172343 AAB CG ALDA E-mail: rccalameda1@ uscg. mil
18	Sentosa	Singapore	IOR POR	Port Operations Control Centre	POCC, 21st Storey, Tanjong Pagar Complex 7B Keppel Rd. Singapore 089055 Singapore	Tel.:+65 622 65539, 632 52493, 632 52394 Fax:+65 622 79971, 622 45776 Telex:+87 20021 RS20021 E-mail: pocc@ mpa. gov. sg

Continued

No.	LES	Country	Ocean Region(s)	MRCC	Address	Contact Details
19	Southbury	United States	AOR-E AOR-W	USCG Norfolk	Commander (ACC) Atlantic Area United States Coast Guard 431 Crawford St. Portsmouth VA 23704 United States	Tel.:+1 757 3986321 Fax:+1 757 3986392 Telex:+230 127775 USCG RCC NYK E-mail: d05-smb-lantcmdctr@uscg.mil
20	Tangua	Brazil	AOR-E	(M)RCC Brazil SALVAMAR	Commando de Operacoes Navais Salvavar Brasil Praca Barao de Ladario S/N Edificiia Almirante Tamanadare 7 Andar Rio de Janeiro R.J. Brazil 20.091-000	Tel.:+55 21 21046056 Fax:+55 21 21046038 Inmarsat-C:471009910 E-mail: mrccbrazil@con.mar.mil.br
21	Thermopylae *	Greece	AOR-E	(J)RCC Piraeus	Ministry of Mercantile Marine 150 G Lambraki Ave Piraeus GR 185 18 Greece	Tel.:+30 210 411 2500, 422 0772 Fax:+30 210 413 2398, 411 5798 Telex:+601 0211588 RCC GR + 601 0211254 RCC GR E-mail: jrccpgr@mail.yen.gr
22	Yamaguchi	Japan	IOR POR	Japan Coast Guard	Operations Centre 2-1-3 Kasumigaseki Chiyoda-ku Tokyo 100-8918 Japan	Tel.:+81 3 359 19000 Fax:+81 3359 182701 E-mail: op@kaiho.mlit.go.jp

* (M)RCCs associated with INMARSAT LES that have been declared operational on Search and Rescue Network (SARNET). SARNET is a communication broadcast system to allow international RCCs to exchange or seek SAR information by using Inmarsat-C EGC FleetNET service. (M)RCC Turku (Finland), (M)RCC Gothenburg (Sweden), (M)RCC Madrid (Spain), RCC Bermuda, (M)RCC Riga (Latvia), (M)RCC Rejkjavik (Iceland) are not associated with Inmarsat LESs but have also been declared operational on SARNET.

Appendix 8   Introduction of Admiralty List of Radio Signals

Admiralty List of Radio Signals provides information on all aspects of Maritime Radio Communications, helping bridge crews to manage communications and comply with all reporting regulations throughout a voyage.

For clarity and convenience, this publication is split across six volumes; with contents ranging from Maritime Radio Station listings to Maritime Safety Information Services worldwide. You can find full details on the contents of each volume and its corresponding parts below.

Volume 1 (NP281)—Maritime Radio Stations (Parts 1 & 2)

Split across two publications, Volume 1 includes radio details for:

- Global Maritime Communications
- Satellite Communication Services
- Coastguard Communications
- Maritime TeleMedical Assistance Service (TMAS)
- Radio Quarantine and Pollution reports
- Anti-Piracy Contact Table

Volume 2 (NP282)—Radio Aids to Navigation, Differential GPS (DGPS), Legal Time, Radio Time Signals and Electronic Position Fixing System (Parts 1 & 2)

Split across two publications, Volume 2 includes radio details for:

- Listing of VHF Radio Direction-finding Stations
- Radar Beacons (Racons and Ramarks)
- Known operational Automatic Identification System (AIS)
- Aids to Navigation (AtoN)
- Radio beacons transmitting DGPS corrections
- International Standard and Daylight Saving Times and Dates
- International Radio Time Signal Broadcast details

Volume 3 (NP283)—Maritime Safety Information Services (Parts 1 & 2)

Split across two publications, Volume 3 includes radio details for:

- Maritime Weather Services
- Safety Information broadcasts
- Worldwide NAVTEX and SafetyNET information
- Submarine and Gunnery Warning details (Subfacts and Gunfacts)
- Radio-Facsimile Stations, frequencies and weather map areas

Volume 4 (NP284)—Meteorological Observation Stations

This volume includes:

- All Met Observation Stations listed worldwide

Volume 5 (NP285)—Global Maritime Distress and Safety System (GMDSS)

This volume includes:

- Worldwide communication requirements for distress, search and rescue
- Extracts from SOLAS and ITU Regulations
- Distress and SAR (incorporating MRCC and MRSC contacts)
- Worldwide NAVTEX and Maritime Safety Information

Volume 6 (NP286)—Pilot Services, Vessel Traffic Services and Port Operations (Parts 1-8)

Split across eight publications, Volume 6 includes radio details for:

- Detailed Pilot information, contact details and procedures
- Vessel Traffic Service information, contact details and procedures
- National and International Ship Reporting Systems
- Port information, contact details and procedures